Fourth Edition

THE TRAGEDY OF VIETNAM

Fourth Edition

THE TRAGEDY OF VIETNAM

Patrick J. Hearden
Purdue University

PEARSON

Boston Columbus Indianapolis New York San Francisco Upper Saddle River
Amsterdam Cape Town Dubai London Madrid Milan Munich Paris Montreal Toronto
Delhi Mexico City Sao Paulo Sydney Hong Kong Seoul Singapore Taipei Tokyo

Editorial Director: Craig Campanella
Publisher: Charlyce Jones Owen
Editorial Assistant: Maureen Diana
Senior Marketing Manager: Maureen Prado
  Roberts
Marketing Assistant: Samantha Bennett
Managing Editor: Ann Marie McCarthy
Creative Art Director: Jayne Conte
Cover Designer: Suzanne Behnke

Cover Photo: © Nicholas Pitt / Almay
Operations Specialist: Renata Butera
Media Editor: Alison Lorbor
Media Project Manager: Tina Rudowski
**Composition and Full-Service Project
  Management:** TexTech International Pvt Ltd
Printer and Binder: Courier Westford
Cover Printer: Courier Westford

Library of Congress Cataloging-in-Publication Data

Hearden, Patrick J.
  The tragedy of Vietnam / Patrick J. Hearden.—4th ed.
    p. cm.
  Includes bibliographical references and index.
  ISBN-13: 978-0-205-74427-5 (alk. paper)
  ISBN-10: 0-205-74427-3 (alk. paper)
    1. Vietnam War, 1961–1975—United States.   2. United States—Foreign
relations—Indochina.   3. Indochina—Foreign relations—United States.
4. United States—Foreign relations—1945–1989.   I. Title.
  DS558.H42 20
  959.704'3373—dc23
                                                        2011016155

10 9 8 7 6 5 4 3 2 1

ISBN-10: 0-205-74427-3
ISBN-13: 978-0-205-74427-5

In Memory of My Father

One day, in another faraway place, other teenage Americans may fight and die for a reason as criminal as our mere reluctance to discuss Vietnam. For if we do not speak of it, others will surely rewrite the script.

AN AMERICAN VETERAN OF THE VIETNAM WAR, 1984

CONTENTS

PREFACE

Since the fall of Saigon to communist forces in 1975, Americans have exhibited a continuing interest in the Vietnam War. Many have been disturbed because the conflict was not only the longest military struggle in American history but also the first war that the United States ever lost. And the consequent blow to the American ego has given birth to a large body of polemical literature that focuses on the issue of what went wrong. Some writers have blamed American military leaders for failing to devise an effective strategy to defeat the enemy on the battlefield. Others have criticized politicians in Washington for imposing restrictions on American commanders who were responsible for achieving victory in Vietnam. Still others have argued that the news media eroded public support on the home front for the American war effort. In addition to the numerous books and articles that attempt to find a scapegoat for the failure of Americans to accomplish their objectives in Southeast Asia, library shelves abound with volumes that center their attention on the question of how the United States fought the Vietnam War.

Yet while many works offer excellent descriptions of the American military experience in Vietnam, few accounts address the two vital questions concerning the role that the United States played in the conflict: Why did the United States become entangled in Vietnam in the first place? And why did Americans sustain their involvement in Vietnam for a quarter of a century? American writers ignore these twin issues only at the peril of their country. For unless the American people receive adequate answers to these crucial questions, the United States may well be condemned to repeat in another part of the world the disaster that befell it in Southeast Asia. Indeed, more than a third of a century after the fall of Saigon, the bitter debates concerning American military operations in Iraq and Afghanistan dramatize the need for people throughout the United States to learn the lessons of the Vietnam War.

This study examines the key decisions that resulted in the tragic American entanglement in Vietnam. In the process, it grapples with the following pivotal queries: Why did President Franklin D. Roosevelt abandon his commitment to liquidate the French empire in Southeast Asia? Why did President Harry S. Truman bankroll the French expeditionary force in Indochina? Why did President Dwight D. Eisenhower block general elections to determine the future of Vietnam? Why did President John F. Kennedy rapidly expand the number of American military advisers in Vietnam? Why did President Lyndon B. Johnson dispatch U.S. combat troops to Vietnam? And why did President Richard M. Nixon extend the American military campaign into Cambodia and Laos?

This investigation uncovers the fundamental causes of the escalating American involvement in Indochina. While the personality traits and party affiliations of those wielding power in Washington changed, the evidence shows that the broad U.S. policy to prevent the spread of communism in Southeast Asia remained the same. Yet the documents also reveal that American leaders were not primarily concerned with extending the blessings of political liberty to the Vietnamese people. Rather, the records demonstrate that the basic reasons for the tragedy that unfolded in Vietnam were rooted in a bipartisan commitment to maintain an international order that American policymakers deemed essential to the survival of free enterprise in the United States.

WHAT'S NEW TO THE FOURTH EDITION

The addition of a set of three primary documents at the end of each chapter has significantly improved the fourth edition of this book. Besides offering strong evidence supporting the main arguments presented in the text, these documents provide students with revealing sources that can be used in the preparation of written assignments. The documents cover many important subjects in the following sequence:

- Chapter 1—the economic motivation for the establishment of the French Indochina Empire in the late nineteenth century, the founding of the Indochinese Communist Party in 1930, and the Vietnamese Declaration of Independence in 1945.
- Chapter 2—the economic and strategic considerations underlying the American decision in 1950 to help finance the French war effort in Indochina.
- Chapter 3—the Final Declaration on Indochina of the Geneva Conference in 1954, the subsequent American-directed covert operations in Vietnam, and the American hopes in 1955 that noncommunist countries in Southeast Asia would become large markets for Japanese exports.
- Chapter 4—the American involvement in the plot lunched by South Vietnamese generals in 1963 to overthrow the Diem regime in Saigon.
- Chapter 5—the Gulf of Tonkin Resolution in 1964 and the reasoning that led to the American decision in 1965 to begin a sustained program of bombing North Vietnam.
- Chapter 6—the debate in 1965 over the wisdom of dispatching American combat troops to South Vietnam and the discussion in 1968 about the desirability of deescalating the American military involvement in Indochina.
- Chapter 7—the Vietnamization policy in 1969, the secret peace negotiations in Paris in 1972, and the confidential American promise in 1973 to provide economic aid for the post-war reconstruction of North Vietnam.
- Chapter 8—the Senate committee report in 1993 on the controversial MIA/POW issue, the Free Trade Agreement in 2000 between the United States and the Socialist Republic of Vietnam, and the American vision for the emergence of a peaceful and prosperous Asia-Pacific Economic Community in the early twenty-first century.

ACKNOWLEDGMENTS

My students at Purdue University deserve special thanks for listening attentively and asking thoughtful questions while my ideas on the deepening American entanglement in Vietnam were developed in the classroom.

Several historians gave me the benefit of their critical judgment and friendly encouragement. Thomas J. McCormick of the University of Wisconsin helped me gain a better understanding of the economic factors underlying the American intervention in Vietnam. Gunther E. Rothenberg of Purdue University shared with me his keen insights into the strategic problems that the United States encountered in Southeast Asia. Walter LaFeber of Cornell University and Mark A. Kishlansky of Harvard University read a draft of the entire manuscript and made many valuable suggestions for revising the content.

Gaylord Nelson kindly provided me with a candid explanation of the pressure that was exerted on him and other members of the U.S. Senate in August 1964 to vote for the Gulf of Tonkin Resolution.

Useful stylistic comments offered by James M. Hall, John L. Larson, William C. Lloyd, and J. Michael Thorn helped make my work more readable. Finally, I would like to thank the following reviewers for their comments: Timothy S. Brown, Northeastern University; Sheri David, Nevada Community College; Richard Filipink, State University of New York at Fredonia; Adolph H. Grundman, Metropolitan State College of Denver; Clifford W. Haury, Piedmont Virginia Community College; Gerald Herman, Northeastern University; Michael Kennedy, High Point University; Meredith Lair, George Mason University; Tom Lairson, Rollins College; Joong Jae Lee, University of Wisconsin, Platteville; Leonard L. Lewane, Blue Ridge Community College; James Olson, Sam Houston State University; Joseph Palermo, California State University, Sacramento; Anne Paulet, Humboldt State University; David Skidmore, Drake University; Robert R. Tomes, St. John's University; and Nancy Beck Young, University of Houston.

Patrick J. Hearden
Purdue University

ACRONYMS

APEC	Asia-Pacific Economic Cooperation
ARVN	Army of the Republic of Vietnam (South Vietnamese army)
ASEAN	Association of Southeast Asian Nations
CIA	Central Intelligence Agency
CMAG	Chinese Military Advisory Group
DMZ	Demilitarized Zone
DRV	Democratic Republic of Vietnam
EDC	European Defense Community
ERP	European Recovery Program
FBI	Federal Bureau of Investigation
JCS	Joint Chiefs of Staff
MAAG	Military Assistance Advisory Group
MACV	Military Assistance Command, Vietnam
MIA	Missing in Action
NATO	North Atlantic Treaty Organization
NLF	National Liberation Front
NSC	National Security Council
NVA	North Vietnamese Army (People's Army of Vietnam)
OPLAN 34 A	Operations Plan 34 Alpha
OSS	Office of Strategic Services
POW	Prisoner of War
PRC	People's Republic of China
PRG	Provisional Revolutionary Government
ROTC	Reserve Officers' Training Corps
SEATO	Southeast Asia Treaty Organization
SRV	Socialist Republic of Vietnam
SVN	South Vietnam (Republic of Vietnam)
UN	United Nations
VC	Vietcong
VCP	Vietnamese Communist Party
WTO	World Trade Organization

Map of Southeast Asia

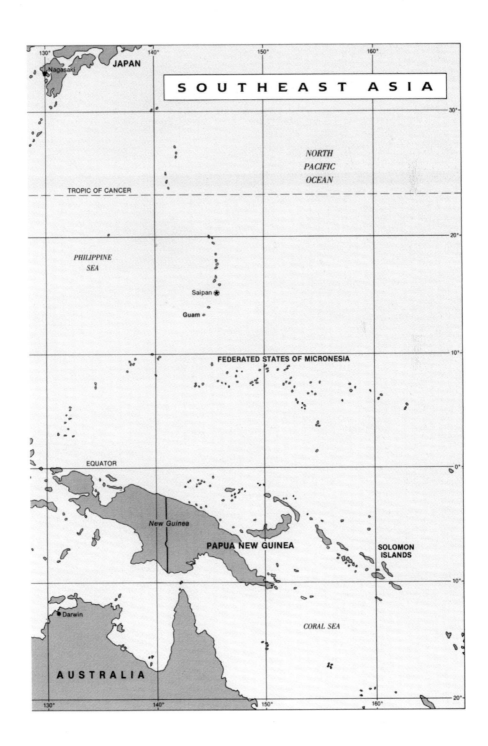

The French Indochina Empire

*Social stability in this industrial age clearly depends on outlets
for industrial goods.... The European consumer-goods market is
saturated; it is necessary to reach into other parts of the world for
new consumers, or, at the dawn of the twentieth century, modern
society will be bankrupt and will suffer destruction by some
cataclysm whose consequences can scarcely be imagined.*

JULES FERRY, FRENCH STATESMAN, 1890

THE EMERGENCE OF VIETNAM

More than 2,000 years ago, the Vietnamese people emerged as a distinct ethnic group possessing a common language and a resilient culture. Their long historical journey began with the establishment of flourishing agricultural settlements on the fertile alluvial soil deposited by the Red River flowing down from the mountains to the sea. The cultivation of rice on the triangular plain at the mouth of this river provided the economic basis for the development of a social structure composed of a small number of prominent landlords and a large mass of ordinary peasants. But while agriculture served as the foundation of their feudal society, the Vietnamese did not limit themselves to harvesting the resources of the land. Since the vast majority of inhabitants of the Red River valley lived within fifty miles of the coast, they were able to supplement their basic diet of rice with fish and salt gathered from the ocean. And these three staples—rice, fish, and salt—continued to be the principal sources of food for the Vietnamese people throughout their tumultuous history.

In 111 B.C., the Chinese invaded the region inhabited by the Vietnamese, and during the next 1,000 years, Vietnam remained a Chinese colony. After defeating the indigenous Vietnamese population, the conquerors from China introduced new agricultural methods into the rich Red River Delta. The Chinese brought plows and draft animals to work in the rice paddies. They also brought sophisticated systems of irrigation and flood control. These agricultural innovations resulted in the intensification of rice cultivation, and the consequent increase in food production led to a population boom. As their agricultural base widened and their numbers swelled, the Vietnamese found that their very survival depended on their ability to harness the vital water of the Red River. Thus, they banded together to build the dams, dikes, and canals needed to obtain greater rice yields to satisfy their expanding nutritional requirements.

In addition to introducing efficient agricultural techniques into the Red River basin, the imperial authorities from China established a mandarin system to administer the Vietnamese territory under their rule. The Chinese proconsuls governing Vietnam appointed a few native landlords to hold minor bureaucratic posts in the new regime. Acting as public officials and civil servants, the local mandarins helped run their country in the interest of China. These indigenous functionaries also adopted the Chinese language and embraced Confucian principles emanating from China. But while these servants of power readily absorbed the morals and aped the lifestyle of their foreign taskmasters, the great bulk of the Vietnamese people continued to toil in the rice fields, where they clung to their traditional customs and values. As a result, a fundamental division developed between the mandarins residing in the provincial towns and the peasants living in the surrounding countryside.

The upper-class members of Vietnamese society, although quick to embrace the trappings of Chinese culture, slowly began to harbor a strong desire for political autonomy. While they continued to enjoy their social and economic privileges, the mandarins gradually came to resent their political subservience to outside authorities. As their discontent steadily mounted, they began to regard the heavily taxed peasants as indispensable allies if they were ever to throw off the yoke of Chinese oppression. These urban Vietnamese leaders eventually reverted to speaking their native language and to honoring ancient practices in an effort to restore their ties with their rural neighbors. After mobilizing the masses into a powerful resistance force, the mandarins launched a determined struggle to achieve national independence. A long series of violent and bloody confrontations ensued. Finally, in 939 A.D., the Vietnamese rebels defeated the Chinese imperialists and drove them out of their homeland. Henceforth, the smaller Vietnamese dragon would no longer pay tribute to the Chinese colossus to the north.

The great victory against China marked the beginning of 900 years of growth and development for Vietnam as an independent country. Shortly after winning their emancipation from foreign domination, the triumphant Vietnamese established a stable and effective government. The new Vietnamese regime revolved around a strong monarch who exercised sovereign authority over his subjects. A long line of emperors lived in the city of Hanoi, which sat strategically along the banks of the Red River, and on the death of each ruler, the royal prerogative was passed on to his eldest son. Although Vietnam evolved as a unified nation with a central government based on a hereditary monarchy, the country nevertheless suffered from considerable political turmoil due to the haughtiness of the large landlords and native mandarins. These two troublesome groups did not always passively submit to the mandate of the monarchs, and they frequently rebelled when an emperor interfered with their exploitation of the peasants. As a result, Vietnam was constantly plagued by feudal dissension that sometimes erupted into full-scale civil war.

Besides suffering from these internal disturbances, Vietnam also fell victim to repeated invasions from China. But the Vietnamese, taking advantage of their climate and geography, were able to repel each Chinese intrusion. "When the enemy is away from home for a long time and produces no victories and families learn of their dead," explained General Tran Hung Dao, who defeated the Chinese in 1284, "then the enemy population at home becomes dissatisfied and considers it a Mandate from Heaven that their armies be recalled. Time is always in our favor. Our climate, mountains and jungles discourage the enemy; but for us they offer sanctuary and a place from which to attack." The Chinese invaded once again in 1406, and after rapidly conquering Vietnam, they ruthlessly exploited the vanquished population. But the Vietnamese, under the leadership of Le Loi, soon revolted against the despotic Chinese. Realizing that he lacked the manpower to engage the Chinese in large battles, Le Loi employed hit-and-run tactics to wear down the gargantuan enemy. Small rebel units under his command would make sudden thrusts against Chinese troops, then quickly dissolve into the jungle to prepare for yet another surprise attack. These guerrilla tactics ultimately proved successful, and in 1428, the Chinese withdrew their forces from Vietnam.

After winning their independence from their northern neighbor, the energetic Vietnamese embarked on their own program of empire building. They gradually began expanding beyond the Red River area, and during the next 400 years, they moved southward, step by step, along the seacoast until they reached all the way down to the Gulf of Siam. This Great March to the South was propelled by an economic imperative. The Vietnamese needed more land in order to raise more rice to feed their growing population. Rice could be cultivated in abundance in only two accessible places: along the narrow strip of coastal lowlands stretching from one end of the Indochina peninsula to the other and along the floodplains of the rivers flowing from the mountains down to the ocean. Driven by their hunger for land, the Vietnamese advanced down the coast in spurts, jumping from one river valley to the next. After each move, these vigorous pioneers established new settlements and harvested more rice until they outgrew their food supply and the time came to make yet another bound to the south.

Armies of ravenous Vietnamese peasants spearheaded these recurrent imperial thrusts. Whenever an increase in their numbers created a need for additional rice fields, the pastoral Vietnamese became aggressive soldiers who pushed back weaker peoples from their expanding southern frontier. And after conquering sufficient living space, the peasants exchanged their swords for plows and settled down to farming once again. This intermittent pattern of territorial aggrandizement, repeated over and over, came at the expense of two adjoining dominions. The militant Vietnamese first attacked the kingdom of Champa, and within a few hundred years, this once flourishing state ceased to exist. The Vietnamese then pressed farther south against the sprawling empire of Cambodia, and by 1800, they had succeeded in expelling the Khmers from the coveted Mekong River basin. Thus, the Vietnamese had gained control of the second of the two great rice-producing regions of Indochina.

After the Great March to the South had run its course, Vietnam was shaped like an elongated S extending for more than 1,200 miles between the ninth and twenty-sixth parallels. The country has often been pictured as two baskets of rice at the opposite ends of a bamboo pole carried on the back of a peasant. The baskets of rice are the two rich alluvial deltas formed by the Red and Mekong rivers, and the bamboo pole is the long chain of mountains, with peaks ranging from about 10,000 feet in the north to around 4,000 feet in the south. These mountains form a vast watershed that serves as a boundary separating Vietnam from Laos and Cambodia. Eighty percent of the geographical area of Vietnam is covered by bush, forest, or heavy jungle, and these highlands are sparsely populated by different ethnic tribes that were forced out of the fertile valleys below by the Khmers and Vietnamese. The vast majority of Vietnamese live at an altitude of less than 900 feet in the coastal lowlands and floodplains that together constitute the remaining 20 percent of the country.

The great leapfrogging movement southward, while providing the Vietnamese with essential farmland, also intensified their political difficulties. For many centuries, Vietnamese monarchs had sat on the throne in Hanoi and ruled over the people of the Red River valley. As the Vietnamese population extended farther and farther to the south, however, the emperors exercised less and less control over their migrating subjects. Settlements established at great distances from the seat of empire in Hanoi came to enjoy a considerable amount of political autonomy. Ultimately, rival factions rebelled against dynastic authority, and as a consequence, Vietnam was divided into two parts. The separate governments that emerged in the northern and southern halves of the country depended on the support of the great landlords and provincial mandarins, and these two groups were therefore allowed to line their pockets by collecting high land rents and excessive taxes from the peasants. But this economic exploitation provoked a series of peasant uprisings.

More and more, the forces of revolt in Vietnam were expressions of peasant discontent rather than articulations of elite ambition. While the peasants took up arms against their oppressors with increasing frequency, however, their sporadic outbursts remained unsuccessful for a long time because they lacked adequate leadership. But finally, in 1772, a local insurrection assumed the dimensions of a national revolution. The rebellion, led by three brothers from the village of Tay Son in the Mekong River valley, drew support from the upstart merchants in the nearby villages and the distressed peasants in the surrounding rice paddies. The ranks of the rebels continued to swell, and in 1786, their leaders succeeded in bringing the northern and southern parts of the country back together once more. Although the Tay Son rulers were overthrown in 1802 and a new monarchy was established at Hué in central Vietnam, the country remained united under a single government, and the Vietnamese people maintained their strong sense of national identity.

THE ESTABLISHMENT OF FRENCH RULE

Despite their long history of militant nationalism, the Vietnamese had already become a target of Western imperialism. The European economic penetration began during the sixteenth century, when Portuguese ships brought enterprising traders to Vietnamese ports, and following closely in their wake were commercial adventurers disembarking from Dutch and British vessels. After establishing several trading posts in Vietnam, these agents of empire gradually turned their attention to more lucrative areas of exploitation elsewhere in Southeast Asia. But the French exhibited a more persistent determination to harvest the wealth of Vietnam when they entered the scramble for Asian riches during the seventeenth century. The French were driven by a potent mixture of economic ambition and religious enthusiasm. Gallic merchants, spurred by a desire for profit, and Catholic missionaries, stirred by a sense of piety, joined forces, and in 1664, they organized both the French East India Company and the Society of Foreign Missions. Hoping that trade would follow the cross, the merchants offered to pay the cost of transporting men of the cloth to Vietnam. The transaction proved to be mutually satisfying. Besides introducing French commodities throughout Vietnam, the missionaries preached their Christian gospel wherever they could find an audience.

The Vietnamese, however, often responded with suspicion and hostility toward the proselytizing endeavors of the missionaries from France. Their negative reaction was rooted in the fundamental tension that exists between the Christian commitment to individual sanctity and the Confucian concern for social stability. While the teachings of the Christian church stress personal salvation and devotion to biblical precepts, the philosophy of Confucius places greater emphasis on communal welfare and respect for parental authority. Vietnamese leaders feared that it would be difficult to maintain control over peasants who fell under the spell of Catholicism. Convinced that the spread of Christianity would disrupt their community, government officials in Vietnam frequently jailed Catholic converts and deported French missionaries. These measures of religious repression had a dampening effect, and as a consequence, in 1800 there were less than 30,000 Christians living in Vietnam.

During the first half of the nineteenth century, Catholics in France began urging their government to take military action to prevent religious persecution in Vietnam. Their propaganda campaign drew support from an aggressive group of naval officers who were more interested in extending the reach of French sea power than in expanding the bounds of Christendom. But the government in Paris paid little attention to pleas for the deployment of military force in Vietnam until growing numbers of French merchants and manufacturers started to demand protection for their overseas commerce. Adding their voice to this mounting expansionist chorus was a new breed of nationalists who began promoting the idea that France had a mission to bring the blessings of civilization to backward areas around the world. But while these cultural chauvinists were moved by impulses of national pride, the influential business interests were motivated more by desires for personal enrichment. And their appetite for Asian trade intensified after the Opium Wars ended in 1842 and China was forced to open its doors to British and American exports.

Succumbing to the pressure exerted by the commercial imperialists, the French government decided to authorize a military assault on Vietnam. Fourteen warships and 2,500 soldiers left France in 1858 with orders to take the city of Tourane on the coast in the central part of Vietnam. The French forces encountered only limited native resistance, but when many of the invading troops died from the scourge of tropical diseases, policymakers in Paris quickly withdrew their beleaguered warriors. Yet the undaunted French attacked Vietnam again three years later with even greater military strength. This time, the French struck with seventy gunboats and 3,500 men against the city of Saigon and the surrounding area in the southern part of Vietnam. After breaking the local resistance in a succession of bloody battles, the French extracted a very favorable treaty in 1862 from the humiliated Vietnamese government. Emperor Tu Duc agreed not only to give the French possession of three Vietnamese provinces adjacent to Saigon but also to open three ports in Vietnam to French traders and to permit Catholic missionaries to propagate their faith throughout the country.

Emperor Tu Duc felt compelled to sue for peace and accept such harsh terms because his government lacked the popular support needed to offset French technological superiority. Many public officials and petty bureaucrats, after being appointed to administrative positions by Tu Duc, had became indifferent to the needs of the Vietnamese people. And while his army was fighting in southern Vietnam against the foreign invaders, peasants in northern Vietnam were rebelling against corrupt mandarins. Tu Duc did not have enough troops to repel the French and at the same time to suppress the peasant uprising. Thus, he was confronted with a difficult dilemma. And when Tu Duc opted to make peace with his foreign enemies in order to wage war against his own subjects, he was forced to grant the French valuable concessions. In brief, Vietnam had fallen prey to French imperialism because the country was plagued not only by technical inferiority but also by class antagonism.

After obtaining possession of the area around Saigon, the French pressed ahead with their quest for empire on the Indochina peninsula. A series of successful military campaigns between 1863 and 1867 enabled the French to complete their conquest of the Mekong River Delta and then to establish a protectorate over Cambodia. While digesting these distant acquisitions during the next decade and a half, the French rapidly developed their industrial base at home. The demands for overseas markets grew louder as business profits were plowed back into manufacturing plants, and in 1883, the French government sent another expeditionary force to Vietnam. After French troops penetrated the Red River valley and bombarded the imperial capital at Hué, the Vietnamese quickly capitulated and signed a treaty that virtually ended their independence. The French completed the creation of their Indochina empire ten years later when they took control of Laos.

The acquisition of these colonies in Indochina provoked a great debate over the issue of empire within France. On the one hand, socialists and humanitarians argued that an imperial policy would mean economic enslavement rather than cultural improvement for the colonial people. These critics also charged that imperialism would benefit only a few big businessmen and colonial administrators, while the great majority of French citizens would have to pay the cost of empire with the blood and money needed to maintain metropolitan control over distant territories. On the other hand, special business interests provided strong backing for a program of imperialism. Bankers and manufacturers viewed colonial areas not only as sources of raw material for French industry but also as markets for French capital and commodities. Narrowly preoccupied with their economic self-interest, these business groups hoped that overseas colonies would provide immediate opportunities for profitable enterprise.

The most influential proponents of imperialism, however, exhibited a broad concern about the long-run functioning of the entire French political economy. These system-conscious leaders noted that domestic industries were turning out more goods than the home market could absorb, and they pointed out that French manufacturers would have to continue dismissing workers unless they could obtain foreign markets for their surplus commodities. Fearing that the twin problems of overproduction and unemployment were creating the material conditions for a social revolution, these elite cosmopolitans concluded that the preservation of capitalism depended on a policy of imperialism. Jules Ferry, who served as the French prime minister twice between 1880 and 1885, was a strong exponent of this argument. Ferry repeatedly advocated a program of overseas economic expansion in order to avoid the danger of a radical social upheaval. "Social stability in this industrial age," he declared, "clearly depends on outlets for industrial goods." Along with their allies in the business community, prominent politicians such as Ferry convinced the government in Paris to make a concerted effort to consolidate French control of Indochina.

Having won the heated controversy over the colonial question, the French imperialists realized the need to rationalize their Indochina empire. Vietnam, Cambodia, and Laos did not generate enough revenue to pay for their own domination when they first became colonies. Since the empire remained in the red for many years, the citizens of metropolitan France had to bear a heavy tax burden to provide salaries for the civil servants and armed forces sent to rule the colonial population. The members of the French National Assembly soon came to understand that administering the far-flung empire was not a money-making operation. But on the assumption that the colonies would pay off in the future, the legislators continued appropriating funds, year after year, to run them. Finally, the French government gave Paul Doumer the challenging job of transforming the Southeast Asian colonies from financial liabilities into profitable possessions. As the governor-general of French Indochina between 1896 and 1902, Doumer strove to put the empire in the black by transferring the cost of imperial administration from the French taxpayers to the colonial subjects. He also began building a modern transportation network to pave the way for the economic exploitation of the colonies.

Doumer ruthlessly imposed a new tax system to accomplish his two basic objectives in Indochina. First, to meet the expenses of administering Vietnam, Cambodia, and Laos, the governor-general created three distinct local budgets that depended exclusively on the direct taxation of the people living in each respective colony. Second, Doumer established a general budget to defray the costs of developing the whole Indochina empire. He generated revenue for the general budget by placing a high tariff on goods imported into the colonies and by organizing state-controlled monopolies that sold licenses for the production and distribution of opium, alcohol, and salt. Most of the money raised through the indirect tax on these three items and through the customs duties went for the construction of roads, bridges, railroads, and harbors. Hence, Doumer began establishing an infrastructure in Indochina to facilitate both the extraction of raw materials from the Southeast Asian colonies and the importation of manufactured products from the mother country back in Europe.

The French also established a new land policy to promote the economic exploitation of Vietnam. Most of the arable land seized during the conquest of the Mekong Delta and most of the additional tracts opened to tillage by the construction of canals and the drainage of marshes were sold to rich French colonists and wealthy Vietnamese natives. At the same time, many Vietnamese peasants lost their small plots because they could not pay high tax levies imposed by French officials along with high interest charges on loans made by large landlords. If the Vietnamese peasants owned their own land, the French authorities reasoned, they would eat almost all the rice they produced. Therefore, very little would be left to sell abroad at a profit. The French wanted large quantities of rice made available for shipment to the huge rice-consuming populations in China and Japan. And they got what they wanted. Between 1880 and 1930, the amount of rice land under cultivation in the Mekong Delta more than quadrupled. Rice exports simultaneously soared, and by the start of World War II, Vietnam was the third-largest rice-exporting country in the world.

Besides accounting for this spectacular rise in rice exports, the French land policy generated a vast pool of cheap labor in Vietnam. Hordes of landless peasants did much of the dirty and dangerous work required to expand the exchange of products between the colony and the metropolis. The French used large numbers of Vietnamese natives to build railroads, work in coal mines, and toil on rubber plantations. During the 1930s, big French corporations invested heavily in the development of rubber plantations in the area around Saigon. The huge Michelin firm alone was responsible for almost 45 percent of all the rubber produced in Indochina. The landless peasants endured terrible working conditions on the rubber plantations, where disease ran rampant. In fact, the death rate for the native rubber workers was four times higher than for the rest of the Vietnamese population. Because most peasants would rather go hungry than submit themselves to such horrendous working conditions, the French imposed a system of forced labor to obtain the large gangs of Vietnamese workers needed for gathering latex from rubber trees.

Despite the rapid growth in rubber production in Vietnam, no local rubber industry developed in the colony. Large quantities of raw latex were sent to France to be converted into rubber tires and other articles. These finished products were then shipped back to Vietnam and elsewhere to be sold at a handsome profit. French authorities refused to allow a local rubber industry to take root in Vietnam because they wanted their rubber factories to remain in Europe and thereby provide employment and prosperity for their home population. Nor did they permit the development of any other industries in their Indochina empire. The French subscribed to the traditional imperial theory that held industrial countries have a built-in advantage when trading with agrarian regions because the process of manufacturing adds labor costs to the value of the final product. Believing that colonies should ship low-priced raw materials to their mother country and buy back high-priced factory goods, policymakers in Paris kept their Indochinese possessions on the agricultural half of an imperial relationship with industrial France. In other words, they were determined that their Indochina empire should continue serving as a farm vis-à-vis the French city.

In addition to prohibiting the development of colonial industry, French policymakers tried to prevent foreign competitors from exporting manufactured articles to Vietnam, Cambodia, and Laos. The French sought to establish sheltered markets in their Southeast Asian possessions by placing discriminatory import duties and transit charges on goods coming into them from the United States and other foreign countries. American consular officials reported from Saigon that the United States was having great difficulty selling merchandise in Vietnam. They explained that compared with their French rivals, American exporters had to pay higher tariffs to land their wares in Vietnam and higher railroad freight rates to transport them to the interior of the colony. In 1939, the last year of normal trade before World War II disrupted the colonial regime, more than 55 percent of all Vietnamese imports came from France, while less than 5 percent of the total came from the United States. As these figures indicate, the French had succeeded in closing the doors of their Indochina empire against foreign competition and in monopolizing the markets of their Southeast Asian colonies.

The Bank of Indochina, the real master of French colonial policy, had achieved its economic objectives. Jointly owned by finance capitalists in Paris and the French government, the Bank of Indochina became the key institution where businessmen and statesmen worked hand in hand, arranging colonial affairs for the economic benefit of metropolitan France. The colonies in Southeast Asia, operating under the dominion of this partly private and partly public institution, became both ready sources of raw materials for French manufacturers and protected markets for their surplus industrial goods. These colonies also produced revenue to pay the cost of imperial administration and thereby provide relief for the French taxpayers. And because the bank succeeded in keeping the Indochina empire in the profit column, anticolonial sentiment in France subsided. But while fewer and fewer people in France raised their voice against the evils of imperialism, more and more of their subjects in Vietnam joined the ranks of a vigorous anticolonial movement.

THE ROOTS OF NATIONALISM AND COMMUNISM

From the very outset, the Vietnamese fought against the French colonization of their country. Although Emperor Tu Duc had ceded the provinces around Saigon in 1862, local Vietnamese partisans continued to resist the French military intrusion. Rebel bands employed hit-and-run tactics to harass the French army, and these small guerrilla units were both elusive and resilient. Even after their country had become a formal French protectorate in 1883, many Vietnamese kept on fighting against the imposition of French authority in the name of their humiliated emperor. Tu Duc had died just before the treaty of surrender was signed at Hué, and in announcing his death, the imperial court declared that he "was killed by sorrow over seeing foreigners invade and devastate his empire and he died cursing the invader." Vietnamese patriots were urged to "keep him in your hearts and avenge his memory." Since many answered this call to action, it took the French another ten years to subdue the native guerrillas and pacify their country.

During the last decade of the nineteenth century, the French set out to destroy the national identity of their Vietnamese subjects. They referred to the Vietnamese people as Annamites, and the actual name of their country ceased to exist in French writings. Vietnam was divided into three separate entities. The northern portion of Vietnam, encompassing the Red River Delta, became Tonkin. The central region of the country, containing the long strip of coastal lowlands, was called Annam. The southern part of Vietnam, embracing the Mekong River Delta, became Cochinchina. Then, after partitioning Vietnam, the French created the Indochinese Union, which was composed of these three distinct units along with Cambodia and Laos. Consequently, the Vietnamese found themselves submerged in a grouping of states that were governed in the interest of their French masters.

The imperial rule imposed by the French sowed the seeds of peasant discontent deep in Vietnamese soil. By the 1930s, only 2 percent of the population in Cochinchina owned 45 percent of the arable land, while in Tonkin, only 9 percent of the people owned 52 percent of the land under cultivation. The large and often absentee landlords forced the peasants to pay excessive rents for the right to cultivate their small plots in the rice fields. The peasants also suffered at the hands of the Vietnamese natives appointed by French governors to serve as bureaucrats in low-level administrative positions. Many such political collaborators, coming as they did from families that had previously converted to Catholicism, practiced the religion of their rulers. These functionaries not only collected taxes to support the French regime, they also coerced the landless to work

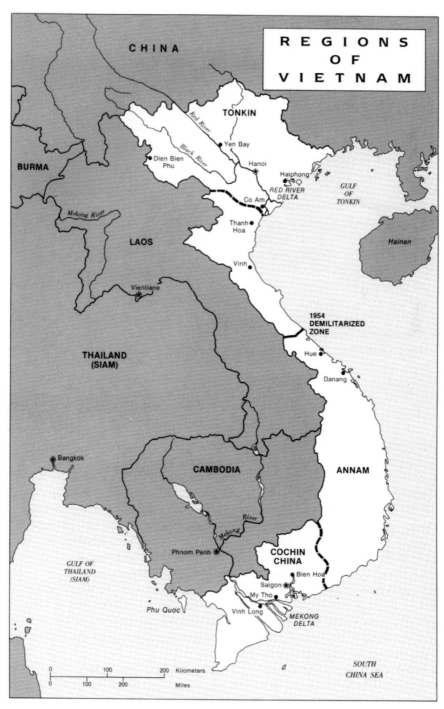

Regions of Vietnam.

on the deadly French rubber plantations. In addition, corrupt mandarins often embezzled funds to supplement their regular salaries. "On our side," admitted a candid French official, "we have only Christians and crooks."

Besides angering the great mass of exploited peasants, French colonial policy also aroused the wrath of many upper-class members of Vietnamese society. Whereas the British depended largely on native inhabitants to maintain control over the entire subcontinent of India, the French refused to give the indigenous population a major role in administering their Indochina empire. So while only 5,000 civil servants from England ruled 325 million Indians in 1925, it took an equal number of civil servants from France to manage a mere 30 million Vietnamese. Not only did the French style of colonial administration make it difficult for ambitious Vietnamese natives to obtain attractive positions in the government bureaucracy, the French policy of retarding the development of colonial industry also meant that there were few employment opportunities for talented and educated Vietnamese in the business community. And even when aspiring natives did get jobs commensurate with their abilities, they usually received two or three times less pay than French colonists doing the same work. More disturbing still was the situation at the University of Hanoi, where a Vietnamese professor received lower wages than a French janitor.

Life in the French empire could be especially frustrating and humiliating for young Vietnamese men of wealthy origins. The sons of Vietnamese landlords and merchants frequently traveled to Paris to complete their formal education, and some earned advanced degrees in science, medicine, and law at the University of Paris and other French institutions of higher learning. They also enjoyed the liberal atmosphere of the Latin Quarter, where they could openly debate political issues and read socialist literature criticizing French imperialism. But a very painful experience awaited these young Vietnamese scholars when they returned home. The colonial police force regarded them as potential subversives and confiscated any of their books that might be tainted by some kind of European radicalism. These returning Vietnamese students likewise discovered that they could not find jobs in either business or government that matched their educational achievement. And after they had been addressed in Paris with the formal *monsieur* used for normal adults, colonial bureaucrats addressed them with the familiar *tu* as if they were children or servants.

More than anything else, the question of colonial education became the focal point in the conflict between the opposing forces of Vietnamese nationalism and French imperialism. Hoping to destroy the cultural identity of Vietnamese students, the French authorities prohibited the use of traditional Chinese characters in the schools of Tonkin, Annam, and Cochinchina. But many native teachers went on strike in protest against the French effort to undermine the coherence of Vietnamese culture. Occurring in the midst of this confrontation, the Japanese victory over Russia in 1905 had a strong impact on Vietnamese nationalists. They learned that a yellow Asian people, if armed with Western scientific and technical knowledge, could defeat a white European power. Vietnamese nationalists quickly concluded that their students needed exposure to Western ideas, and in 1907, they established the Free School of Tonkin in Hanoi. The French, however, regarded their attempt to modernize Vietnamese thought as an act of political subversion. After only eight months, they closed the school and arrested the teachers.

Although the French crushed the Free School of Tonkin, they could not prevent Phan Boi Chau from keeping the Vietnamese national resistance movement alive during the first quarter of the twentieth century. Chau was the driving force among the Vietnamese scholars who believed that Eastern peoples needed Western knowledge to defend themselves against European imperialism. In 1905, he organized an underground service to send gifted Vietnamese students to Japan, where they could study Western science and technology. During the next three years, some 200

Vietnamese students participated in what they called "the exodus to the East." Chau also advocated the formation of a transnational alliance to put an end to white rule throughout the Far East, and in 1908, he helped create the East Asia League. Composed of nationalists representing several different Far Eastern countries, the organization began to lay the foundations for a pan-Asiatic movement against European domination.

Yet if Phan Boi Chau provided the campaign against imperialism with dynamic leadership, his brand of nationalism was doomed to fail. Chau did not go beyond the political demands of the wealthy landlords and upper-class intellectuals who were frustrated and humiliated by French policies. These two elite groups wanted freedom from French dominion, but they had no interest in making any sweeping changes in the Vietnamese social structure. Opposed to a radical redistribution of wealth, they never developed a program that addressed the fundamental economic needs of the peasant masses. Chau remained tied to the great landlords and urban intellectuals. Unable to transcend his upper-class orientation, he appealed to the privileged minority rather than the oppressed majority. Chau ultimately failed because his resistance movement could not free Vietnam from colonial bondage without the support of the lower class.

Among the Vietnamese nationalists, only the communists were able to rally the masses in a drive to expel the French from their homeland. The communists aimed to offset the technological superiority possessed by the French colonists with the numerical strength of the Vietnamese peasants. The Vietnamese communists had dual objectives. They were determined not only to burst the shackles of colonialism but also to solve the problem of landlordism. After achieving their immediate nationalist goal of home rule, the communists intended to implement their long-range program aimed at creating a more equitable social order. They planned to divide the large estates of the great landlords into small plots and to distribute them to the landless peasants. Thus, the communists promised the peasants that they would have a better life after the French were thrown out of their country.

Ho Chi Minh emerged as the indisputable father of Vietnamese communism. Born in 1890 in a small village in central Vietnam, he grew up in a family of modest means. His father had studied hard to climb above his peasant origins and become a public official, but he lost his administrative job because of his sympathy for Phan Boi Chau and other Vietnamese nationalists. As a boy, Ho heard stories from his elders about how the arrogant French colonists had mistreated the Vietnamese people. Ho attended school in the old imperial capital of Hué, and his nationalist feelings grew stronger while he studied in this great center of Vietnamese culture. After teaching for a brief time, Ho decided to leave Vietnam, and in 1912, at the age of twenty-two, he got a job as a kitchen boy on a French freighter. Ho spent the next two years sailing around the globe, but when World War I began, he left the ship to find work in England. While living in London, he joined a group of Asian students and workers who were supporting the Irish struggle for national independence. Then, in 1917, Ho decided to move to France, where he could deal with the problems of his own country.

Ho Chi Minh plunged into the vortex of world politics when he arrived in Paris. The United States had already entered the Great War, as it was known then, and American statesmen were planning to use their influence to shape the peace settlement. In his famous Fourteen Points speech delivered in 1918, President Woodrow Wilson announced that the United States stood for the democratic principle of national self-determination. Ho was excited about what Wilson had said. He hoped that the concept of home rule would be applied to the black, brown, and yellow people living in the colonial areas of the world and not just to the white people residing in Europe. Fast becoming the leading figure of the Vietnamese community in Paris, Ho drafted a petition calling for self-government for Vietnam. He intended to hand his petition to Wilson at the Versailles Peace Conference in 1919, but the president refused to see him. Ho was deeply disappointed when he discovered the wide gap that existed between Wilsonian rhetoric and American diplomacy.

After being rebuffed by Wilson and his European allies at Versailles, Ho became more deeply involved in radical politics in France. The shock waves of the Bolshevik Revolution in Russia were beginning to split the French Socialist Party into rival factions. Although Ho was not interested in many of the subtle points that were driving French socialists and communists apart, he was keenly concerned about their respective attitudes toward the issue of colonial independence. When the socialists refused to join with the communists in supporting Lenin's demand for the immediate emancipation of all colonial areas, Ho decided that he would be a communist rather than a socialist. Ho helped found the French Communist Party in 1920, and he quickly became its leading expert on the colonial question by repeatedly attacking every aspect of French imperialism in both public addresses and newspaper articles. As a delegate of the French Communist Party, Ho traveled to Moscow in 1924 to participate in an international meeting of communists and to speak for the liberation of the colonial masses around the world.

The leaders of the Comintern promptly dispatched Ho Chi Minh to China, where Chiang Kai-shek and the nationalists were cooperating with Mao Zedong and the communists. Ho went directly to Canton, which was a major center for young Vietnamese political exiles. While living in Canton between 1925 and 1927, he helped organize an Eastern alliance against Western imperialism called the League of Oppressed Peoples of Asia. Ho also trained hundreds of Vietnamese students in Canton to become radical activists, and some were infiltrated back into Vietnam to form a hard-core political cadre. Pham Van Dong, who eventually became Ho's most trusted deputy, stood out among those who were sent home to recruit their compatriots and to agitate against the French. Ho had to leave Canton in 1927 because Chiang broke with Mao and began attacking communist enclaves in China. But Ho slipped into Hong Kong in 1930, and there, together with his radical followers, he established the Indochinese Communist Party.

By then, hundreds of young Vietnamese communists, after receiving their training in either Russia or China, had returned to their native land to foment a revolution against the old colonial order. These communist agents advanced a radical program that addressed the basic economic grievances of the downtrodden Vietnamese peasants and workers. Their social reform program held out the promise of lower taxes and land distribution for the peasants along with the prospect of higher wages and better medical care for plantation workers. The communists decided to provoke a peasant rebellion in 1930, but the uprising failed miserably. The French brutally smashed the rebels in a great bloodbath that left an estimated 10,000 Vietnamese peasants dead. This White Terror, as the Vietnamese called it, taught the communists a bitter lesson. Realizing that they were not yet ready to challenge French military power, the communists decided to go underground in order to make preparations for a successful revolt from below. But their opportunity did not come until the winds of World War II swept across the Pacific and loosened the bonds of French colonialism in Indochina. Then, in May 1941, after traveling abroad for more than a quarter of a century, Ho Chi Minh returned to Vietnam to lead the forces of revolution.

THE RISE OF THE VIETMINH

In December 1941, half a year after Ho Chi Minh's return to Vietnam, the Japanese launched a surprise attack on Pearl Harbor as part of their drive to establish a new order in East Asia. Their quest for empire, which had begun ten years earlier, was based on economic necessity. The narrow chain of Japanese islands did not provide an adequate natural resource base to support the dense urban population living on them. Thus, it was essential for the Japanese to export manufactured goods in order to pay for the foodstuffs needed to feed their people and the raw materials required to sustain their industries. But after the onset of the Great Depression in 1929, the United States and European countries began erecting high tariffs against Japanese products. Policymakers in Tokyo responded by looking for Asian markets that Japan could monopolize, and in 1931, they invaded Manchuria and set up a puppet state called Manchukuo. Then, the Japanese promptly turned Manchuria into an exclusive sphere of economic influence whose doors were closed against American and European commodities.

The Japanese had visions of a vast empire that extended far beyond the borders of Manchuria, however. Their desire to monopolize the entire China market of more than 400 million consumers was disclosed after Japanese and Chinese troops exchanged shots in July 1937 at the Marco Polo Bridge. Japan seized on the skirmish as an excuse for making further conquests on the Asian mainland, and this aggression provoked a determined Chinese resistance. As the invaders pushed deep into the Middle Kingdom, they quickly assumed control of every major seaport, railroad, and industry in northern China. The Japanese were eager to extend their authority over the rest of China as well, and in November 1938, Tokyo boldly announced plans for the creation of a Greater East Asia Co-Prosperity Sphere. With Japan serving as the industrial core and her Asian satellites accepting their inferior role as producers of foodstuffs and raw materials in this new order, the Land of the Rising Sun would enjoy as much economic self-sufficiency as either the United States or the British Empire.

It soon became evident that the Japanese included French Indochina in their grandiose dreams of economic hegemony in the Far East. When Nazi Germany defeated metropolitan France in June 1940, the Japanese imperialists cast covetous eyes on the French possessions in Southeast Asia, and they immediately grasped this golden opportunity to extort valuable economic and strategic concessions from the vanquished European nation. Shortly after surrendering to Hitler, the pro-Nazi government at Vichy in the German-occupied part France agreed to close the Tonkin border adjacent to China and to allow Japan to place inspectors along the French Indochina Railroad to make sure that trains did not carry supplies to the Chinese resistance forces. Three months later, in September 1940, the distressed French gave Japan permission to station 25,000 soldiers in Tonkin. Finally, in May 1941, the French agreed that all the rubber, rice, and coal available for export from their Indochinese colonies would be reserved for the Japanese occupation troops or shipped to the Japanese home islands.

This readiness to collaborate with the Japanese occurred even though the French still had a large military force deployed in Indochina. After learning that the United States would not come to their aid, policymakers in France decided not to spill Gallic blood defending their Southeast Asian protectorates against Japan. And while their home government was capitulating to pressure exerted by Tokyo, the French colonists in Indochina were cooperating fully with the occupational authorities sent from Japan. Not wanting to be bothered with the problems of colonial administration, the Japanese asked the local French officials to continue running the affairs of Vietnam, Cambodia, and Laos. But the Japanese insisted that they must have access to the raw materials and foodstuffs produced in the French possessions and that none of these resources could be sent to the Chinese armies fighting against Japan. Yielding to these demands, the French willingly administered their Indochina empire for the economic and strategic benefit of Japan.

The Vietnamese communists, by contrast, were determined to resist the Japanese occupation of their country. In May 1941, Ho Chi Minh summoned the Central Committee of the Indochinese Communist Party to discuss the need for a broad national front to fight against both the old French enemy and the new Japanese foe. This historic meeting, held at Ho's headquarters in a remote cave in the mountains near the Chinese border, gave birth to the Revolutionary League for the Independence of Vietnam (better known as the Vietminh—meaning Vietnamese nationalist). Although the leadership of the organization was firmly in communist hands, the Vietminh included all shades of nationalist opinion. Ho and his comrades downplayed their radicalism in order to attract conservatives to their nationalist cause. Their pragmatic agrarian program, for example, promised that patriotic landlords could keep their property and that only treasonous landowners would have their holdings confiscated and distributed to landless peasants. Rather than discussing their ultimate goal of building a communist utopia, the leaders of the Vietminh emphasized their immediate aim of ousting the foreign adversaries. After receiving support from members of every social class, Ho issued a call in September 1941 for his countrymen to take up arms in order to create an independent Vietnamese republic.

Following his decision to employ military force, Ho asked Vo Nguyen Giap to build an army for the Vietminh. General Giap had a unique background. He was politically active during his youth, and in 1933, at the age of twenty-one, he had joined the Indochinese Communist Party. After earning a law degree from the University of Hanoi, he taught history in a Vietnamese school and studied the guerrilla tactics used by the Chinese communists. Giap promptly set about organizing and training guerrilla units in the jungle-covered mountains of northern Tonkin. In this remote mountainous region, far from the French and Japanese soldiers down in the Red River valley, he began the difficult task of recruiting mountain tribesmen. The Vietnamese had historically regarded the ethnic peoples living in the mountains as savages, but Giap demanded that his troops overcome their traditional ethnocentric attitudes. He realized that it was critical for the Vietminh to maintain friendly relations with the mountain tribes not only to get them to join his army but also to keep them from telling the French and Japanese the whereabouts of his training centers. Giap successfully wooed many tribesmen by promising that they would have autonomy in areas traditionally under their control after the foreigners were expelled from the country.

Giap gradually expanded his base of operations deep in the mountains of northern Tonkin. After winning the support of numerous tribesmen, he began recruiting village chiefs and training Vietnamese peasants in the art of guerrilla warfare. Giap instructed his Vietminh forces to strike with superior numbers against tiny and isolated French outposts, to capture guns and supplies, and then to melt back into the jungle before making another surprise attack. But while the Vietminh guerrillas began to overrun small French garrisons in 1944, they avoided any major battles where the French could use their superior firepower to greater advantage. Giap spent most of his time during World War II recruiting troops and training them to capture weapons and ammunition. He concentrated on strengthening the Vietminh forces in the hope that when that war ended, they would be able to emerge triumphant.

In the meantime, Ho Chi Minh crossed over the border into southern China in order to obtain support for his resistance movement. Ho wanted to get Vietnamese exiles to return to their homeland and join the ranks of the Vietminh. He also hoped to receive economic aid from the warlords who controlled southern China. When Ho arrived in China in August 1942, however, the warlords arrested and imprisoned him. Hoping that someday they could dominate Indochina, the warlords tried to organize their own Vietnamese independence movement. But the group backed by the Chinese lacked able leadership and popular support, and consequently, it could not provide information about Japanese plans and operations in Indochina. Realizing that only the Vietminh could give them what they wanted, the warlords released Ho from prison and began supplying him with money in exchange for intelligence about the Japanese. The Chinese subsidy helped the Vietminh establish a strong underground network throughout Tonkin, where they continued preparing for their chance to seize power.

They did not have to wait long before what remained of French authority in Indochina came to an abrupt end. Most French colonists in Indochina had been actively collaborating with the Japanese since 1940, when their native country fell under the shadow of the swastika. But many Frenchmen underwent a change of heart at the end of 1944, when they heard that American forces under General Douglas MacArthur were in the process of reconquering the Philippines. As rumors spread that the Americans would soon liberate Indochina, General Charles de Gaulle decided that his Free French troops should prepare for military action. During the first two months of 1945, de Gaulle parachuted French agents and arms into Vietnam with orders to attack the Japanese as soon as American soldiers hit the beaches. But the French plans were a poorly kept secret, and on March 9, the Japanese moved suddenly to nip the uprising in the bud. Despite the presence of almost 100,000 French troops in Indochina, the Japanese met with little resistance. Most of the French soldiers were quickly disarmed and imprisoned, while about 5,000 of them fled from the Japanese and straggled into China. The Japanese coup ended all pretense of French sovereignty in Indochina.

The American military and intelligence personnel stationed in southwestern China had not until then showed much interest in the activities of the Vietminh. But almost immediately after the Japanese takeover of French Indochina in March 1945, American army officers made a deal with Ho Chi Minh. The Americans agreed to provide the Vietminh with communications equipment, medical supplies, and small arms, and in return, Ho offered to give the United States information about Japanese troop movements and to help rescue downed American pilots. The Office of Strategic Services (OSS) also established a friendly relationship with the Vietminh. A small OSS team, headed by Archimedes Patti, parachuted into northern Tonkin on July 16 to make contact with General Giap at his mountain redoubt. After reporting to Washington that 85 percent of the people living in Tonkin supported the Vietminh, Patti and his fellow OSS officers began helping Giap train his forces for operations against the Japanese. But the principal effect of this brief American association with the Vietminh was political rather than military in nature. It appeared as if Ho and Giap had formed an alliance with the United States, so their prestige among the Vietnamese people was greatly enhanced.

The Vietminh also gained popularity because of their militant actions during a ghastly famine that engulfed northern Vietnam. To satisfy their military requirements, the Japanese had forced many Vietnamese peasants to raise jute, hemp, and castor beans rather than food crops. Adverse weather conditions and widespread flooding in the Red River Delta during 1945 exacerbated the food shortage in Tonkin. Yet the Japanese continued requisitioning their rice quotas, which were stored in huge granaries in anticipation of an Allied invasion. During the ensuing famine, an estimated 2 million of the 10 million inhabitants of the northern half of Vietnam died. This massive starvation produced a deep hatred for the Japanese oppressors and provoked the Vietnamese peasants to fight for their very survival. When the famine became acute, Vietminh soldiers led hungry peasants who succeeded in breaking into some of the storage depots and distributing the rice to their starving countrymen. Their action in seizing the granaries marked the Vietminh as the patriotic champions of the Vietnamese peasants.

Then, in August 1945, along with the blast of atomic bombs over Hiroshima and Nagasaki, the great opportunity for the Vietminh to lead a revolution in Vietnam suddenly came. On August 16, two days after Japan surrendered to the United States, Ho Chi Minh called for a general uprising. Ho aimed to mobilize the masses throughout Vietnam and then welcome the Allied troops when they arrived to disarm the Japanese. On August 19, the Vietminh marched into Hanoi and occupied the government buildings without firing a shot. The Japanese offered no resistance, and there were no Vietnamese reprisals. While bright red Vietminh flags fluttered over Hanoi,

Ho Chi Minh (1890–1969), President of the Democratic Republic of Vietnam, 1946. Laure Albin-Guillot/Roger-Violet/The Image Works.

throngs of happy people paraded down the streets proclaiming Vietnamese independence and chanting death to the French. The revolt spread with incredible speed. Revolutionary committees quickly took over provincial governments, and within just six days, the Vietminh had gained control of the entire country. Red flags flapped over every part of Vietnam, and in a burst of exuberance Saigon, was renamed the City of Ho Chi Minh.

The Vietminh thereupon decided to dispose of Emperor Bao Dai and set up their own government in Hanoi. Bao Dai had functioned as a puppet under the French and as a figurehead in the new client administration that the Japanese installed after their March coup. His willingness to serve foreign rulers discredited him in the eyes of his countrymen. And when thousands of angry peasants stormed into the royal capital of Hué, the Vietminh pressured the besieged emperor to abdicate his throne. Bao Dai promptly yielded, and on August 30, he turned over the royal seal to a revolutionary committee. The Vietminh then established the Democratic Republic of Vietnam (DRV). The new regime received widespread and enthusiastic support, and the Vietnamese people were delighted when the charismatic Ho Chi Minh became their president. And it was with a show of warmth and affection that they referred to their frail and gentle leader as Uncle Ho.

The great revolution of August 1945 filled Ho with hope for the future of his country. On September 2, speaking before a crowd of 500,000 people assembled in Hanoi, Ho proclaimed

Vietnamese independence. Wearing a faded khaki suit and rubber sandals, he began his address by quoting from the American Declaration of Independence. "We hold these truths to be self-evident," he told his cheering audience, "that all men are created equal." Ho concluded his speech by appealing to the United States to acknowledge the independence of Vietnam. Four years earlier, in August 1941, President Franklin D. Roosevelt and Prime Minister Winston Churchill had met off the coast of Newfoundland to discuss Anglo-American war aims, and in the highly publicized Atlantic Charter, they pledged to restore self-government to all people who had been forcibly deprived of home rule. Although Ho had been bitterly disappointed at Versailles when Woodrow Wilson failed to make good on his rhetoric, he hoped that this time American leaders might abide by their promise to support the democratic principle of national self-determination. Because the French had collaborated with the Japanese and the Vietminh had worked with the Americans, Ho thought that perhaps the United States might prevent the French from recovering their Indochina empire.

DOCUMENT 1-1
Jules Ferry on Colonialism and the Preservation of Capitalism

Jules Ferry, twice the prime minister of France between 1880 and 1885, argued that the preservation of capitalism depended on a policy of colonialism.

Colonial policy is the child of industrialization. For wealthy nations where capital abounds and accumulates fast, where industry is continually expanding, and where even agriculture must be mechanized in order to survive, exports are essential for national prosperity….Had it been possible to establish, among the leading industrial nations, some kind of rational division of labor, based on the natural resources and social aptitudes of the different producing countries, so that certain of them might engage in cotton and metallurgical manufacture, others in alcohol and sugar-refining industries, and still others in woolen and silk production, Europe might not have had to seek markets for its products in lands beyond its borders….

But today every nation wants to do its own spinning and weaving, forging and distilling. All of Europe refines sugar and tries to export it. With the arrival of the industrial giants, the United States and Germany, with a regenerated Italy, a Spain enriched by the investment of French capital, an enterprising Switzerland, and a growing Russia, the entire west has plunged down a slope from which there can be no return.

Beyond the Vosges and across the Atlantic, protectionism has increased the volume of manufactured goods, suppressed former outlets, and thrust the countries of Europe into a fierce competition for markets. To protect their home markets, nations have raised their tariff barriers…. The likely effect will be increased domestic competition and a general lowering of prices, profits, and wages.

The Protectionist system, unless accompanied by a serious colonial policy, is like a steam engine without a safety valve. An excess of capital invested in industry not only reduces profits on capital but also impedes the rise of wages. This is not an abstract law, but a phenomenon made of flesh and bones, driven by passions and willfulness. Social stability in this industrial age clearly depends on outlets for industrial goods. The economic crisis that has weighed so heavily on the workingmen of Europe since 1877, with its prolonged and frequent strikes, has simultaneously struck France, Germany, and England with a marked and persistent drop in exports. Europe is like a commercial firm whose business has been shrinking for a number of years. The European consumer-goods market is saturated; it is necessary to reach into other parts of the world for new consumers, or, at the dawn of the twentieth century, modern society will

(continued)

DOCUMENT 1-1   Continued

be bankrupt and will suffer destruction by some cataclysm whose consequences can scarcely be imagined....

Colonial policy is an international manifestation of the eternal laws of competition....

France is not weak....Because it is strong, this great military state can support ten thousand men in Indochina. Because France is strong it must not abandon it role and its rights as a great power.... A nation cannot be a great power by remaining bound to its own shores....

Without compromising the security of the country, without sacrificing its past traditions and future aspirations, the Republicans have, in less than ten years, given France four kingdoms in Asia and Africa.... If the Republic had declared, like the doctrinaires of the Radical school, that the French nation ends at Marseilles, to whom would Tunisia, Indochina, Madagascar, and the Congo belong today?

Source: Jules Ferry, *Le Tonkin et la Mere-Patrie* (Paris: Victor-Harvard, 1890), 40–43 and 47–48. Parts of this document have been reprinted with a slightly different translation in Harvey Goldberg, *French Colonialism: Progress or Poverty?* (New York: Rinehart and Company, 1959), 2–4.

DOCUMENT 1-2

Appeal on the Founding of the Indochinese Communist Party, February 18, 1930

An appeal made on February 18, 1930 by Ho Chi Minh on the occasion of the founding in Hong Kong of the Communist Party of Indochina.

Workers, peasants, soldiers, youth and pupils!
Oppressed and exploited compatriots!
Sisters and brothers! Comrades!

Imperialist contradictions were the cause of the 1914–1918 World War. After this horrible slaughter, the world was divided into two camps: One is the revolutionary camp including the oppressed colonies and the exploited working class throughout the world. The vanguard force of this camp is the Soviet Union. The other is the counter-revolutionary camp of international capitalism and imperialism whose general staff is the League of Nations.

During this World War, various nations suffered untold losses in property and human lives. The French imperialists were the hardest hit. Therefore, in order to restore the capitalist forces in France, the French imperialists have resorted to every underhanded scheme to intensify their capitalist exploitation in Indo-China. They set up new factories to exploit the workers with low wages. They plundered the peasants' land to establish plantations and drive them to utter poverty. They levied many heavy taxes. They imposed public loans on our people. In short, they reduced us to wretchedness....

However the French imperialists' barbarous oppression and ruthless exploitation have awakened our compatriots who have all realized that revolution is the only road to life, without it they will die out piecemeal. This is the reason why the Vietnamese revolutionary movement has grown ever stronger with each passing day: The workers refuse to work, the peasants demand land, the pupils strike, the traders boycott. Everywhere the masses have risen to oppose the French imperialists.

The Vietnamese revolution has made the French imperialists tremble with fear. On the one hand, they utilize the feudalist and comprador bourgeois in our country to oppress and exploit our people. On the other, they terrorize, arrest, jail, deport and kill a great number of Vietnamese revolutionaries. If the French imperialists think that they can suppress the Vietnamese revolution by means

DOCUMENT 1-2 Continued

of terrorist acts, they are utterly mistaken. Firstly, it is because the Vietnamese revolution is not isolated but enjoys the assistance of the world proletarian class in general and of the French working class in particular. Secondly, while the French imperialists are frenziedly carrying out terrorist acts, the Vietnamese Communists, formerly working separately, have now united into a single party, the Communist Party of Indo-China, to lead our entire people in their revolution.

Workers, peasants, soldiers, youth, pupils!
Oppressed and exploited compatriots!

The Communist Party of Indo-China is founded. It is the Party of the working class. It will help the proletarian class to lead the revolution in order to struggle for all the oppressed and exploited people. From now on we must join the Party, help it and follow it in order to implement the following slogans:

1. To overthrow French imperialism, feudalism and the reactionary Vietnamese capitalist class.

2. To make Indo-China completely independent.
3. To establish a worker-peasant and soldier government.
4. To confiscate the banks and other enterprises belonging to the imperialists and put them under the control of the worker-peasant and soldier government.
5. To confiscate the whole of the plantations and property belonging to the imperialists and Vietnamese reactionary capitalist class and distribute them to poor peasants.
6. To implement the 8 hours working day.
7. To abolish public loans and poll tax. To waive unjust taxes hitting the poor people.
8. To bring back all freedoms to the masses.
9. To carry out universal education.
10. To implement equality between man and woman.

Source: *Ho Chi Minh, Selected Works* (Hanoi: Foreign Languages Publishing House, 1961), vol. II, 145–148.

DOCUMENT 1-3

Declaration of Independence of the Democratic Republic of Vietnam, September 2, 1945

The Declaration of Independence of the Democratic Republic of Vietnam proclaimed by Ho Chi Minh on September 2, 1945, before a large crowd in Hanoi.

All men are created equal. They are endowed by their Creator with certain inalienable rights, among these are Life, Liberty and the pursuit of Happiness.

This immortal statement was made in the Declaration of Independence of the United States of America in 1776. In a broader sense, this means: All the peoples on the earth are equal from birth, all the peoples have a right to live, to be happy and free.

The Declaration of the French Revolution made in 1791 on the Rights of Man and the Citizen also states: "All men are born free and with equal rights, and must always remain free and have equal rights."

Those are undeniable truths.

Nevertheless, for more than eighty years, the French imperialists, abusing the standard of Liberty, Equality and Fraternity, have violated our Fatherland and oppressed our fellow-citizens. They have acted contrary to the ideals of humanity and justice.

In the field of politics, they have deprived our people of every democratic liberty.

(continued)

DOCUMENT 1-3 Continued

They have enforced inhuman laws. They have set up three distinct regimes in the North, the Centre and the South of Viet Nam, in order to wreck our national unity and prevent our people from being united.

They have built more prisons than schools. They have mercilessly slain our patriots; they have drowned our uprisings in rivers of blood.

They have fettered public opinion; they have practiced obscurantism against our people.

To weaken our race they have forced us to use opium and alcohol.

In the field of economics, they have fleeced us to the backbone, impoverished our people and devastated our land.

They have robbed us of our rice fields, our mines, our forests and our raw materials. They have monopolized the issuing of bank-notes and the export trade.

They have invented numerous unjustifiable taxes and reduced our people, especially our peasantry, to a state of extreme poverty.

They have hampered the prospering of our national bourgeoisie; they have mercilessly exploited our workers.

In the autumn of 1940, when the Japanese fascists violated Indo-China's territory to establish new bases in their fight against the Allies, the French imperialists went down on their bended knees and handed over our country to them.

Thus, from that date, our people were subjected to the double yoke of the French and the Japanese. Their sufferings and miseries increased. The result was that from the end of last year to the beginning of this year, from Quang Tri province to the North of Viet Nam, more than two millions of our fellow-citizens died from starvation. On the 9th of March, the French troops were disarmed by the Japanese. The French colonists either fled or surrendered, showing that not only were they incapable of "protecting" us, but that, in the span of five years, they had twice sold our country to the Japanese.

On several occasions before the 9th of March, the Viet Minh League urged the French to ally themselves with it against the Japanese. Instead of agreeing to this proposal, the French colonists so intensified their terrorist activities against the Viet Minh members that before fleeing they massacred a great number of our political prisoners detained at Yen Bay and Cao Bang.

Notwithstanding all this, our fellow-citizens have always manifested towards the French a tolerant and humane attitude. Even after the Japanese putsch of March 1945, the Viet Minh League helped many Frenchmen to cross the frontier, rescued some of them from Japanese jails and protected French lives and property.

From the autumn of 1940, our country had in fact ceased to be a French colony and had become a Japanese possession.

After the Japanese had surrendered to the Allies, our whole people rose to regain our national sovereignty and to found the Democratic Republic of Viet Nam.

The truth is that we have wrested our independence from the Japanese and not from the French.

The French have fled, the Japanese have capitulated, Emperor Bao Dai has abdicated. Our people have broken the chains which for nearly a century have fettered them and have won independence for the Fatherland. Our people at the same time have overthrown the monarchic regime that has reigned supreme for dozens of centuries. In its place has been established the present Democratic Republic.

For these reasons, we, members of the Provisional Government, representing the whole Vietnamese people, declare that from now on we break off all relations of a colonial character with France; we repeal all the international obligations that France has so far subscribed to on behalf of Viet Nam and we abolish all the special rights the French have unlawfully acquired in our Fatherland.

The whole Vietnamese people, animated by a common purpose, are determined to fight to the bitter end against any attempt by the French imperialists to reconquer their country.

We are convinced that the Allied nations which at Teheran and San Francisco have acknowledged the

DOCUMENT 1-3 Continued

principles of self-determination and equality of nations will not refuse to acknowledge the independence of Viet Nam.

A people who have courageously opposed French domination for more than eighty years, a people who have fought side by side with the Allies against the fascists during these last years, such a people must be free and independent.

For these reasons, we, members of the Provisional Government of the Democratic Republic of Viet Nam, solemnly declare to the world that Viet Nam has the right to be a free and independent country—and in fact is so already. The entire Vietnamese people are determined to mobilize all their physical and mental strength, to sacrifice their lives and property in order to safeguard their independence and liberty.

Source: *Ho Chi Minh, Selected Works* (Hanoi: Foreign Languages Publishing House, 1961), vol. II, 17–21.

Chronological List of Main Events

111 BC	The Chinese invasion of Vietnam
939 AD	The end of the Chinese occupation of Vietnam
1800	The completion of the Great March to the South
1858	The beginning of the French conquest of Indochina
1890	The birth of Ho Chi Minh
1930	The organization of the Indochinese Communist Party
1940	The beginning of the Japanese occupation of Vietnam
1941	The formation of the Vietminh
1945	The establishment of the Democratic Republic of Vietnam

Study Questions

1. What military tactics did Le Loi employ to induce the Chinese to withdraw their troops from Vietnam?
2. What policies did Paul Doumer implement in an effort to turn the French colonies in Southeast Asia into profitable possessions?
3. Why was Ho Chi Minh more successful than Phan Boi Chau in organizing a national resistance movement to free Vietnam from the clutches of French imperialism?
4. Would the French have been able to maintain their Indochina empire if the Japanese had not embarked on a military program to dominate East Asia?

2

The Dream of a Pax Americana

Continuing, or even maintaining, Japan's economic recovery depends upon keeping Communism out of Southeast Asia, promoting economic recovery there and in further developing those countries, together with Indonesia, the Philippines, Southern Korea and India as the principal trading areas for Japan.

JOINT REPORT OF THE STATE AND DEFENSE DEPARTMENTS, 1950

BLUEPRINTS FOR A NEW WORLD ORDER

Even before the United States formally entered World War II, American leaders began making plans for the creation of a peaceful and prosperous international order after hostilities ceased. President Franklin D. Roosevelt and his State Department advisers hoped to establish a liberal capitalist world system based on the principle of equal commercial opportunity. Confident that the United States would emerge from the conflict with a preponderance of military and economic power, they aimed to promote an open door policy that would give all industrial countries equal access to raw materials and commodity markets around the globe. American leaders realized that Great Britain would no longer be able to rule the world in the interest of free trade, and they believed that the United States should be prepared to fill the power vacuum. Just as the last century had belonged to England, they hoped that an Allied victory over the Axis would mark the dawn of an American century. In short, they envisioned the establishment of a Pax Americana that would replace the Pax Britannica and thereby sustain the capitalist epoch.

One nightmare, however, haunted American leaders when they contemplated the nature of the postwar world. Following the stock market crash on Wall Street in 1929, the United States had plunged into the decade-long Great Depression. Businessmen shut down plants and laid off workers because of a lack of demand for consumer goods, and as unemployment increased and household spending declined, more companies closed their doors. President Roosevelt launched his New Deal program to counteract the vicious circle, but economic recovery did not come until the onset of World War II. When the shooting started in Europe in 1939, American factories began receiving orders for a vast array of weapons and munitions from both the U.S. government and the Allied nations. The stimulus of military spending turned the wheels of industry and created jobs for those without work. Though pleased about the wartime prosperity, Roosevelt and his advisers feared that when the demand for military hardware declined at the end of the war, the twin problems of overproduction and unemployment would return to plague the United States.

Top government officials and corporate executives who participated in the decision-making process understood that there were two different ways of avoiding a postwar depression in the United States. Either they could plan the American economy so that domestic production would match the requirements of the home market, or they could obtain foreign markets to absorb the surplus output of the farms and factories in the United States. American policymakers rejected the option of centralized economic planning to create an internal balance between supply and demand because they believed that excessive governmental controls would destroy the essentials of free enterprise. Fearing that an extension of New Deal regulations would undermine entrepreneurial freedom by taking management decisions out of private hands, American leaders chose the alternative of overseas commercial expansion to solve the problem of domestic overproduction. And their belief that political liberty depended on economic freedom reinforced their determination to open new frontiers in the markets throughout the world in hopes of preserving capitalism in the United States.

President Roosevelt and Secretary of State Cordell Hull also hoped to promote world peace by liberalizing international commerce. During the Great Depression, many manufacturing nations had erected high tariff walls around both their internal and their colonial markets. The consequent decline in the volume of world trade had a particularly harmful impact on countries that did not have enough natural resources to sustain themselves in economic isolation. Germany and Japan, after being denied access to essential foodstuffs and raw materials, led a group of these "have-not nations" in an attempt to redivide the world in order to satisfy their material needs. Although American policymakers assumed that the Allies would defeat the Axis drive to partition the planet into exclusive spheres of influence, they feared that a resumption of economic nationalism in the postwar era would sow the seeds for yet another global conflict. They were therefore intent on establishing a liberal international trading system after the war so that "have-not nations" such as Germany and Japan could achieve prosperity by engaging in peaceful commerce rather than military conquest.

During their postwar planning sessions between 1941 and 1945, State Department officials drafted blueprints for the creation of a peaceful and prosperous international capitalist utopia. They carefully advanced a multidimensional economic program embracing the following five key points: (1) the extension of American loans to underwrite the economic reconstruction of industrial countries that had been devastated by the long military ordeal, (2) the reintegration of Germany into the global economy, (3) the limitation of armaments in order to permit small countries to devote their sparse resources to economic rehabilitation rather than military preparation, (4) the reduction of American tariffs in order to allow foreign countries to increase their exports to the United States and thereby earn dollars that they could use to purchase American products, and (5) the modification of the European imperial preference systems to give all nations equal access to raw materials and commodity markets in colonial areas such as British Malaya, Dutch Indonesia, and French Indochina.

The architects of the new world order spent much of their time in the State Department discussing the dangers of colonialism. Stanley Hornbeck, Leo Pasvolsky, and others pointed out not only that the continuation of colonial monopolies in the postwar period would undermine American economic interests but that imperial preferences might even provoke dynamic "have-not nations" into taking aggressive actions that would culminate in World War III. These State Department experts also noted that continued colonial exploitation might stimulate a wave of revolutionary upheavals throughout the Third World. They were particularly worried that the imperial policies of the British, Dutch, and French in the Far East would give rise to a strong anticolonial movement under the banner of "Asia for the Asians." Many nationalists, noncommunist as well as communist, were talking about the need for a united Asian crusade to end European rule in the Far East. American diplomats feared that such a pan-Asiatic movement would threaten the economic interests of the United States along with the other industrial countries around the world.

Disturbed by such dismal prospects, the postwar planners in the State Department sponsored an ambitious trusteeship scheme to solve the troublesome problem of colonialism. They proposed that all dependent areas should be administered by either a single trustee country or a group of trustees acting under the auspices of the United Nations (UN). These trustees would be responsible for helping the colonial peoples under their guardianship attain political maturity. By progressively introducing measures of self-government in dependent regions, the trustees were to prepare their wards for eventual independence. The plan also called on the trustee nations to promote economic development in colonial areas for the benefit of both the native populations and the rest of the world. The trustees would therefore be required to open the territories under their tutelage to the trade and investments of all countries, regardless of their size. Under Secretary of State Sumner Welles stressed this point when he told his subordinates in the State Department that the issue of equal access to natural resources and commodity markets was "the keystone of the whole structure of trusteeship for dependent areas."

President Roosevelt gave the trusteeship proposal strong support. He liked to point out that during the last four decades the United States had been preparing the Philippine Islands for self-government, and he frequently suggested that the American treatment of the Philippines should serve as a model for the European powers to emulate. Roosevelt believed that colonial peoples should go through an interim period of international guardianship until they were ready for independence. He thought that the training period might be as short as a decade or so for advanced areas like Indochina—and as long as a century or more for backward regions like Borneo. Although he was a gradualist with regard to the decolonization question, Roosevelt emphasized the need for the European powers to fix definite timetables for granting independence to their wards. He insisted that dependent peoples should not be held in tutelage after they were able to stand on their own feet. In a nutshell, Roosevelt regarded the trusteeship interval as a transitional stage along the road from the colonialism of the past to the self-determinism of the future.

President Roosevelt and his counselors in the State Department also planned to establish an international security system based on the Big Four police powers. After disarming their Axis enemies at the end of the war, the United States, Great Britain, Soviet Russia, and China were to cooperate with each other in maintaining world peace. Although China was weak and divided, American leaders insisted that the disorganized Asian giant must be included in the Big Four. They hoped that China would eventually become an important trading partner, military ally, and valuable political associate that would support American positions in the United Nations. Their grand strategy called for Russia and Britain to shoulder most of the burden for keeping the peace in Europe, while the United States would assume primary responsibility for maintaining security in the Western Hemisphere and the Pacific Ocean. Realizing the need for distant naval and air bases, American policymakers decided that the United States would have to maintain complete control of the islands that had been taken from Japan during the sweep across the Pacific.

At first, Secretary Hull and his aides in the State Department did not think that France would play a major strategic role in the postwar world. Although the French had a huge army on the European continent when World War II began, they surrendered to Germany within six weeks after Hitler launched his *blitzkrieg* against the western front. Then, they quickly began collaborating with both the Germans in Europe and the Japanese in Indochina. As a result, American diplomats regarded France as a third-rate power. They not only viewed the French with contempt because of their anemic war record, they also blamed them for having caused an arms race in Europe. The United States had tried to get France to enter into an arms limitation agreement after World War I, but the French, wanting to maintain military superiority on the continent, had refused. Many smaller European countries then followed the French in building up their military forces. Recalling that Hitler had used the French refusal to disarm as an excuse for rearming Germany, American policymakers reasoned that France should be disarmed when the current conflict ended.

In addition, during their early deliberations, neither President Roosevelt nor his State Department advisors thought that Indochina should be returned to France after the war. American leaders issued public statements to the contrary in an effort to get the French to resist their Nazi oppressors. But they made it quite clear in their private conversations that Indochina should be administered by international trustees. "There is a great moral question involved here," Under Secretary Welles observed in August 1942, "and it is a question that will shape and color the history of the world after this war is over." However, when Great Britain registered strong objections to their decolonization plans, State Department officials concluded that only the areas taken from enemy countries during the two world wars should be placed under international trusteeship. They believed that the Allied nations should continue managing their colonies while preparing them for independence and permitting them to trade freely with all countries. But the president insisted that France should be treated differently from the other colonial powers. During a discussion with Hull in January 1944, Roosevelt firmly stated that France must not be allowed to regain possession of Indochina. "France has milked it for 100 years," he declared. "The people of Indochina are entitled to something better than that."

American leaders hoped that their Russian allies would support their plans for the postwar era. After crossing through Eastern Europe, the German Wehrmacht had penetrated deep into the Soviet Union. Millions of Russians were dying in defense of their homeland, and the Nazi armies were destroying thousands of Soviet factories. Seeking to reduce Russian fears about a future German invasion, American officials indicated that the United States would participate in policing the postwar world. They also thought that they might be able to win Soviet cooperation in Eastern Europe by offering American loans for Russian economic reconstruction. But the apprehension grew in Washington that the Russians would attempt to dominate the countries of Eastern Europe in order to satisfy their own security needs. As they became increasingly concerned about the likelihood of Soviet expansion on the European continent if both Germany and France were disarmed, American leaders began thinking that France should resume her traditional position as a principal European power. And by November 1944, they concluded that it would be necessary to rearm France with American weapons.

After reversing himself with regard to the issue of French militarism, President Roosevelt also began changing his mind about the question of French colonialism. Roosevelt wanted to postpone making a final decision concerning Indochina until the peace settlement following the war, but after the Yalta Conference in February 1945, evidence was growing that the Soviet Union aimed to dominate Poland and other countries in Eastern Europe. In a discussion with the American ambassador in Paris on March 13, General Charles de Gaulle pointed to the Russian menace to Europe in an attempt to blackmail the United States into supporting the restoration of the French empire in Indochina. "The Russians are advancing apace," de Gaulle warned. "When Germany falls they will be upon us. If the public here comes to realize that you are against us in

Indochina there will be terrific disappointment and nobody knows to what that will lead. We do not want to become Communist; we do not want to fall into the Russian orbit, but I hope that you do not push us into it." On the next day, Roosevelt told one of his close advisers that he would agree to let the French retain their colonies in Indochina with the proviso of independence as the ultimate goal.

Although Roosevelt died a month later and Vice President Harry S Truman entered the White House, there was no sharp break in American policy toward Indochina. The State Department assumed the difficult task of attempting to reconcile American objectives in Europe and Asia. On the one hand, American diplomats thought that the United States should allow the French to keep their Indochina empire in order to maintain France as a military ally in the event of future Russian aggression in Europe. On the other hand, they believed that the United States should urge the French to grant local autonomy in their Southeast Asian possessions in order to prevent bloodshed in Vietnam. The State Department adopted these views on April 30 in a key policy paper that held the United States should not oppose the restoration of French authority in Vietnam, Laos, and Cambodia but that American officials should seek assurance of French intentions to establish self-government in Indochina. A few days later, at the first meeting in San Francisco to create the United Nations, Secretary of State Edward R. Stettinius told the French ambassador that the United States had never questioned the sovereignty of his country in Indochina.

THE FIRST INDOCHINA WAR

The French were eager to reestablish control over their Indochina colonies. Although Germany had delivered a sharp blow to their national pride by defeating and occupying their country, the French did not want to reassert their imperial authority simply because of a psychological need to compensate for the humiliation they had suffered at the hands of Hitler. Cosmopolitan French leaders were prompted by rational calculations rather than emotional feelings. The influential directors of the Bank of Indochina, hoping to safeguard their huge investments, demanded protection for French economic interests in Vietnam. Concerned about maintaining the cohesion of their overseas empire as a whole, policymakers in Paris subscribed to the "tenpin theory," which held that if one French colony won its independence, nationalism would be encouraged elsewhere in their empire. If the first tenpin tumbled, it would strike others, and they in turn could bring down the whole stand. More specifically, should Vietnam fall to the forces of nationalism, the French might lose not only their economically less important colonies in Southeast Asia (Cambodia and Laos) but also their more valuable possessions in North Africa (Morocco, Tunisia, and Algeria).

Following the Japanese surrender in August 1945, the French received quiet assistance from the Truman administration when they decided to dispatch an expeditionary force to reconquer Vietnam. President Truman refused to recognize the Democratic Republic of Vietnam founded by Ho Chi Minh, and his State Department advisers indicated that the American government had no thought of opposing the restoration of French rule in Indochina. But the United States did not merely acquiesce in the French endeavor to destroy the DRV and regain their Indochina empire. Although State Department officials published a statement promising that their country would not participate in the forceful reimposition of French authority in Indochina, American policymakers acted in ways that ran counter to their public posture of neutrality. The United States permitted the French not only to keep without payment the American military equipment and supplies that had been furnished to General de Gaulle before the Japanese capitulation but also to use these materials in Indochina after all the American insignia had been removed. In addition, the United States provided a large number of ships for the transport of French troops and American weapons to Vietnam.

While the American government attempted to conceal these actions, Great Britain openly supported the French campaign to recolonize Indochina. The Allied powers had agreed, at the Potsdam Conference in July 1945, that after the war, the responsibility for disarming and repatriating the Japanese troops in French Indochina would go to the British in the region south of the sixteenth parallel and to the Chinese in the area north of that parallel. The first British troops arrived in Saigon on September 12, and a small detachment of French soldiers accompanied them. General Douglas D. Gracey, the commander of the British forces, promptly ordered the Vietnamese inhabitants of Saigon to turn over their weapons. When the Vietminh called a general strike in protest on September 17, General Gracey responded by proclaiming martial law, suspending all Vietnamese newspapers, and banning demonstrations of any kind. Gracey also released from prison and armed 1,400 French soldiers who had been interned by the Japanese after their March coup. The French troops immediately took over the public buildings in Saigon and stormed down the streets looking for Vietnamese to beat.

The brutal French rampage set the stage in southern Vietnam for the outbreak of a war for national liberation. The Vietminh called a general strike on September 24, and it soon became difficult to get food and supplies into Saigon. With insufficient British and French troops to restore order and expand his control beyond the city, General Gracey decided to use the Japanese soldiers he had been sent to disarm. Gracey threatened to treat Japanese officers as war criminals if they refused to order their men to help subdue the Vietminh. When the first military units arrived from France on October 5, they joined with the British and Japanese in cracking the blockade around Saigon and then in driving through the Mekong Delta. The Vietminh retreated into the highlands and resorted to guerrilla tactics. The Japanese, after suffering heavy casualties in the intense fighting, were gradually disarmed and replaced by reinforcements from France. As their numbers grew, the French were able to administer the larger cities and provincial towns in southern Vietnam. But they could not prevent the Vietminh guerrillas from controlling the surrounding countryside.

In northern Vietnam, by contrast, the Vietminh exercised firm control of urban as well as rural areas. The government established by Ho Chi Minh in Hanoi following the revolution in August 1945 enjoyed widespread public support. Even Catholic priests backed the Vietminh regime after Ho initiated a reformist rather than a communist program. Besides allowing native landlords who had not collaborated with the foreign enemies to keep their large holdings, the Vietminh wiped out the salt monopoly, abolished the forced labor system, reduced land taxes, legalized unions, and instituted an eight-hour workday. Gambling and prostitution were banned, the use of opium and alcohol was prohibited, and free classes were set up to teach the illiterate masses how to read and write. In addition to introducing these social and economic reforms, the Vietminh established a system of universal suffrage to bring more people into the political process. All men and women over eighteen years of age were given the right to vote on both the local and the national level.

Vietminh efforts to implement this liberal program in northern Vietnam were suddenly disrupted on September 9, however, when the first Chinese forces arrived in Hanoi to disarm the Japanese. General Lu Han, a warlord from southern China, led between 125,000 and 150,000 troops into famine-stricken Tonkin. Swarming down from China like a ravenous horde of human locusts, these soldiers plundered and looted everything in their path. Their officers were even more destructive. Establishing a new exchange rate between the Chinese dollar and the Vietnamese piaster, General Lu Han made Chinese money worth three times more in Hanoi than at home. The Chinese then began using their overvalued currency to buy local businesses and property at little cost to themselves. Unlike the British in the south, Lu Han had no intention of helping the French regain control of northern Vietnam. Instead, he was willing to let the Vietminh govern Tonkin while his army gouged the whole region. Lu Han and his cohorts in southern China viewed the occupation of northern Vietnam as an opportunity to impose their own long-range program of economic exploitation in Indochina.

The nationalist government in China headed by Generalissimo Chiang Kai-shek, however, had different ideas. Uninterested in controlling any part of Indochina on a permanent basis, Chiang viewed the Chinese occupation of northern Vietnam as a chance to extract political concessions from France. The Generalissimo succeeded in working out a deal with the French on the last day of February 1946. The French agreed to relinquish their old imperial right of extraterritoriality in China, and in return, Chiang agreed to allow French troops to replace Chinese forces in Tonkin. A week later, after Chiang had put pressure on him, Ho Chi Minh signed an ambiguous treaty with the French. Ho agreed to permit 15,000 French soldiers to land peaceably in northern Vietnam, with the understanding that they would be gradually withdrawn during the next five years. For their part, the French agreed to recognize the Democratic Republic of Vietnam as a free state, but only on the condition that it would remain part of the French Union. Finally, both parties agreed that there would be a referendum in Cochinchina to determine whether it would be reunited with the rest of Vietnam or remain a separate state in the French Union.

Ho Chi Minh had signed this unpalatable treaty with the French in order to get the Chinese out of Vietnam. When many of his comrades accused him of making a bad deal, Ho answered his critics with a lesson in geopolitics. "You fools," he lectured. "Don't you realize what it means if the Chinese remain? Don't you remember your history? The last time the Chinese came, they stayed a thousand years. The French are foreigners. They are weak. Colonialism is dying. The white man is finished in Asia. But if the Chinese stay now, they will never go. As for me, I prefer to sniff French shit for five years than to eat Chinese shit for the rest of my life." But the French had no intention of abiding by the provisions of their agreement with Ho. Realizing that the vast majority of the peasants would vote for reunification with the rest of Vietnam, they refused to hold a plebiscite in Cochinchina. The French also revealed their true colors when they rejected a Vietminh request for a cease-fire in southern Vietnam.

Hoping to avoid a war with France, Ho Chi Minh traveled to Paris in the spring of 1946 to do what he could to work out a peaceful settlement. But during the ensuing discussions, neither side would abandon their basic aims. The French were not interested in making peace if it meant losing their Indochina empire, and Ho was not willing to make peace if it meant sacrificing the independence of his country. "If we must fight, we will fight," Ho warned his French hosts. "You will kill ten of our men and we will kill one of yours. Yet, in the end, it is you who will tire." Ho left Paris empty-handed after months of fruitless negotiations, and when he arrived home in the autumn of 1946, he found that both his compatriots and their French adversaries were preparing for a military showdown. While the French continued building up their troop strength in Vietnam, General Vo Nguyen Giap increased the size of his regular army from 30,000 to 60,000 men. The clash soon came. On November 23, the French navy shelled Vietminh positions in the port of Haiphong, and when the Vietminh army attacked French troops in Hanoi on December 19, a general war erupted.

After he had ignored repeated pleas from Ho Chi Minh for American support for Vietnamese independence, President Truman decided to assist France. The Cold War against the Soviet Union had begun to unfold, and Truman, along with his advisers in the State Department, chose not to exert pressure on Paris to make concessions that might end the bloodletting in

Indochina for fear that France would refuse to help check the spread of Russian influence in Europe. Their Europe-first mentality was reinforced by their increasing concern about the communist leadership of the Vietminh. But while American policymakers preferred French colonialism over Vietnamese communism, they did not want to be charged with sponsoring Western imperialism in the Far East. Thus, they tried to camouflage American aid for the French military campaign in Vietnam by channeling most of it indirectly through metropolitan France. The United States sent France huge amounts of money and large quantities of weapons, ostensibly for French economic reconstruction and European strategic protection. But American officials realized that the French were using a considerable portion of this military and financial assistance to sustain their war effort in Indochina.

Even with the aid they were receiving from the United States, however, the French still could not defeat the Vietminh. Beginning in December 1946, General Giap launched a series of intense attacks against French positions in the principal towns of Tonkin. But his poorly armed troops were no match for the overwhelming French firepower, and they were quickly driven out of the urban areas. The Vietminh then turned to guerrilla warfare in the north, as they had done earlier in the south, fighting chiefly at night when it was hard for the French to bomb them from the air or batter them with heavy ground artillery. Their hit-and-run tactics frustrated the French, who had difficulty separating the guerrilla forces from the general population. The Vietminh frequently infiltrated villages and fired at French troops, and the French often responded by destroying the villages and killing many innocent civilians. As a result, more and more enraged peasants either joined the guerrillas or at least gave them information about French movements. So although the French were able to exercise their authority in most of the cities and towns throughout Vietnam, the Vietminh controlled over half the countryside and over half the population.

Even so, the French were determined to crush the Vietminh. In October 1947, they mounted a major offensive against the Vietminh base area in the mountains north of Hanoi. The French captured large stores of Vietminh food and ammunition, yet they could not destroy their elusive foe. The guerrillas easily disappeared into the jungle when they heard the distant roar of French tanks and trucks rumbling along the narrow roads. Not only were the gains minimal, the costs were prohibitive. As the overextended French soldiers retreated slowly down the roads winding through the jungle-covered mountains of northern Tonkin, the Vietminh staged ambush after ambush, and the French suffered heavy casualties: over 1,000 killed and over 3,000 wounded. The Vietminh were encouraged by their success, and early in 1948, they increased their attacks on isolated French outposts and exposed French convoys.

Unable to win a decisive battlefield victory, the French soon began to search for a political solution to their troubles in Indochina. They ultimately decided to install a puppet government in Vietnam under former Emperor Bao Dai with the hope of uniting all noncommunist nationalists behind the new regime. Bao Dai had fled to Hong Kong after the establishment of the Democratic Republic of Vietnam, but the French succeeded in persuading him to return home and assume the appearance of power. In an agreement with Bao Dai in June 1948, the French declared their recognition of Vietnamese independence within the framework of the French Union. Yet the status of Cochinchina remained unsettled, and Vietnamese nationalists were skeptical about French intentions. In a second agreement with Bao Dai in March 1949, the French promised that Cochinchina would be reunited with Annam and Tonkin, but they stipulated that both the military affairs and the foreign relations of Vietnam must remain in their hands. Because the French were not willing to grant Bao Dai real independence, most noncommunist nationalists refused to back his regime. And since many of these conservatives concluded that they had no alternative but to follow Ho Chi Minh, the Vietminh achieved complete control of the Vietnamese resistance movement.

The Cold War confrontation between capitalism and communism reached into East Asia while Bao Dai was struggling to establish his authority in Vietnam. In October 1949, after their victory over the nationalists in the Chinese civil war, Mao Zedong and his communist associates founded the People's Republic of China (PRC). American policymakers assumed that Mao would institute a dictatorship in Beijing and impose severe restrictions on Western trade and investment in China, as Joseph Stalin had done in the Soviet Union. But they had different expectations about how the Chinese communists would behave toward neighboring countries. On the optimistic side, some hoped that conflicting national interests would keep the Chinese and Russians from forming a gigantic communist bloc. On the pessimistic side, others feared that Mao would join hands with Stalin and promote the spread of communism throughout the Far East. The apprehensions of the pessimists grew in January 1950 when both the PRC and the Soviet Union established official diplomatic relations with the Democratic Republic of Vietnam.

Determined to contain the cancer of communism, President Truman formally recognized the Bao Dai government in February 1950 even though it lacked popular support. He also responded favorably when French officials said that they needed more American money to sustain their war effort in Indochina. Secretary of State Dean G. Acheson worried that every franc the French spent in Vietnam would mean one less franc they could use to maintain their military strength in Europe. Along with his desire to help France stand as a bulwark against the Soviet Union, Acheson hoped to use financial aid as a lever to compel the French not only to approve American plans to rearm West Germany but also to grant independence to the Bao Dai regime. But the French leaders reacted to pressure from Washington by warning that without an increase in American assistance, they might have to withdraw from Vietnam. Although the French remained intransigent, President Truman approved a $15 million aid package on March 10 to underwrite French military operations in Indochina. That seemingly small step, however, marked a major shift in American policy as the United States began providing overt rather than covert support for French colonialism.

THE CRISIS OF WORLD CAPITALISM

The decision by the Democratic administration of Harry Truman to give the French overt support grew out of concerns over a profound dislocation in the international economic system following World War II. The United States had enormously expanded its industrial capacity during the war, and American leaders realized the need for an enlarged export trade to avoid falling back into the depths of a depression. They also understood that the industrial countries of Europe needed to import capital goods from the United States to get their devastated factories running once again. But the European nations, victors and vanquished alike, did not have enough dollars to pay for the vital products that they needed to buy from the United States. American leaders referred to this global economic disequilibrium as the "dollar gap" in world trade. The United States was exporting far more than it was importing, and as the American export surplus grew, the dollar gap widened. In fact, the trade imbalance ballooned from $7.8 billion in 1946 to $11.6 billion a year later.

European countries responded to their shortage of dollars by resorting to a wide range of controls over their international economic transactions. They aimed to conserve their dollars by using them only for essential capital goods and not for less important products. European nations not only limited the amount of their currency that could be converted into dollars for the purchase of American merchandise, they also erected high tariffs to protect their domestic industries from American competition. Besides impeding the flow of trade across the Atlantic with monetary restrictions and customs barriers, Europeans entered into bilateral barter arrangements that violated the principle of equal economic opportunity and closed more doors against American commerce. Government officials and business leaders in the United States feared that if the dollar gap remained unsolved, these measures of economic nationalism would become permanent and thereby shatter the American dream of a liberal capitalist international community.

The Marshall Plan, formally called the European Recovery Program (ERP), was the major American response to the crisis of world capitalism. Between 1948 and 1952, the United States provided the nations of Western Europe with $17 billion in grants for the renovation of their war-torn industries. Policymakers in Washington decided to give rather than loan the money because if the Europeans had to repay huge debts to the United States, they would have fewer dollars available to purchase American commodities. But while they did not demand any monetary compensation, American leaders insisted that countries receiving ERP funding must cut wages, lower taxes, reduce social welfare spending, and deflate their currencies. The basic goal of the Marshall Plan was not only to modernize the industries of Western Europe but also to make them competitive in the markets of the world. If the Europeans lowered the price of their industrial products and regained their ability to sell abroad, they could earn foreign exchange needed to buy American goods.

The State Department assumed the difficult task of convincing Congress about the need for the European Recovery Program. When the time came each year for Congress to appropriate funds for European recovery, State Department officials asserted that the Marshall Plan was only a temporary measure required to meet an emergency and claimed that the program was a great success. Industrial production was increasing in the nations of Western Europe, but these countries did not have adequate export markets where they could acquire dollars needed to purchase American merchandise. After giving repeated assurances about the success of the Marshall Plan, however, Secretary Acheson and his colleagues in the State Department realized that Congress could not be expected to make additional appropriations to extend the program. Acheson explained the situation to President Truman in February 1950: "Put in its simplest terms the problem is this: As ERP is reduced, and after its termination in 1952, how can Europe and other areas of the world obtain the dollars necessary to pay for a high level of United States exports, which is essential both to their own basic needs and to the well-being of the United States economy? This is the problem of the 'dollar gap' in world trade."

Before the dollar gap had created a serious international economic crisis, many government officials and business leaders hoped that China would become a golden market for the United States. They were captivated by the vision of a New China, containing 400 million customers, emerging from the ashes of World War II as a modern nation under the conservative leadership of Chiang Kai-shek. In their eyes, El Dorado beckoned from across the Pacific. But to keep the potentially vast China market free from the danger of foreign domination, the United States needed to declaw the Japanese dragon. General Douglas MacArthur was therefore commissioned to occupy Japan as soon as the war came to a close. Between 1945 and 1947, the American occupational authorities disarmed Japan and purged the military caste to prevent the old warlords from ever again threatening the peace of the Far East. The American authorities also aimed during the first two years of the military occupation to destroy the *zaibatsu* system of family capitalism in Japan and thereby render the interlocking monopolies less capable of manufacturing the sinews of war.

When it became evident that Mao Zedong and his communist followers would emerge triumphant in China, however, the United States quickly reversed the course of its occupational policy in Japan. Beginning in 1947, American administrators in that country shifted their emphasis away from political reform and toward economic recovery. Policymakers in Washington decided that the Japanese industrial structure should be rebuilt so that Japan could replace China as a large market for American products. They wanted Japan to be part of the trilateral core in a new liberal capitalist world system: The United States would be the major workshop in the Western Hemisphere; Western Europe would be a regional workshop centered around West Germany; and Japan would be the industrial workshop in the Far East. American policymakers also decided that the Japanese should be rearmed so that Japan could replace China as an important military ally of the United States. They wanted Japan to serve as the sheet anchor in an island chain of American military bases around the Asian rim. In short, Japan was to play a key role as a junior economic and strategic partner in the evolving Pax Americana.

The United States implemented the so-called Dodge Plan in 1949 in an effort to promote the postwar reconstruction of Japan. Like the Marshall Plan for Western Europe, the basic goal of the Dodge Plan was to revive industrial production in Japan and to make Japanese goods competitive in world markets. The United States did not, however, funnel billions of dollars into Japan for industrial renovation. Unlike the Europeans, the Japanese were forced to finance their own economic rehabation. In addition, the Dodge Plan required severe cuts in wages and social welfare services and the reinvestment of profits in plant modernization. It also demanded a balanced budget as well as the suppression of labor strikes to keep inflation down and prices low. But the Dodge Plan failed for the very same reason that the Marshall Plan proved inadequate. Although their industrial output increased, the Japanese lacked export outlets where they could acquire foreign exchange needed to purchase American goods. Thus, Japan, like the countries of Western Europe, continued to suffer from a large dollar deficit.

The State Department advocated a massive increase in military spending as a short-run solution to the dollar gap problem. If American corporations received large orders from the armed forces of the United States, they would be able to run profitably despite a drop in civilian demand for their commodities in countries suffering from a shortage of dollars. Companies in Western Europe and Japan, moreover, would be able to earn dollars if they could sell military equipment to the United States. Under the Mutual Defense Assistance Program, conceived by diplomats in Washington, the offshore procurement of armaments for the rapidly expanding American military forces would replace foreign economic aid as a way of funneling dollars to Western Europe and Japan. State Department officials succeeded in persuading Congress to appropriate funds for a vast military buildup by playing up public fears of an international communist conspiracy to dominate the whole world. But the Mutual Defense Assistance Program was intended more as an interim solvent for the global economic crisis than as a check against the exaggerated Red Menace.

The State Department simultaneously called for the reintegration of colonial areas into a liberal international trading system as the long-run solution to the dollar gap problem. Before World War II, an important triangular trade pattern had evolved: The United States used dollars to buy raw materials from colonial areas, which in turn used these dollars to purchase industrial goods from European countries, which then used the same dollars to pay for American products. For example, the United States purchased large quantities of rubber and tin from British Malaya with dollars, and British Malaya bought manufactured articles from Great Britain with these dollars, and finally, the Great Britain paid for American commodities with the same dollars. State Department officials hoped to reestablish this kind of triangular trade flow in order to restore international economic equilibrium, and they succeeded in getting federal funds earmarked for increasing the production of foodstuffs and raw materials in colonial areas. The precedent for this form of economic assistance was set in February 1950, when the Export-Import Bank received authorization to lend Indonesia $100 million to buy American equipment needed for the development of natural resources.

American policymakers believed that the expansion of primary commodity production in Southeast Asia was particularly important for the restoration of Japanese prosperity. They hoped that Japan would be able not only to obtain foodstuffs and raw materials in Southeast Asia without paying dollars for these essential imports but also to earn dollars by exporting manufactured goods to Southeast Asia. American leaders thought that in some parts of Southeast Asia, the introduction of more irrigation would allow the cultivation of two rice crops per year instead of the prevailing single crop. And if these areas doubled their rice yield, they might also double their purchases of industrial products from Japan. Aiming to stimulate mineral and agricultural production throughout Southeast Asia, American economic experts estimated that by 1955, the region could absorb more than 50 percent of Japan's total exports. China had been Japan's most important market in the Far East before World War II, but after China fell to communism in 1949, American diplomats feared that Japan, if denied access to noncommunist markets in Southeast Asia, might become economically dependent on Red China and be lured into making a political accommodation with the communist bloc. Thus, they hoped that Southeast Asia would become Japan's major market in the Far East.

Although the economic task of increasing the production of primary commodities in that part of the world would not require a large amount of American capital, the United States faced a more difficult problem: Southeast Asia lacked political stability. Communist rebels and conservative nationalists were challenging colonial rule in French Indochina, British Malaya, and the Dutch East Indies. Regarding the military pacification of the region as a prerequisite for the economic revival of Japan, American policymakers concluded that the United States would have to help contain the rising tide of revolution in Southeast Asia. Before the Japanese or anyone else could walk the commercial streets of Southeast Asia, they repeatedly argued, those streets would have to be made safe from communism. A joint report, made by the Departments of State and Defense in January 1950, went to the heart of the matter: "Continuing, or even maintaining, Japan's economic recovery depends upon keeping Communism out of Southeast Asia, promoting economic recovery there and in further developing those countries, together with Indonesia, the Philippines, Southern Korea and India as the principal trading areas for Japan."

Concerned about Japan's need for noncommunist markets in Southeast Asia, officials in both the State Department and the Pentagon regarded French Indochina as vitally important to the political stability of the entire region. They realized that Vietnam, Cambodia, and Laos could absorb only a small amount of Japanese goods, but they perceived these French colonies as the linchpin in the Great Crescent that stretched along the Asian rim from Japan all the way to India. French Indochina, while possessing little intrinsic commercial value for Japan, occupied a key strategic position between Red China to the north and the vast Malaya Archipelago to the south. Following the fall of China to communism in 1949, American policymakers subscribed to what came to be called the "domino theory," which held that if the Vietminh defeated the French in Indochina, communism would spread throughout the whole region. Guerrilla forces in other parts of Southeast Asia not only would be encouraged by the success of their neighbors in overcoming European colonialism, they would also be able to obtain weapons from nearby communist countries. American leaders therefore feared that if the Vietnam domino fell to communism, it would tip over others until finally the whole row would be knocked down.

Such dire prospects generated a debate in the State Department over the wisdom of supplying direct American aid for the French military campaign in Indochina. A few State Department officials were pessimistic about the chances for a French victory because the Vietminh had widespread backing. Noting that the French were fighting against a large portion of the Vietnamese population, these skeptics concluded that the French would ultimately lose even if they received a massive dose of American financial and technical assistance. But Secretary of State Acheson and most of his top aides argued that the United States should back the French and Bao Dai even if the odds were heavily against them. While acknowledging that Bao Dai lacked popular support, they assumed that he was the only alternative to Ho Chi Minh, who Acheson and his followers noted aimed to establish a communist government in Vietnam after he achieved his nationalist aspirations. They feared that if the French were driven out of Vietnam, the rest of Southeast Asia would be in grave danger of succumbing to the forces of communism. They also worried that the French would object to American plans to include West Germany in a multilateral European military force if the United States refused to subsidize their war effort in Indochina.

Secretary Acheson and his colleagues in the State Department were determined to resist not only the expansion of Russian influence in Europe but also the spread of indigenous communism in Southeast Asia. They understood that communism was not monolithic and that all communist leaders did not take orders from Moscow. Marshal Tito, for example, had established an independent communist regime in Yugoslavia that remained free from Soviet domination. And although Acheson admitted in May 1949 that Vietnam might in fact develop as a "National Communist State on the pattern of Yugoslavia," he thought that the United States should explore that possibility "only if every other avenue closed." While clearly preferring the puppet Bao Dai to a Titoist Ho Chi Minh, Acheson envisioned three different scenarios for the Indochina War: (1) The Vietminh might defeat the French and become tools of the Kremlin; (2) the Vietminh might win and establish an independent communist government in Vietnam that would remain free from Russian control; or (3) the French might emerge victorious and stamp out the germ of communism before it infected the whole region. Given these choices, Acheson and his associates favored French colonialism rather than either international or indigenous communism.

The State Department believed that it was imperative for economic reasons to prevent any kind of communism from sweeping across Southeast Asia. American diplomats feared that even if Asian communists steered clear of Soviet political influence, they would follow the Russian model for economic growth. By emphasizing industrial development rather than the production of primary commodities, communist countries in Southeast Asia would become more self-sufficient and less dependent on foreign commerce. Thus, the spread of economic nationalism along with indigenous communism would restrict the opportunity for Japan and the capitalist countries of Western Europe to exchange manufactured goods for foodstuffs and raw materials produced in Southeast Asia. Prompted by such thoughts, the State Department decided in February 1950 to recommend direct American financial support for the French war effort in Indochina. Acheson and his colleagues urged that the United States should furnish money but not soldiers so that the war could be fought with American equipment and French troops. As already noted, President Truman gave his approval on March 10 to the proposal to provide the French with $15 million for their military operations in Indochina.

The Korean War began three months later. In June 1950, communist North Korea launched a surprise attack across the boundary running along the thirty-eighth parallel in an effort to conquer noncommunist South Korea. President Truman promptly dispatched American combat troops to lead a United Nations military campaign to defend South Korea. After UN forces under the command of General Douglas MacArthur pushed the invaders back above the thirty-eighth parallel, Truman authorized an advance northward to unify Korea along capitalist lines. But Mao Zedong ordered human wave assaults, under Russian air cover, against UN ground troops as they moved close to the Chinese border. General MacArthur quickly retreated below the thirty-eighth parallel. During the long stalemate that followed, the president directed MacArthur to employ a limited war strategy designed to keep South Korea from falling into communist hands without risking a nuclear conflict with the Soviet Union. But MacArthur wanted to drop atomic bombs on China and liberate North Korea from communist domination. When the general publicly criticized his boss in April 1951 for refusing to expand the scope of the war, Truman fired him, and finally, in July 1953, a cease-fire agreement brought the fighting to an end.

The American involvement in the Korean War, just as in the Vietnam conflict, grew out of a determination to draw the line against the spread of communism into Southeast Asia. Although more than 30,000 American servicemen were killed in Korea, the war helped policymakers in Washington achieve several of their objectives: It prevented the South Korean domino from falling into the clutches of communism; it made it easier to obtain larger and larger appropriations from Congress to fund the French struggle against the Vietminh; and it provided an opportunity to send more and more dollars to Japan for the purchase of military equipment for American soldiers fighting in Korea. But President Truman and his State Department advisers continued to regard Japanese economic integration with Southeast Asia as the permanent remedy for the dollar gap in Japan. They also continued to worry that the Japanese would be pulled into the communist political and economic orbit if they were denied access to noncommunist markets in Southeast Asia. "Communist control of all Southeast Asia," a State Department memorandum warned in March 1952, "would remove the chief potential area for Japanese commercial development, and would so add to the already powerful mainland pulls upon Japan as to make it dubious that Japan could refrain from reaching an accommodation with the Communist bloc."

THE BAO DAI REGIME

The U.S. government, while sponsoring military action to keep the doors of Southeast Asia open to Japan and other industrial countries, advocated a political solution to the conflict in Indochina. Realizing that French colonialism was fanning the flames of Vietnamese communism, American officials repeatedly urged the French to make political concessions to Bao Dai to help him broaden his base of support. They hoped that if Bao Dai had more autonomy, he would be able to woo the noncommunist Vietnamese nationalists who were backing Ho Chi Minh. In August 1950, the Policy Planning Staff in the State Department concluded that the only hope for peace lay in getting the French to set a definite date for granting independence to Indochina. The Joint Strategic Survey Committee similarly reasoned in October 1950 that a French military victory would provide only a temporary solution to the hostilities in Indochina. Even if the French defeated the Vietminh, the committee warned, there would be renewed outbreaks of guerrilla warfare unless the French satisfied the Vietnamese demand for self-government. Thus, the committee concluded that a permanent solution to the war in Indochina depended on the ability of Bao Dai to win the hearts and minds of the Vietnamese people.

The United States and France, however, had fundamentally different objectives in the Far East. American policymakers regarded the establishment of a viable noncommunist regime in Vietnam as an essential part of their plans to incorporate Southeast Asia into an expanding liberal capitalist world system. The French, in sharp contrast, wanted to maintain their monopoly over the markets of Indochina. Washington never threatened France with a cutoff in military aid, however, even though the French were fighting against communism in order to perpetuate their colonial empire. American leaders feared that the French would withdraw their forces from Indochina if the United States stopped funding their war against the Vietminh. They also worried that the French would continue opposing American plans for West German rearmament if France lacked sufficient resources to maintain a strong army in Europe. Realizing their leverage in Washington, the French would not relinquish their imperial rule over Indochina. Nor would they permit the small American Military Assistance Advisory Group (MAAG) to participate in strategic planning in Vietnam. Despite their continued refusal to comply with the wishes of their benefactors in the United States, the French obtained increasingly large amounts of American military aid with no strings attached.

The fall of China to communism in 1949 significantly altered the strategic situation in Indochina. Although Ho Chi Minh did not want Chinese combat troops stationed in Vietnam, he did want Chinese military assistance. And in April 1950, two months after he had traveled to Beijing to meet with Mao Zedong and his comrades, Ho asked the Chinese to send military advisers as well as large quantities of weapons and supplies to help General Giap defeat the French army in Vietnam. Mao promptly ordered the formation of the Chinese Military Advisory Group (CMAG), and he also began furnishing the Vietminh with rifles, machine guns, mortars, howitzers, bazookas, munitions, clothes, medicine, and food. Determined to keep open the vital supply routes from China, Ho decided in June 1950 to launch a military campaign to eliminate the string of French forts along the Chinese border. He asked Beijing to dispatch the CMAG and a senior military advisor to coordinate the whole operation. After his arrival in Vietnam a month later to serve as the top Chinese military advisor to the Vietminh, General Chen Geng prepared an overall plan for the border campaign. Ho and Giap approved the battle plan, and in September 1950, Vietminh forces began attacking the isolated French military posts near the northern frontier of Tonkin. The French garrisons fell one by one as many of their defenders fled in panic. During the fighting, the French lost some 6,000 soldiers and abandoned 11,000 tons of ammunition.

The Truman administration was alarmed about the crushing French defeat. Responding to urgent requests from Paris for help, President Truman promptly agreed to provide an additional $33 million in military aid for the French forces in Indochina. Secretary of State Acheson thought that the French needed more than money, however, and in January 1951, he told his colleagues that the only daylight he could see lay in the possibility of building a strong and effective Vietnamese national army to help the French. Besides expressing concern about the deteriorating military situation, American leaders worried about political conditions in Vietnam. They knew that the Bao Dai regime, largely composed of wealthy landlords, did not represent the interests of the great mass of Vietnamese peasants. Therefore, during the next two years, the Truman administration tried to buy popular support for Bao Dai by supplying more than $50 million in economic and technical assistance to help buttress his puppet government.

While American leaders were pessimistic about circumstances in Vietnam, General Giap responded with optimism to his impressive victories in northern Tonkin. He and his Chinese advisers mistakenly concluded that his Vietminh forces were now strong enough to embark on a general offensive to drive the French out of the Red River valley. In January 1951, Giap led his regular troops down from their mountain retreat and launched a large-scale attack against French positions around the town of Vinh Yen, located only about twenty-five miles from Hanoi. Giap adopted the human wave tactic that the Chinese had used successfully during their initial offensive in Korea. But the French superiority in aviation and artillery proved decisive. The Vietminh lost more than 6,000 soldiers during the battle. Yet the French also suffered large losses, and their narrow victory would not have been possible without the use of American technology. The terrifying napalm bombs and the 105-millimeter howitzers that the French had obtained from the United States enabled them to avoid being overwhelmed by the Vietminh.

Giap was not deterred by his close defeat, however. He had yet to learn that napalm flames made human wave assaults a deadly and futile undertaking. Still confident that the Vietminh could take Hanoi, Giap directed two major attacks in the spring of 1951 against French positions in the Red River Delta. The results were similar to those in the battle around Vinh Yen. The

French defenders used American firepower to repulse the Vietminh attackers, and both sides sustained high losses. But while the French enjoyed a brief emotional uplift after the smoke cleared, they were unable to follow up their narrow victories over the Vietminh. And the bloody encounters convinced Giap and the Chinese Military Advisory Group that the Vietminh troops were not yet ready for a general offensive against the French. Once again, the Vietminh reverted to hit-and-run tactics, and the French once more found themselves blindly stabbing at empty spaces in the jungles of Vietnam.

General Jean de Lattre de Tassigny, the commander of the French Expeditionary Corps in Indochina, had already decided to construct a chain of defensive fortresses around the entire Red River valley. Completed in the late spring of 1951, the de Lattre Line was designed to cut off the Vietminh guerrillas from their sources of food, money, and manpower in the Tonkin Delta. But the de Lattre Line leaked like a sieve. The Vietminh walked right past the dispersed French forts at night, and by the end of 1953, the rebels controlled more than half of the villages in the Red River valley. In the meantime, de Lattre organized troops that were not engaged in static defense into mobile groups to pursue the guerrillas into the highlands. But these motorized French units, dependent on American tanks and trucks, became prisoners of the roads. The heavily equipped forces could not catch the lightly armed rebels before they disappeared into the dense jungles. Worse yet, the Vietminh coaxed the slow-moving French pursuers into one ambush after another.

The Vietminh guerrillas had one crucial advantage over the French: The great majority of the Vietnamese population sympathized with their struggle for national independence. Their evasions and ambushes succeeded because the peasants rarely informed the French about their movements. The strength of the Vietminh rebels rested on their ability to mobilize the masses. At night, the Vietminh dominated the entire countryside, including areas nominally under French

Vietminh soldiers preparing for combat against the French on January 20, 1951.
Peter Newark Military Pictures/The Bridgeman Art Library International.

control. The guerrillas were therefore able to collect taxes in the form of rice, recruit soldiers, gather information about French plans, and terrorize their opponents. In fact, the Vietminh succeeded in organizing the bulk of the Vietnamese population in their war for national liberation. While many young men joined the rebel ranks, their parents and children often made booby traps and other primitive weapons to help defeat the French.

Viewed as authentic nationalists whose ultimate aims could not be achieved until after they had fulfilled the immediate aspirations of the Vietnamese people, Ho Chi Minh and his comrades in the Democratic Republic of Vietnam did not act at all like Bao Dai and his unsavory cohorts. Vietminh agents collected a rice tax to support their cause rather than to enrich themselves. The top Vietminh leaders led spartan lives, and not even their worst enemies accused them of corruption. At the same time, the high officials in the Bao Dai regime lived in luxury at the expense of the Vietnamese people. Bao Dai himself was receiving a personal allowance in excess of $4 million a year from the U.S. government, and he was transferring large sums of money into French and Swiss banks so that he would still be wealthy if someday he were run out of Vietnam. The pathetic figurehead was little more than a playboy who especially enjoyed having illicit affairs with beautiful French women. Realizing his own position in Vietnam, he once defended one of his blonde playmates when reporters penetrated her facade. "That girl is really good in bed," Bao Dai insisted. "She is only plying her trade. I'm the real whore."

Since large amounts of American supplies as well as dollars continued to go down the drain in Vietnam, General de Lattre traveled to Washington in September 1951 to plead for more military assistance. The United States promptly began shipping the French army in Indochina over 130,000 tons of equipment, including 53 million rounds of ammunition, 200 aircraft, 650 combat vehicles, and 14,000 automatic weapons. But many of these arms and materials were either destroyed by besieged French units or captured by the Vietminh. Between December 1951 and February 1952, for example, General Giap directed a series of vicious attacks against French strongholds around Hoa Binh, located in the highlands southwest of Hanoi. The Vietminh quickly cut off both the water and the land routes to Hoa Binh, and the French lost many men and armaments attempting to reopen their lines of communication. While de Lattre lay dying from cancer in Paris, the decision was made in Indochina to abandon Hoa Binh. The French completed the evacuation with relatively light casualties, but they blew up 150 tons of supplies and ammunition because they lacked the means to transport these materials back to the Red River Delta.

At this point, despite their readiness to continue making major contributions to the French war chest, American leaders were not about to dispatch U.S. ground forces to Vietnam. The Joint Chiefs of Staff had their hands full in Korea, and they argued firmly against getting entangled in a second war on the Asian mainland. Always mindful of their worldwide strategic responsibilities, these military authorities did not want the United States to endanger the security of Europe by becoming overextended in the Far East. Many American leaders thought that Indochina might even have to be abandoned if the Chinese decided to send soldiers to help the Vietminh fight the French. But President Truman and his top advisers refused to write off Indochina. In June 1952, Truman approved a National Security Council (NSC) plan calling for the bombardment of Chinese cities and the blockade of Chinese coasts if Chinese troops swarmed into Vietnam. It was thus decided that in the event of Chinese armed intervention in Indochina, the American reaction should be limited to naval and aerial attacks against China and that the United States should avoid becoming bogged down in another Asian ground war.

The Chinese Military Advisory Group, in the meantime, proposed that the Vietminh launch a campaign against weak French positions in northwestern Tonkin and thereby open the way for a later thrust into northern Laos. After endorsing the plan, Ho Chi Minh made a secret trip to

Beijing in September 1952 to consult with Chinese leaders about a broad strategy for winning the war. The Chinese suggested that the Vietminh should first seize northwestern Tonkin and northern Laos and then move south to capture the Red River Delta. Ho agreed. On October 14, General Giap and his forces began their offensive, and by December 10, they had gained control of a vast mountainous area in northwestern Tonkin. American leaders now realized that the war had reached a stalemate. And after Dwight D. Eisenhower won the presidential election in November 1952, he met with Dean Acheson to discuss the Indochina question. The outgoing secretary of state warned him that a strong body of opinion in France regarded Indochina as a lost cause. So after his inauguration in January 1953, it would be up to President Eisenhower and John Foster Dulles, selected to replace Acheson as secretary of state, to try to figure out a way to break the military deadlock in Vietnam before the French lost their will to carry on the war.

DOCUMENT 2-1

State Department Policy Statement on Indochina prepared on September 27, 1948

A. Objectives

The immediate objective of US policy in Indochina is to assist in a solution of the present impasse which will be mutually satisfactory to the French and the Vietnamese peoples, which will result in the termination of the present hostilities, and which will be within the framework of US security.

Our long-term objectives are: (1) to eliminate so far as possible Communist influence in Indochina and to see installed a self-governing nationalist state which will be friendly to the US and which, commensurate with the capacity of the peoples involved, will be patterned upon our conception of a democratic state as opposed to the totalitarian state which would evolve inevitably from Communist domination; (2) to foster the association of the peoples of Indochina with the western powers, particularly with France with whose customs, language and laws they are familiar, to the end that those peoples will prefer freely to cooperate with the western powers culturally, economically and politically; (3) to raise the standard of living so that the peoples of Indochina will be less receptive to totalitarian influences and will have an incentive to work productively and thus contribute to a better world economy; and (4) to prevent undue Chinese penetration and subsequent influence in Indochina so

that the peoples of Indochina will not be hampered in their developments by the pressure of an alien people and alien interests.

B. Policy Issues

To attain our immediate objective, we should continue to press the French to accommodate the basic aspirations of the Vietnamese: (1) unity of Cochinchina, Annam, and Tonkin, (2) complete internal autonomy, and (3) the right to choose freely regarding participation in the French Union. We have recognized French sovereignty over Indochina but have maintained that such recognition does not imply any commitment on our part to assist France to exert its authority over the Indochinese peoples. Since V-J Day, the majority people of the area, the Vietnamese, have stubbornly resisted the reestablishment of French authority, a struggle in which we have tried to maintain insofar as possible a position of non-support for either party.

While the nationalist movement in Vietnam (Cochinchina, Annam, and Tonkin) is strong, and though the great majority of the Vietnamese are not fundamentally Communist, the most active element in the resistance of the local peoples to the French has been a Communist group headed by Ho Chi Minh. This group has successfully extended its

(continued)

DOCUMENT 2-1 Contiuned

influence to include practically all armed forces now fighting the French, thus in effect capturing control of the nationalist movement.

The French on two occasions during 1946 attempted to resolve the problem by negotiation with the government established and dominated by Ho Chi Minh. The general agreements reached were not, however, successfully implemented and widespread fighting subsequently broke out. Since early 1947, the French have employed about 115,000 troops in Indochina, with little result, since the countryside except in Laos and Cambodia remains under the firm control of the Ho Chi Minh government. A series of French-established puppet governments have tended to enhance the prestige of Ho's government and to call into question, on the part of the Vietnamese, the sincerity of French intentions to accord an independent status to Vietnam.

1. Political

We have regarded these hostilities in a colonial area as a detriment not only to our long-term interests which require as a minimum a stable Southeast Asia but also detrimental to the interests of France, since the hatred engendered by continuing hostilities may render impossible peaceful collaboration and cooperation of the French and the Vietnamese peoples. This hatred of the Vietnamese people toward the French is keeping alive anti-western feeling among oriental peoples, to the advantage of the USSR and the detriment of the US.

We have not urged the French to negotiate with Ho Chi Minh, even though he probably is now supported by a considerable majority of the Vietnamese people, because of his record as a Communist and the Communist background of many of the influential figures in and about his government.

Postwar French governments have never understood, or have chosen to underestimate, the strength of the nationalist movement with which they must deal in Indochina. It remains possible that the nationalist movement can be subverted from Communist control but this will require granting to a non-Communist group of nationalists at

least the same concessions demanded by Ho Chi Minh. The failure of French governments to deal successfully with the Indochinese question has been due, in large measure, to the overwhelming internal issues facing France and the French Union, and to foreign policy considerations in Europe. These factors have combined with the slim parliamentary majorities of postwar governments in France to militate against the bold moves necessary to divert allegiance of the Vietnamese nationalists to non-Communist leadership.

In accord with our policy of regarding with favor the efforts of dependent peoples to attain their legitimate political aspirations, we have been anxious to see the French accord to the Vietnamese the largest possible degree of political and economic independence consistent with legitimate French interests. We have therefore declined to permit the export to the French in Indochina of arms and munitions for the prosecution of the war against the Vietnamese. This policy has been limited in its effect as we have allowed the free export of arms to France, such exports thereby being available for reshipment to Indochina or for releasing stocks from reserves to be forwarded to Indochina....

D. Policy Evaluation

The objectives of US policy towards Indochina have not been realized. Three years after the termination of war a friendly ally, France, is fighting a desperate and apparently losing struggle in Indochina. The economic drain of this warfare on French recovery, while difficult to estimate, is unquestionably large. The Communist control in the nationalist movement has been increased during this period. US influence in Indochina and Southeast Asia has suffered as a result.

The objectives of US policy can only be attained by such French action as will satisfy the nationalist aspirations of the peoples of Indochina. We have repeatedly pointed out to the French the desirability of their giving such satisfaction and thus terminating the present open conflict. Our greatest difficulty in talking with the French and in stressing what should and what should not be done has been our inability to suggest any practical solution of the

DOCUMENT 2-1 Contiuned

Indochina problem, as we are all too well aware of the unpleasant fact that Communist Ho Chi Minh is the strongest and perhaps the ablest figure in Indochina and that any suggested solution which excludes him is an expedient of uncertain outcome. We are naturally hesitant to press the French too strongly or to become deeply involved so long as we are not in a position to suggest a solution or until we are prepared to accept the onus of intervention. The above considerations are further complicated by the fact that we have an immediate interest in maintaining in power a friendly French government, to assist in the furtherance of our aims in Europe. This immediate and vital interest has in consequence taken precedence over active steps looking toward the realization of our objectives in Indochina.

We are prepared, however, to support the French in every way possible in the establishment of a truly nationalist government in Indochina which, by giving satisfaction to the aspirations of the peoples of Indochina, will serve as a rallying point for the nationalists and will weaken the Communist elements. By such support and by active participation in a peaceful and constructive solution in Indochina we stand to regain influence and prestige.

Some solution must be found which will strike a balance between the aspirations of the peoples of Indochina and the interests of the French. Solution by French military reconquest of Indochina is not desirable. Neither would the complete withdrawal of the French from Indochina effect a solution. The first alternative would delay indefinitely the attainment of our objectives, as we would share inevitably in the hatred engendered by an attempted military reconquest and the denial of aspirations for self-government. The second solution would be equally unfortunate as in all likelihood Indochina would be taken over by the militant Communist group. At best, there might follow a transition period, marked by chaos and terrorist activities, creating a political vacuum into which the Chinese inevitably would be drawn or would push. The absence of stabilization in China will continue to have an important influence upon the objective of a permanent and peaceable solution in Indochina.

We have not been particularly successful in our information and education programs in orienting the Vietnamese toward the western democracies and the US. The program has been hampered by the failure of the French to understand that such informational activities as we conduct in Indochina are not inimical to their own long-term interests and by administrative and financial considerations which have prevented the development to the maximum extent of contacts with the Vietnamese. An increased effort should be made to explain democratic institutions, especially American institutions and American policy, to the Indochinese by direct personal contact, by the distribution of information about the US, and the encouraging of educational exchange.

Source: *United States Vietnamese Relations, 1945–1967: Study Prepared by the Department of Defense*, Printed for the use of the House Committee on Armed Services (Washington, D.C., Government Printing Office, 1971), Book 8, 144–148.

DOCUMENT 2-2

Problem Paper prepared by a Working Group in the State Department on February 1, 1950

Military Aid for Indochina

I. The Problem

Should the United States provide military aid in Indochina and, if so, how much and in what way.

II. Assumption

a. There will not be an effective split between the USSR and Communist China within the next three years.

(continued)

DOCUMENT 2-2   Continued

b. The USSR will not declare war on any Southeast Asian country within the next three years.

c. Communist China will not declare war on any Southeast Asian country within the next three years.

d. The USSR will endeavor to bring about the fall of Southeast Asian governments which are opposed to Communism by using all devices short of war, making use of Communist China and indigenous communists in this endeavor.

III. Facts Bearing on the Problem

1. When the Mutual Defense Assistance Act of 1949 was being written, the question of providing military aid to Southeast Asia was examined and it was decided not to include specific countries in that area, other than the Republic of the Philippines.

2. The attitude of Congress toward the provision of military and economic aid to foreign countries recently has stiffened due to both economy and to policy considerations.

3. At the same time, the Congress has shown considerable dissatisfaction with policies which are alleged to have contributed to the Communist success in China and which are involved in the current United States' approach to the question of Formosa.

4. Section 303 of the Mutual Defense Assistance Act of 1949 makes available to the President the sum of $75 million for use, at the President's discretion, in the general area of China to advance the purposes and policies of the United Nations.

5. Section 303 funds are unrestricted in their use.

6. The British Commonwealth Conference recently held in Colombo recognized that no SEA (South East Asia) regional military pact now exists due to divergent interest and that such an arrangement was now unlikely.

7. Communism has made important advances in the Far East during the past year.

8. Opposition to Communism in Indochina is actively being carried on by the three legally-constituted governments of Vietnam, Cambodia and Laos.

9. Communist-oriented forces in Indochina are being aided by Red China and the USSR.

IV. Discussion

1. Indochina has common border with China and Burma, thus making it subject to invasion by Red China.

2. Its population is some 27 million concentrated in the delta regions of the Mekong and Red Rivers. Of the total population, Chinese account for between 600,000 and a million, concentrated largely in the cities.

3. Indochina has an agricultural economy based principally on rice of which it is an exporter. World War II and its aftermath seriously disrupted the national economy. The country presently has an annual trade deficit of about $85 million.

4. There are three subdivisions of Indochina: Vietnam, Laos, and Cambodia. An agreement was signed March 8, 1949, between France and Vietnam which provides for the latter to become an Associated State within the French Union. Ratification of the Agreement, followed by the recognition of Vietnam by the West, is expected in the near future. French policy aims at making Laos and Cambodia Associated States within the French Union at the same time.

5. Government stability is poor in Indochina. In Vietnam, less than one-third of the country is controlled by the legal government with the French in control of the major cities; in Cambodia and Laos, the French maintain order but unrest is endemic. Before World War II Indochina was made up of four French Protectorates (Tonkin, Annam, Laos and Cambodia) and the colony of Cochinchina. It was occupied after the war by Chinese troops in the north (Tonkin) and by British and later French in the south. In 1946 a (nationalist coalition) government headed by the Moscow-trained Communist agent Ho Chi Minh consented to the return to the north (Tonkin) of the French upon promises of independence

DOCUMENT 2-2   Continued

within the French Union. French negotiations with Ho were broken off following the massacre of many foreigners in Tonkin and Cochinchina in December 1946 by Ho's forces. Hostilities have continued to date.

6. The French are irrevocably committed in Indochina and have sponsored Bao Dai as a move aimed at achieving non-Communist political stability. It was a case of backing Bao Dai or accepting the Communist government of Ho Chi Minh. This latter alternative was impossible not only because it would obviously make their position in Indochina untenable but would also open the door to complete Communist domination of Southeast Asia. Such a Communist advance would have severe repercussions in the non-Communist world.

7. Military operations in Indochina represented a franc drain on the French treasury of the equivalent of approximately $475 million in 1949. This constitutes nearly half of the current French Military Budget.

8. Ho Chi Minh, a Moscow-trained Communist, controls the Viet Minh movement which is in conflict with the government of Bao Dai for control of Vietnam. Ho actually exercises control of varying degree over more than two-thirds of Vietnam territory and his "government" maintains agents in Thailand, Burma and India. This Communist "government" has been recognized by Communist China and the USSR.

9. Most Indochinese, both supporters of Bao Dai and those of Ho Chi Minh, regard independence from the French as their primary objective. Protection from Chinese Communist imperialism has been considered, up to now, a secondary issue.

10. Unavoidably, the United States is, together with France, committed in Indochina. That is, failure of the French Bao Dai "experiment" would mean the communization of Indochina. It is Bao Dai (or a similar anti-Communist successor) or Ho Chi Minh (or a similar Communist successor); there is no other alternative. The choice confronting the United States is to support the French in Indochina or face the extension of Communism over the remainder of the continental area of Southeast Asia and, possibly, further westward. We then would be obliged to make staggering investments in those areas and in that part of Southeast Asia remaining outside Communist domination or withdraw to a much-contracted Pacific line. It would seem a case of "Penney wise, Pound foolish" to deny support to the French in Indochina.

11. The US plans on extending recognition to the newly-created states of Vietnam, Laos and Cambodia, following French legislative action which is expected in early February 1950.

12. Another approach to the problem is to apply the practical test of probability of success. In the present case we know from the complex circumstances involved that the French are going to make literally every possible effort to prevent the victory of Communism in Indochina. Briefly, then, we would be backing a determined protagonist in this venture. Added to this is the fact that French military leaders such as General Cherriere are soberly confident that, in the absence of an invasion in mass form Red China, they (the French) can be successful in their support of their anti-Communist governments in Indochina.

13. Still another approach to the problem is to recall that the United States has undertaken to provide substantial aid to France in Europe. Failure to support French policy in Indochina would have the effect of contributing toward the defeat of our aims in Europe.

V. Conclusions

a. Significant developments have taken place in Indochina since the Mutual Defense Assistance Act of 1949 was drawn up, these changes warranting a reexamination of the question of military aid.

b. The whole of Southeast Asia is in danger of falling under Communist domination.

c. The countries and areas of Southeast Asia are not at present in a position to form a regional

(continued)

DOCUMENT 2-2 Continued

organization for self-defense nor are they capable of defending themselves against military aggressive Communism, without the aid of the great powers. Despite their lack of military strength, however, there is a will on the part of the legal governments of Indochina toward nationalism and a will to resist whatever aims at destroying that nationalism.

d. The French native and colonial troops presently in Indochina are engaged in military operations aimed at delaying the expansion southward of Communism from Red China and of destroying its power in Indochina.

e. In the critical areas of Indochina France needs aid in its support of the legally-constituted anti-Communist states.

VI. Recommendations

1. The United States should furnish military aid in support of the anti-Communist nationalist governments of Indochina, this aid to be tailored to meet the deficiencies toward which the United States can make a unique contribution, not including United States troops.

2. This aid should be financed out of funds made available by Section 303 of the Mutual Defense Assistance Act of 1949.

Source: Department of State, *Foreign Relations of the United States*, 1950, vol. VI, 711–715.

DOCUMENT 2-3
Paper on Indochina prepared in the State Department on March 27, 1952

Draft—Indochina Section of NSC Paper

Problem: To determine the policy of the United States toward the countries of Southeast Asia, and in particular, the courses of action which may be taken by the United States to strengthen and coordinate resistance to Communism on the part of the government and peoples of the area.

Assumption: That identifiable Chinese Communist aggression against Southeast Asia does not take place.

Analysis:

Importance of Indochina

The strategic importance of Indochina derives from its geographical position as a key to the defense of mainland Southeast Asia; its economic value as a potential large scale exporter or rice; and its political importance as an example of Western resistance to Communist expansion.

a. It is generally accepted that should Indochina fall to Communist control, Thailand and Burma could be expected to make their own accommodation with the Communist bloc....

b. The problem of whether or not the loss of Indochina would be followed by the loss of Malaya and Indonesia as well as Thailand and Burma is of major importance is assessing the *economic* importance of maintaining the Western position in Indochina. If Indochina's loss to the Communists were accompanied by the loss of Thailand and Burma alone, Western losses would consist primarily of the loss of valuable sources of exportable rice surpluses. The loss of these rice exporting areas would impose a two fold pressure on Japan by removing simultaneously a source of food and a potential field for Japanese export development. The loss of these rice surplus countries would thus create real difficulties for the continued maintenance of a Western oriented Japan. Finally, the control of these three rice surplus countries by the Communists would provide them with an economic advantage of far greater importance to them than the loss of the area may be to the free world.

DOCUMENT 2-3 Continued

If, however, the loss of Indochina were accompanied by the loss of Malaya and Indonesia as well, the West would suffer economic losses of major importance, and the Western orientation of Japan would be seriously jeopardized. Malaya and Indonesia are major sources of tin and rubber. Malaya is an important source of dollar earnings for the UK. Indonesia is an important secondary source of oil for the West. Communist control of all of Southeast Asia would remove the chief potential area for Japanese commercial development, and would so add to the already powerful mainland pulls upon Japan as to make it dubious that Japan could refrain from reaching an accommodation with the Communist bloc.

Present Situation in Indochina

5. In the long run, the security of Indochina against Communism will depend upon the development of native governments able to command the support of the masses of the people and national armed forces capable of relieving the French of the major burden of maintaining internal security. The Vietnamese Government has been slow to assume its responsibilities and has continued to suffer from a lack of strong leadership. It has had to contend with: (a) lingering Vietnamese suspicion of any French-supported regime, combined with the apathetic and "fence-sitting" attitude of the bulk of the people; (b) the difficulty, common to all new and inexperienced governments, of training the necessary personnel and building an efficient administration; (c) the failure of factional and sectional groups to unite in a concerted national effort; and (d) the relatively ineffective character of Bao Dai's administration.

Efforts to create a National Vietnamese Army—an essential prerequisite to growth in political stature of the Vietnamese Government and to an ultimate non-Communist solution in Indochina—have made some progress, and Vietnamese units have performed creditably in recent engagements. Plans call for the expansion of the army from its present strength of 120,000 to 150,000. However, it will take considerable time before the planned forces are organized, trained, and equipped in battalion units, and even longer before effective divisional units can be put in the field. Progress in the formation of the army is retarded by lack of capable officers at all levels of command, French budgetary difficulties, shortages of equipment, and the apathetic attitude of the population. At the same time, differences of opinion between the Vietnamese leaders and the French, particularly over who will exercise control over the Vietnamese Army, have prevented in the past full cooperation and maximum progress in the army's development. Delay in establishing a Vietnamese Army under Vietnamese control has been a contributing factor in limiting popular support of the Vietnamese regime.

The military situation in Indochina continues to be one of stalemate. Increased U.S. aid to the Franco-Vietnamese forces has been one important factor in enabling them to withstand recent Communist attacks. However, Chinese aid to the Viet Minh in the form of logistical support, training, and technical advisers is increasing at a comparable rate. In the absence of intervention by important forces other than those presently engaged, and provided French will and effort remain undiminished, the prospect is for a continuation of the present stalemate.

Possibilities of Diminuation of French Will or Effort

The French Government is increasingly concerned over France's ability to maintain its position in Indochina. There is a growing official feeling in France that it cannot simultaneously support presently projected military efforts in both Europe and Asia without greater U.S. aid. If the French were unable, by remaining in Indochina, to secure financial assistance for both their European and Indochinese operations, and were forced to choose between the two, they would probably view their Indochinese commitment as of lesser importance. Moreover, there has been a growing popular feeling that the distant and costly Indochinese war offers few rewards even if won. This feeling is increasing political pressure for some alleviation of the French burden in Indochina.

(continued)

DOCUMENT 2-3 Continued

Strong factors, however, still hold the French to their present commitments. These include: (a) the intangible but powerful factor of prestige; (b) the knowledge that withdrawal from Indochina would have repercussions elsewhere in the French Union; (c) the concern over the fate of French nationals and investments in Indochina; (d) the official feeling that no settlement with the Viet Minh or with Communist China could be achieved that would reserve any French Interests in Indochina; and (e) the physical and technical difficulties of a withdrawal operation.

On balance it appears probable that the French will continue the effort to maintain their position in Indochina, but will attempt to alleviate their burden by insisting that the U.S. undertake an increased share of financial responsibility for the defense of the area. The French may, in due course, also press for U.S. armed assistance, either directly, or through the UN, and may also press for U.S. or international support. The French will probably attempt to convince the U.S. that the alternatives to U.S. assumption of an important share of at least financial support for the Indochina operation will be either French withdrawal, or a negotiated settlement with the Viet Minh which would be tantamount to acceptance of a Communist Indochina. It is, however, quite possible that if the French are unsuccessful in securing greater U.S. financial assistance they will in fact seriously consider withdrawal from Indochina, or, as a more likely alternative, will explore the possibilities of extricating themselves as gracefully as possible from their Indochina entanglement through a negotiated settlement with the Communists, following an achievement of a truce similar to that now being sought in Korea.

Considerations Affecting U.S. Assumption of Increased Responsibility for Indochina

Important as the maintenance and development of an anti-Communist position in Indochina is to the interests of the U.S., a U.S. decision to undertake greater responsibility in Indochina should be made only in light of (a) the possibility that any U.S. course of action, short of actual employment of U.S. armed forces, may in the long-run prove inefficacious;

(b) the possibility that a marked improvement in the anti-Communist position in Indochina which threatened to eliminate the Viet Minh might occasion Chinese Communist intervention; (c) the possibility that U.S. assumption of responsibility in Indochina might occasion a rapid and extensive loss of interest in the situation on the part of the French; and (d) U.S. ability to assume increased burdens in Indochina in view of its present world-wide commitments....

U.S. Objectives

In light of the considerations described above, U.S. courses of action with regard to Indochina should be designed to:

a. Enable the French to continue to fulfill French responsibilities for Indochina without sacrificing development of French strength under NATO;

b. Supplement rather than supplant French efforts in Indochina, and minimize any increase of U.S. responsibility for the area;

c. Assist in development of the fullest degree of political and military independence of the Associated States which may be consistent with continuation of French efforts in the area, and assist in the development of stable and competent indigenous governments, strong national armies, and sound economies.

d. Minimize possibilities of Chinese Communist intervention....

Recommendations:

The U.S. should:

1. Continue and increase its military and economic assistance programs for Indochina;

2. Continue to provide substantial financial assistance for the French effort in Indochina either through direct budgetary assistance to France or through assumption of financial responsibility for the Indochinese national armies, or a combination of both.

3. Continue to exert influence to promote constructive political developments in Indochina, and in particular to promote broadening of the base of the governments of the Associated States.

DOCUMENT 2-3 Continued

4. Continue to stress French responsibility for Indochina and oppose any decrease of French efforts in Indochina.
5. The U.S. should not employ U.S. armed forces in Indochina.

6. The U.S. should not exert its influence for the achievement of a truce in Indochina.

Source: Department of State, *Foreign Relations of the United States*, 1952–1954, vol. XIII, pt. 1, 82–89.

Chronological List of Main Events

1945	The abandonment of the trusteeship plan for Indochina
1946	The beginning of the First Indochina War
1948	The establishment of the Bao Dai government
1949	The formulation of the Dodge Plan to rebuild Japan
1949	The fall of China to communism

January 1950	The Russian and Chinese recognition of the Democratic Republic of Vietnam
February 1950	The American recognition of the Bao Dai government
March 1950	The American decision to provide financial support for the French war effort in Indochina
June 1950	The outbreak of the Korean War

Study Questions

1. What was the trusteeship plan?
2. What was the domino theory?
3. Why did the Truman administration decide to help finance French military operations in Indochina?
4. Would Ho Chi Minh have become an Asian Tito if the United States had supported the government that he established in Vietnam in 1945?

America's Mandarin

If we don't assist Japan, gentlemen, Japan is going Communist. Then instead of the Pacific being an American lake, believe me it is going to be a Communist lake.

PRESIDENT DWIGHT D. EISENHOWER, 1954

THE ROAD TO DIEN BIEN PHU

The Republican administration of Dwight D. Eisenhower accepted without modification the basic principles of the Indochina policy bequeathed by the Democrats. When they assumed control of American diplomacy in January 1953, President Eisenhower and Secretary of State John Foster Dulles agreed that the United States should make a concerted effort to prevent the fall of Indochina to communism. They subscribed to the prevailing belief that if the Vietminh were to win in Vietnam, the cancer of communism might spread throughout the entire region. They feared that Japan, if denied access to noncommunist markets in Southeast Asia, might be pulled out of the international capitalist trading network. They also worried that French officials, if deprived of American support for their war effort in Indochina, would continue to balk at proposals for the establishment of a European Defense Community (EDC) that would include West German forces. Eisenhower and Dulles, like Truman and Acheson before them, wanted to expand the liberal capitalist world system and therby enable free enterprise and political liberty to flourish both at home and abroad. Although reluctant to commit American combat forces in Vietnam, they were determined to continue the policy of providing American financial support to buttress the French military campaign in Indochina.

President Eisenhower and Secretary Dulles, however, were alarmed about growing signs of war weariness in France. By the end of 1952, the number of French soldiers killed, wounded, missing, and captured in Indochina since the beginning of the conflict totaled more than 90,000. The French were losing young officers in the jungles and rice paddies of Vietnam faster than they could be replaced with graduates from the military academy at Saint-Cyr. As French casualties continued to climb, public support for what the French had come to call the "dirty war" rapidly waned. Ho Chi Minh's prophecy was coming true. Although the Vietminh were losing about ten men for each French soldier killed in the conflict, more and more French politicians and newspapers began advocating negotiations with the Democratic Republic of Vietnam to stop the loss of lives and francs in Indochina. And as the antiwar sentiment intensified in France, the apprehension grew in Washington that French public opinion might impel the government in Paris to seek a negotiated settlement rather than a military victory in Indochina.

Eisenhower and Dulles were eager to break the stalemate in Indochina before French leaders bowed to public pressure and sued for peace. In March 1953, Dulles informed the French government that the United States believed it was essential for the French to prepare a plan that would lead to a victory in Indochina within two years. Dulles urged the French not only to develop an aggressive military strategy but also to expand the indigenous Vietnamese National Army into an effective fighting force. But Eisenhower and Dulles, like their predecessors, realized that without a French promise to restore home rule in Vietnam after the war, the Vietnamese people would have no reason to help the French win. They likewise understood that a battlefield victory alone would not solve the fundamental political problem in Indochina. In May 1953, therefore, Eisenhower urged the French government to make a clear and unequivocal statement that Indochina would be granted complete independence as soon as the Vietminh were defeated.

The Korean War armistice concluded in July 1953 gave Eisenhower and Dulles additional cause for concern. They feared that the Chinese communists, since their soldiers were no longer engaged in Korea, might intervene in Vietnam. Dulles tried to deter the Chinese in September 1953 by issuing a stern public statement implying that the United States would drop nuclear bombs on China if that country entered the Indochina conflict. Although the Chinese refrained from sending combat troops to Vietnam, they did begin supplying the Vietminh with large numbers of trucks, heavy artillery pieces, and antiaircraft guns, while continuing to furnish them with a array of small arms as well. The cease-fire in Korea, besides generating apprehensions about the Chinese, gave rise to worries in Washington that the Japanese dollar gap would widen because of a decline in American orders for military equipment made in Japan. Determined to keep Southeast Asia open to Japanese trade and investment, Eisenhower and Dulles repeatedly articulated their commitment to preventing the forces of communism from toppling the Indochina dominoes.

In France, however, the Korean War armistice gave added strength to the antiwar movement. If the United States had negotiated a settlement in Korea after failing to achieve a military victory, many French political leaders asked, why should not their country do the same in Vietnam? Such reasoning prompted the French parliament in October 1953 to endorse a resolution that called on the government to explore every possibility for negotiating an end to the fighting in Indochina. In response to this mounting pressure, Prime Minister Joseph Laniel announced on November 12 that if an honorable solution became possible, his government, "like the United States in Korea, would be happy to welcome a diplomatic solution of the conflict." But Laniel did not want to undertake negotiations with the Democratic Republic of Vietnam from a position of weakness. In an attempt to improve his bargaining position before entering into peace talks, he therefore decided to lead France into one final military campaign in Indochina.

General Henri Navarre had already been appointed to command the French Expeditionary Corps in Indochina. At the urging of American military leaders in July 1953, General Navarre prepared a new strategic plan calling for a vast augmentation in the size of the Vietnamese National Army and the deployment of nine additional battalions of French troops in Indochina. Navarre proposed to consolidate his units that were spread out in static defensive positions, to combine them with new reinforcements into a mobile striking force, and to initiate a major offensive to drive the Vietminh out of the Red River Delta. In a secret report to Paris, however, Navarre warned that the Indochina war could not be won in a strict military sense and the best that could be expected was a draw. Navarre and his government hoped to be able to regain the initiative in Indochina during the next two years with the objective of strengthening their battle-field position prior to the beginning of peace negotiations. Yet the French did not dare to disclose their limited war aims when they asked for American financial aid.

American leaders seriously debated whether or not the United States should bankroll the Navarre Plan. Skeptical about French intentions and capabilities, the Joint Chiefs of Staff (JCS) warned that military success in Indochina depended on the establishment of a political climate that would give the Vietnamese people an incentive to support the French and to supply them with intelligence about the Vietminh. But the State Department feared that if Washington refused to finance the Navarre Plan, the French government would negotiate a settlement that would mean "the eventual loss to Communism not only of Indochina but of the whole of Southeast Asia." Finally, after extracting a promise from Paris to pursue the Navarre Plan with vigor, the United States agreed in September 1953 to provide France with an additional $385 million in military assistance. The United States continued to meet the escalating French requests for money and supplies needed to implement the Navarre Plan, and as a result, American aid made up 78 percent of the French military budget in Indochina during fiscal 1954. In fact, between 1950 and 1954, the United States contributed more than $2.6 billion in direct assistance for the French war effort in Indochina.

Despite this enormous support from the United States, however, General Navarre could not achieve his central objective of recovering the initiative in the Red River valley. Bao Dai had previously cautioned the French not to rely on Vietnamese recruits to fight for them. "It would be dangerous to expand the Vietnamese Army," he warned, "because it might defect en masse and go to the Vietminh." Nevertheless, in response to American prodding, the French went ahead and organized a 300,000-man Vietnamese auxiliary army. But this large indigenous military force remained poorly trained, poorly led, and poorly motivated. Few middle-class natives would serve as officers in an army fighting against rather than for Vietnamese independence. Nor were many Vietnamese peasant soldiers willing to risk their lives to protect the puppet government in Saigon. Not surprising to Bao Dai, a major reason for the failure of the Navarre Plan lay in the inability of the Vietnamese National Army to hold areas that the French troops had cleared in the Red River Delta.

Although General Giap wanted to launch a major campaign against the French regulars in the Red River valley, the Chinese Military Advisory Group argued that the main theater should remain in the northwest, where French troops could be drawn into remote areas and annihilated. The CMAG believed that the Tonkin Delta should continue as a secondary theater in which the Vietminh could intensify their guerrilla activities to help pave the way for the eventual conquest of Hanoi. Ho Chi Minh agreed. In September 1953, he directed Giap to focus his efforts in the northwest, and when Giap began moving his troops toward northern Laos, General Navarre took the bait. In November 1953, he decided to parachute 3,000 elite French soldiers onto a plateau just outside Dien Bien Phu, a village near the Laotian border in the northwest corner of Vietnam. Navarre wanted to lure Giap into a large set-piece battle in which French firepower could devastate the Vietminh. General Wei Guoqing, the newly appointed top Chinese military advisor to the Vietminh, encouraged Gaip to accept the challenge. Giap promptly ordered his forces to encircle the isolated French garrison. He hoped to hit Navarre with a crushing blow that would sap the will of the French people to continue supporting the costly struggle in Indochina.

The military situation in Vietnam provoked serious concerns in both the United States and France. Although the French had sent another 10,000 soldiers to reinforce their fortress at Dien Bien Phu, the commander of the American Military Assistance Advisory Group warned in

January 1954 that the French were operating from an inferior defensive position. He estimated that the French forces at Dien Bien Phu had only a 50-50 chance of survival. Worried more about the overall military picture in Indochina, American army staff planners cautioned on February 7 that there was little evidence the French had the ability to bring the war to a successful conclusion. The French defense minister and his service chiefs were equally apprehensive. In fact, after making an inspection tour of the battlefields in Vietnam, they reported that they could hope for nothing better than an improved military position that might strengthen the hand of French diplomats at a future peace conference.

Faced with a steadily deteriorating military situation in Vietnam and a rapidly growing war-weariness at home, the French government decided to negotiate with the Democratic Republic of Vietnam. Prime Minister Laniel insisted in February 1954 that the Indochina issue should be discussed at the Geneva Conference scheduled to begin in April for the purpose of working out a political settlement in Korea. The U.S. government, however, still hoped that France could achieve a military victory in Vietnam. Afraid that the French would consent to peace terms favoring the Vietminh, Secretary of State Dulles sought to prevent a negotiated settlement. But Laniel warned that his country would not participate in the European Defense Community designed to shield the continent from the Soviet menace if the United States tried to block peace talks in Geneva between France and the DRV. Dulles then reluctantly agreed to have the Indochina question added to the agenda of the forthcoming Geneva Conference.

On March 12, the eve of the Battle of Dien Bien Phu, a Joint Chiefs of Staff memorandum summarized American military thinking in the following way: (1) In the absence of a substantial improvement in the French military position in Vietnam, a negotiated settlement would probably be inconsistent with basic American objectives in Southeast Asia; (2) a settlement based on free elections would almost certainly lead to communist control of Indochina; (3) the conquest of the rest of Southeast Asia would inevitably follow the fall of Indochina to the communists unless the Western powers took immediate and effective counteraction; (4) the loss of Southeast Asia to communism would drive Japan into an accommodation with the communist bloc; (5) the United States should therefore urge the French government not to abandon the aggressive prosecution of the war in Vietman until a satisfactory settlement could be achieved; and (6) if the French did surrender any part of Indochina in negotiations with the communists, the United States should not associate itself with such a settlement so that it would remain free to join with other countries in continuing the struggle against the Vietminh without French participation.

On the very next day, March 13, the Vietminh began a massive assault against the French positions at Dien Bien Phu. The Chinese had sent large quantities of ammunition to help the Vietminh prepare for the battle. Moreover, besides training and equipping four Vietminh battalions with antiaircraft guns, the Chinese had furnished Giap with powerful field artillery. The French, while establishing their defenses at Dien Bien Phu, had made a fatal mistake. They had assumed that the Vietminh would be unable to get heavy artillery up the high hills surrounding their fortress in the valley below. But Giap used thousands of Vietnamese porters to carry 105- and 75-millimeter howitzers piece by piece up the hills and to reassemble them in caves impervious to French artillery and strafing. The Vietminh immediately trained their big guns on the strongholds along the perimeter of the garrison and quickly drove the French out. Unable to silence the Vietminh batteries, the French artillery commander committed suicide on the second day of the attack. Then, the Vietminh pulverized the French airstrip and made preparations for an infantry assault on the besieged French bastion.

THE GENEVA PEACE SETTLEMENT

General Paul Ely, the French chief of staff, hurried to the United States while the Vietminh were pounding the French positions at Dien Bien Phu. Upon his arrival in Washington on March 20, General Ely stressed that the French needed more American aircraft if they were to succeed in defending their fortress. He also argued that in the event of Chinese intervention in the Indochina conflict, the French would need direct American air support. Noting that the French chances of holding out at Dien Bien Phu were no better than 50 percent, Ely made it clear that the French wanted additional American military aid to help them bolster their battlefield position before the peace conference opened at Geneva. He also indicated that he had abandoned hope for achieving a military victory in Indochina and thought that France should seek a diplomatic solution at Geneva.

American policymakers were deeply dismayed by the Ely mission. Secretary of State Dulles informed Ely that he and President Eisenhower would not consider deploying American forces in Vietnam until the French not only granted real independence to their Southeast Asian possessions named the Associated States of Indochina but also demonstrated their resolve to achieve a military victory over the Vietminh. Admiral Arthur W. Radford, the chairman of the Joint Chiefs of Staff, had become increasingly impatient with the French failure to create a strong and effective indigenous army in Vietnam. In a conversation with Ely, Admiral Radford proposed that the Military Assistance Advisory Group be expanded so that American personnel could help train the Vietnamese National Army. But Ely replied that French prestige would be undermined if the United States assumed the responsibility for training the native forces in Vietnam.

Despite his disappointment with this response, Radford told Ely that the United States might be willing to make a massive air strike against the Vietminh forces surrounding Dien Bien Phu. The plan, dubbed Operation Vulture, called for the use of sixty B-29 bombers based in the Philippines, escorted by fighter aircraft from the Seventh Fleet. Radford viewed the proposal not simply as a one-time action to improve the French bargaining position at Geneva but rather as the first step in an escalating American campaign to help defeat the Vietminh. And although Radford made no commitments, Ely returned to France with a strong impression that the White House would approve Operation Vulture if his government requested it. But President Eisenhower informed the National Security Council on March 25 that he would agree to American military intervention in Indochina only under the following two conditions: (1) if other nations would join with the United States in the war effort and (2) if Congress would sanction the deployment of American forces in operations against the Vietminh.

Mindful of these stipulations, American military authorities immediately began debating whether or not the United States should drop atomic bombs to relieve the beleaguered French garrison at Dien Bien Phu. The Army War Plans Division argued on March 25 in favor of such an operation. But General Matthew B. Ridgway, the army chief of staff, opposed the idea. Ridgway promptly ordered another study regarding the probable consequences of American military intervention in Indochina. This time, the Army War Plans Division concluded that even with the use of tactical nuclear weapons, American air and naval forces alone could not defeat the Vietminh. The war planners argued that the United States would have to send ground troops—seven American combat divisions if China stayed out of the conflict and twelve divisions if China became involved—in order to assure an ultimate victory in Indochina.

Admiral Radford then asked the Joint Chiefs of Staff to consider the question of committing American air and naval units to save the French forces at Dien Bien Phu. During a meeting on March 31, General Ridgway argued emphatically against the proposed bombing raid. He reasoned that even if Operation Vulture proved successful, a victory at Dien Bien Phu would not decisively affect the overall military situation in Indochina. Yet Radford persisted. On April 2, he asked the JCS to reconsider the issue of an atomic attack against the Vietminh to turn the tide of battle at Dien Bien Phu. Both the chief of naval operations and the commandant of the Marine Corps sided with Ridgway, however. Only the Air Force chief was willing to give even qualified support for the proposed atomic strike. The JCS therefore concluded that the United States should not respond favorably if France requested American military intervention in Indochina.

Nevertheless, the Eisenhower administration proceeded to seek congressional support for possible American military action in Indochina. On April 3, Secretary Dulles invited a bipartisan group of House and Senate leaders to a confidential meeting at the State Department. Dulles showed the senators and representatives a State Department proposal for a congressional resolution empowering the president to use air and naval forces in Southeast Asia. The legislators made it clear, however, that they would not approve American military intervention in Vietnam until Dulles had obtained firm commitments from allied governments to participate in joint combat operations with the United States. Expressing the unanimous feeling of the group, one legislator declared, "We want no more Koreas with the United States furnishing 90 percent of the manpower." It was the sense of the meeting that the United States should not fight alone and that Dulles should attempt to secure cooperation from Great Britain and other nations. If definite commitments for united military action could be obtained, the consensus of the group was that a congressional resolution along the lines Dulles had drafted could be passed.

The meeting reinforced Eisenhower and Dulles in their desire for united action rather than unilateral intervention. On April 4, the French government officially requested that the United States implement Operation Vulture to lift the siege of Dien Bien Phu. But Eisenhower reaffirmed his determination not to authorize military action without congressional approval and British participation. The president said he would also require assurance that the French would continue fighting in Indochina and grant complete independence to the associated states. Dulles thereupon informed the French government on April 5 that the United States had decided against military involvement except on a multilateral basis. In a personal letter to Prime Minister Winston Churchill on the same day, Eisenhower asked Great Britain to join the United States in a coalition of nations to help France defeat the Vietminh. The National Security Council and the President's Special Committee on Indochina also urged that maximum diplomatic pressure should be placed on France in order to prevent its withdrawal from the war.

Eisenhower and Dulles wanted to internationalize the Indochina conflict. During a National Security Council meeting on April 6, the president said that he would seek congressional authorization for intervention if a united military front could be established. Eisenhower and his top advisers agreed that the Joint Chiefs of Staff should prepare contingency plans for military operations in Indochina. After the meeting, Dulles immediately departed for England and France in hopes of organizing a multinational military grouping. However, he was destined to be disappointed. When he arrived in London, Dulles found that the British opposed military action in Indochina until the chances for a reasonable peace settlement had been explored at the Geneva Conference. Then, in Paris, Dulles learned that while the French insisted on maintaining their imperial rule in Indochina, they wanted an American air strike on Dien Bien Phu only to strengthen their negotiating position at Geneva.

This was unacceptable to Eisenhower. Although he advocated united action to prevent the spread of communism in Southeast Asia, Eisenhower refused to consider unilateral intervention on behalf of French colonialism in Indochina. The president was deeply annoyed with the French, and he blamed their military failures on their refusal to grant independence to Vietnam, Cambodia, and Laos. Democratic spokesmen in the Senate gave vent to similar feelings. Senator John F. Kennedy of Massachusetts warned that American military aid would not enable the French to defeat rebel forces that had popular support. Senator Lyndon B. Johnson of Texas agreed and therefore opposed "sending American G.I.s into the mud and muck of Indochina on a blood-letting spree to perpetuate colonialism and white man's exploitation in Asia." Eisenhower felt the same way, and on April 26, he told congressional leaders that it would be a "tragic error to go in alone as a partner of France."

The American decision to scrap Operation Vulture sealed the fate of the French garrison at Dien Bien Phu. Shortly after the battle had commenced in March 1954, Giap ordered human wave assaults in an attempt to achieve a quick victory. When his losses mounted, however, Giap abruptly changed tactics. Hoping that attrition and exhaustion would slowly wear down the enemy, he instructed his troops to dig a vast network of trenches around the French fortress. Beijing dispatched a dozen army engineers, who had gained valuable experience in Korea, to supervise the construction of these trenches. And the Chinese Military Advisory Group taught Vietminh officers how to use snipers to disrupt enemy troop movements and to undermine French morale. Although American military leaders urged that a large number of soldiers be sent to reinforce Dien Bien Phu, General Navarre lacked the necessary manpower because many of his forces were tied down in defensive operations elsewhere in Vietnam and Laos. The Vietminh, in the meantime, tunneled closer and closer until they were able to overrun the last French stronghold at the point of fixed bayonet. Finally, on May 7, the French surrendered after fifty-five days of resistance. This humiliating defeat, which cost Navarre more than 16,000 troops, signaled the end of the French war effort in Indochina.

The Indochina phase of the Geneva Conference began just one day after the last French gun fell silent at Dien Bien Phu. Hoping to turn their great military victory into an equally impressive political triumph at the peace table, Ho Chi Minh and his comrades sought not only to gain control of their entire country but also to bring Cambodia and Laos under their domination. But Red China and the Soviet Union had national interests that outweighed any ideological desires to help the Vietnamese communists achieve their basic aims. Having little concern about affairs in Indochina, the Russians were primarily interested in promoting a reasonable peace settlement in order to assure the survival of a French government that opposed the creation of a European Defense Community with West German participation. And the Chinese had one overriding goal: to bring the peace conference to a successful conclusion so that American policymakers would not send combat troops to Indochina as they had done in Korea. In this way, they hoped to avoid another costly military conflict with the United States and to concentrate on plans for the development of their economy. In addition, the Chinese wanted to prevent the smaller Vietnamese dragon from establishing a strong Indochinese empire on their southern frontier.

As the Geneva Conference got underway, Prime Minister Pham Van Dong, the head of the delegation from the Democratic Republic of Vietnam, demanded that France withdraw completely from his country and let the Vietnamese resolve their own differences. He also insisted that France recognize the Vietminh-backed revolutionaries who were trying to overthrow the royal governments in Laos and Cambodia. But China and the Soviet Union exerted pressure on the DRV to accept a compromise. Leading the Chinese delegation, Foreign Minister Zhou Enlai persuaded Dong to drop his demand that the Pathet Lao and Khmer rebels be seated at the conference and to promise that Vietminh troops would be withdrawn from Laos and Cambodia. He also convinced Dong that Vietnam should be temporarily divided into two relatively equal parts and that general elections should be scheduled to reunify the country. Although Dong argued that the elections should be held only six months after a cease-fire agreement was signed, Foreign

Minister Vyacheslav Molotov, the chief of the Soviet delegation, used his influence to get Dong to agree that the elections should take place a full two years after the armistice.

The cease-fire arrangement, worked out at Geneva in July 1954, provided for the temporary partition of Vietnam along the seventeenth parallel. The accords stressed that the demarcation line should not be "interpreted as constituting a political or territorial boundary." France and the Democratic Republic of Vietnam agreed that a demilitarized zone (DMZ) 10 kilometers wide would be established along the seventeenth parallel and that the Vietminh forces would be regrouped north of the DMZ while the French troops moved south of the buffer area. Both sides also agreed that national elections would be held in July 1956 to reunify the country. Disappointed that the political settlement at Geneva did not reflect their military superiority in Vietnam, the DRV delegates felt betrayed by the Chinese. Pham Van Dong complained to an aide that Zhou Enlai had "double-crossed" them. Realizing that it would be difficult to expel the French from Vietnam without Chinese military aid, Dong and his colleagues had been compelled to settle for half of the loaf at Geneva. They could only hope to get the other half in the future, either by casting ballots or by firing bullets.

Although the United States refused to associate itself with the Geneva Accords, neither President Eisenhower nor Secretary of State Dulles were completely displeased with the results of the conference. They knew that Ho Chi Minh, who had established a communist government in Hanoi to rule northern Vietnam, would easily win if country-wide elections were held in the near future. But they believed that the two-year delay, stipulated in the peace agreements, would give them enough time to build a separate, noncommunist state in southern Vietnam. While his subordinates were attending the conference in Geneva, Dulles told a group of congressmen that the United States would have to assume the responsibility for defending the southern half of Vietnam along with Laos and Cambodia. He also said that in addition to providing economic and military aid to these areas of Indochina, it would be necessary for the United States to organize a strong regional defense association in order to draw the line against the advance of communism in Southeast Asia. Dulles and Eisenhower both hoped that without the burden of supporting French colonialism, the United States would be able to help South Vietnamese conservatives set up a noncommunist government in Saigon.

Their determination to prevent the spread of communism in Southeast Asia was rooted in their continuing desire to keep Japan in the capitalist orbit. Eisenhower and Dulles repeatedly warned that the Japanese might become dependent on Red China if they did not have access to noncommunist markets in Southeast Asia. "Japan's population," Dulles explained in June 1954, "depends for its livelihood upon foreign trade. Trade is offered by the Communists—at a price. The price is that Japan—the only industrial power in Asia—should cease to cooperate with the United Nations and with the United States." A few days later, during a private discussion with several congressional leaders, Eisenhower emphasized the same point. "If we don't assist Japan, gentlemen, Japan is going Communist," he lectured. "Then instead of the Pacific being an American lake, believe me it is going to be a Communist lake."

THE BIRTH OF A CLIENT STATE

Ngo Dinh Diem was the man around whom the United States would struggle to build a new South Vietnamese nation to serve as a bulwark against the spread of communism in Southeast Asia. Diem was born in 1901 and reared in a conservative Vietnamese family with strong religious and political feelings. Back in the seventeenth century, his ancestors had been among the earliest Vietnamese converts to Catholicism. His father, a well-educated mandarin who had come to resent the foreign domination of Vietnam, quit working for the government and began participating in anti-French nationalist activities. Diem inherited from his father a deep hostility toward French imperialism along with a fierce religious fervor. Hence, he grew up to be both an ardent nationalist and a devout Catholic who hated communism. So while Diem wanted to oust the French from his country, he stood against a radical revolution that would alter the traditional economic and political structure of Vietnam. In short, Diem was a Vietnamese patriot with conservative views about government and society.

Like Phan Boi Chau before him, Diem became one of the most prominent noncommunist nationalists in Vietnam. During his youth, Diem never learned to feel comfortable with members of the opposite sex, and while he was attending a Catholic school, the young puritan contemplated becoming a priest. Finally, however, he decided to enter a local French school of law and public administration to prepare himself for a government job. Soon after graduation in 1926, Diem became a provincial governor, and in 1933, Emperor Bao Dai appointed him minister of the interior. But Diem accused the emperor of being a tool of the French, and after only three months, he resigned from his high government post. And when Bao Dai offered to make him prime minister in 1949, Diem rejected the offer because he regarded the emperor as a French puppet. Instead, he created a new political organization to serve as the nucleus for the emergence of a "Third Force" standing between the polar extremes of French colonialism and Vietnamese communism. But the party remained small.

Unable to attract many supporters to his brand of nationalism in Vietnam, Diem looked to the United States for patronage. After leaving home in 1950 and visiting the Vatican, he spent two years living in a Maryknoll seminary in New Jersey. Taking advantage of his location on the east coast, Diem made frequent trips to New York and Washington, where he became acquainted with prominent Catholics such as Francis Cardinal Spellman and Senator John F. Kennedy. His great opportunity soon came. While the statesmen at Geneva were preparing to partition Vietnam, Bao Dai again decided to appoint Diem as prime minister, but this time his authority would be limited to the southern portion of the country. The playboy summoned the puritan to Paris in June 1954 and persuaded him to kneel before a crucifix and swear that he would defend southern Vietnam against both the communists and the French. Diem then hurried back to Vietnam. When he landed at the Saigon airport on June 26, Diem received a warm welcome from a small group composed mostly of Catholics. And the new prime minister expected the South Vietnamese people to obey him just as if he had been appointed by God to govern them. Never willing to abandon the idea that he had a mandate from heaven to rule those living below the seventeenth parallel as he saw fit, Diem typically responded to queries about his policies by saying that he knew what was best for his people.

Even though Diem's paternalistic attitudes ran counter to democratic principles, Eisenhower and Dulles decided to support him. They hoped to keep Vietnam permanently divided and to help Diem establish a noncommunist regime in Saigon. Right after the conclusion of the Geneva Conference, American leaders set out to rebuild the economy of South Vietnam. They were motivated by three considerations. First, if the South Vietnamese people enjoyed prosperity under Diem, they would be less likely to join the communist movement. Second, if the South Vietnamese received financial aid from the United States, they would obtain dollars that could be used to purchase Japanese goods. Third, if South Vietnam became a successful showcase for capitalism, the people living above the seventeenth parallel might be induced to abandon their commitment to communist leaders in the Democratic Republic of Vietnam. While the minimum American goal was to erect a stable capitalist regime in South Vietnam, the maximum American objective was to spark a counterrevolution in the DRV (hereafter referred to as North Vietnam) and thereby roll back the tide of communism to the Chinese border.

Besides promoting economic reconstruction in South Vietnam, Eisenhower and Dulles quietly dispatched Colonel Edward G. Lansdale to Saigon to organize a covert campaign aimed at undermining communism in North Vietnam. Lansdale had served with the Office of Strategic Services during World War II, and later, he advised the president of the Philippines on how to suppress the Huk rebels. Upon his arrival in Vietnam in June 1954, Lansdale used Central Intelligence Agency (CIA) funds to set up the Saigon Military Mission, which was composed of American soldiers and intelligence agents. Lansdale infiltrated small paramilitary units across the demilitarized zone on missions to sabotage railroads and bridges in North Vietnam. These undercover teams not only tried to destroy transportation facilities, they also employed psychological warfare techniques in an effort to foster opposition to the communist government in Hanoi. Likewise, the Sigon Military Mission recruited secret squads of South Vietnamese commandos and trained them to foment unrest among the North Vietnamese. But these clandestine operations failed to stimulate a popular uprising against Ho Chi Minh.

At the same time, Colonel Lansdale and his staff were working to strengthen the Diem regime by encouraging a mass exodus of Vietnamese civilians from the northern to the southern half of their country. Taking advantage of the Geneva Agreements that allowed for the free movement of population within Vietnam, American intelligence operatives directed a propaganda campaign at North Vietnamese Catholics with slogans proclaiming that "Christ has gone South" or that "The Virgin Mary has departed from the North." American agents also spread rumors that the United States might bomb the communists in the north and that the only way to escape atomic destruction was to flee to the south. The propaganda barrage produced tangible results. Between August 1954 and May 1955, more than 800,000 Vietnamese living above the seventeenth parallel migrated below that demarcation line. The U.S. Navy furnished transportation for many of those who chose to leave the north, and the American government provided $282 million to help pay the cost of resettling them in the south.

These political refugees provided a hard-core group of supporters for the Diem government in Saigon. Most were Catholics who had strongly opposed the Vietminh and their struggle for national liberation. In fact, many were either civil servants who had worked under Bao Dai or auxiliary soldiers who had fought for the French. Vietnamese nationalists resented the role that many Catholics had played in the French colonial regime. "Vietnamese Catholics," they complained, "are the claws by which the French crab has been able to crawl across and devour our land." About half of the northern Catholic community moved below the seventeenth parallel, and as a result, the size of the southern Catholic population more than doubled. These Catholics, numbering approximately 1 million, helped Diem maintain political power by serving as both government officials and military officers in the new order emerging in South Vietnam.

While Diem was integrating these Catholics into his regime, Dulles was busy organizing a regional defense association that treated the seventeenth parallel as a permanent political boundary rather than as a temporary line for the regroupment of opposing military forces. Dulles hurried to Manila in September 1954 to persuade other countries to join with the United States in establishing a legal basis for united military action in Indochina. The Manila conference produced the South East Asia Treaty Organization (SEATO) to protect Cambodia, Laos, and southern Vietnam against either an attack from northern Vietnam or internal subversion. Along with the United States, the SEATO alliance included Great Britain, France, the Philippines, Australia, New Zealand, Pakistan, and Thailand. Conspicuous in their absence from the organization were India, Burma, and Indonesia. The SEATO members agreed to consult with one another about how to meet any common danger that might arise in Southeast Asia. But they did not pledge themselves to defend any country or government in the region. After the Senate ratified the

SEATO pact, however, Eisenhower and his successors in the White House claimed that they had congressional sanction for American military intervention to check the spread of communism in Indochina.

In the meantime, the United States maneuvered to block the peaceful reunification of Vietnam. American intelligence sources predicted in August 1954 that the Vietminh would easily win if free elections were held in Vietnam according to the schedule agreed on at Geneva. Two weeks later, the National Security Council concluded that the United States should make every effort to prevent general elections and the reunification of Vietnam under communist rule. The State Department hoped to achieve that goal, however, without publicly admitting that Washington was attempting to undermine the Geneva Accords. Dulles therefore cabled the American embassy in Saigon in April 1955 that Diem should demand election safeguards that the communists would reject. Not wanting the Vietminh to appear as the sole champions of reunification, the NSC decided on May 17 that Diem should agree to consultations regarding proper voting procedures and that the United States should then help him blame the ultimate failure for holding elections on the communists. But Diem refused to discuss the issue with Ho Chi Minh. And on August 9, in response to calls from Hanoi for talks to prepare the ground-work for a political contest, Diem announced that there could be no elections as long as the communists ruled North Vietnam.

President Eisenhower and Secretary Dulles had already decided that the United States should help organize a new South Vietnamese army to buttress the Diem regime. Dulles explained to American military planners that the only purpose for building this army was to help Diem maintain internal security and that any external threat from the North Vietnamese would have to be countered by either American or SEATO forces. Although the Joint Chiefs of Staff were reluctant to assume the task of training an indigenous army for a weak and unstable government, Dulles argued that the best way to strengthen the anticommunist regime in Saigon was to assist in creating an efficient South Vietnamese military force. And he assured American military authorities that a small army of about 50,000 South Vietnamese soldiers would be adequate because its mission would be limited to suppressing political subversion. Eisenhower agreed. "What we want," he told the National Security Council in October 1954, "is a Vietnamese force which will support Diem." Even if American efforts failed to keep Diem in power in South Vietnam, Dulles observed, they would buy time for the United States to help other Southeast Asian dominoes stand firm against the threat of communism.

President Eisenhower decided to send General J. Lawton Collins to South Vietnam as his personal representative to help stabilize the Diem regime. When General Collins arrived in Saigon in November 1954, he was appalled by the chaotic political situation confronting him. Collins found that General Nguyen Van Hinh, the commander of the Bao Dai army, had been openly talking about forming a new government to replace Diem. With French backing, General Hinh was pushing Prince Buu Hoi as his candidate for prime minister. But American officials firmly opposed Buu Hoi because he favored holding elections to reunify Vietnam. They therefore informed General Hinh that in the event of a coup against Diem, the United States would not provide financial support for a new South Vietnamese government. Realizing that his candidate could not survive without American economic aid, Hinh abandoned his plans for a coup. Bao Dai also succumbed to American pressure. Four days after Collins arrived in Saigon, the emperor ordered Hinh to Paris and dismissed him from the army.

Even though Prince Buu Hoi could no longer challenge Diem, General Collins remained concerned about the continuing political instability in South Vietnam. The Cao Dai and Hoa Hao religious sects refused to merge their militias into the regular army, and the Binh Xuyen gang

President Eisenhower and Secretary of State Dulles meeting with Ngo Dinh Diem in May 1957. From National Archives (Still Pictures Branch), U.S. Air Force.

would not give up control of gambling, prostitution, and opium in Saigon. In early March 1955, these three heavily armed factions issued an ultimatum demanding the formation of a new government in South Vietnam. Collins became increasingly alarmed, and on April 9, he cabled Dulles that the United States should replace Diem with a coalition government that could unify the powerful factions. But Dulles replied that any change in political leadership might be for the worse. Thus, Diem continued to receive strong American support. With the help of Colonel Lansdale and the use of large bribes, Diem was able to induce a majority of Cao Dai and Hoa Hao military leaders to rally to his side. Then, Dulles persuaded Diem to attack the Binh Xuyen, and by May 2, his army had succeeded in driving the gangsters out of Saigon.

After extending his control over the religious sects and crushing the Binh Xuyen, Diem moved swiftly to consolidate his political power. He called for a national referendum to determine whether South Vietnam should remain a monarchy with Bao Dai as emperor or become a republic with himself as president. The election was held under the supervision of his own police force in October 1955, and Diem claimed that 98.2 percent of the voters had cast their ballots for him to replace Bao Dai as the chief of state. Fraud was extensive. In many electoral districts, there were more votes recorded for Diem than there were registered voters. American advisers had cautioned Diem that a 60 percent majority would look more credible, but he wanted his victory to appear like a mandate from heaven. Diem thereupon established a dictatorship rather than a democracy in the new Republic of Vietnam (hereafter referred to as South Vietnam). To placate American officials, however, he created a national assembly in March 1956, but this legislative body remained powerless. Diem knew that he could resist American pressure to broaden his political base because Eisenhower and Dulles regarded his government as a crucial element in their campaign to block the expansion of communism in Southeast Asia. So while Diem served as a mandarin under the aegis of the United States, he was a puppet who frequently pulled his own strings.

Despite his refusal to reform, Diem received American aid to build the South Vietnamese army needed to support his regime. The withdrawal of the French Expeditionary Corps from Indochina beginning in March 1955 meant that the Army of the Republic of Vietnam (ARVN) would have to be larger than originally planned. In addition to serving as an internal police force, the South Vietnamese army would have to be strong enough at least to delay an attack from North Vietnam until American or SEATO forces could come to the rescue. The American Military Assistance Advisory Group, headquartered in Saigon, assumed the responsibility for building the ARVN into a force that could shield South Vietnam against a massive communist assault across the seventeenth parallel. To accomplish that objective, the MAAG officers fashioned the ARVN after the American forces that had successfully fought conventional conflicts during World War II and in Korea. The new South Vietnamese army, like the old French Expeditionary Corps, became a heavily equipped, road-bound force. As a result, the ARVN was totally unprepared to cope when an insurgency erupted within South Vietnam.

THE REVOLT IN THE RICE FIELDS

While American military advisers were training South Vietnamese soldiers to repel an external attack, Ho Chi Minh and his comrades in Hanoi were struggling to promote economic reconstruction in the area above the seventeenth parallel. They aimed to transform North Vietnam from a backward agricultural colony into a modern industrial country with a prosperous socialist economy. After nationalizing French companies and converting large businesses into producer cooperatives, Ho traveled to Beijing and Moscow during the summer of 1955 to ask for financial and technical assistance. China agreed to give North Vietnam $200 million for industrial development, and the Soviet Union agreed to furnish $100 million for manufacturing projects. Both countries also promised to provide North Vietnamese students and workers with technical and professional training. Hoping to achieve economic independence, Ho and his colleagues chose to purchase industrial equipment rather than consumer goods with the money they obtained from exporting raw materials. Their decision imposed a low standard of living on the North Vietnamese population for the sake of economic growth. But their austerity program, together with the flow of aid from China and the Soviet Union, helped lay the foundation for the development of heavy industry in North Vietnam.

Following in the footsteps of their Chinese neighbors, the communist dictators in Hanoi launched a land reform program designed to increase agricultural production and to consolidate their political power in North Vietnam. They succeeded in turning the large mass of landless peasants into small farmers with enough acreage to grow surplus crops that could be exchanged for factory goods made in urban areas. They were also successful in destroying the power that wealthy landlords used to dominate the rural population. As the program gained momentum, many landlords and rich peasants were either imprisoned or killed, and their property was confiscated and distributed to poor tenants and sharecroppers. But the property redistribution campaign soon got out of control as landless peasants and overzealous cadres began accusing landowners of crimes that they had not commited. By early 1956, it became clear that the emphasis on class struggle had provoked widespread social unrest in North Vietnam. Ho Chi Minh publicly admitted that mistakes had been made in implementing the land reform program, and he promptly ordered the release of thousands of innocent landholders from prison.

In the meantime, while the North Vietnamese were largely pulling themselves up by their own bootstraps, the South Vietnamese continued to depend on American financial support. The United States gave the Saigon government almost $1 billion between 1955 and 1959, yet South Vietnam remained economically underdeveloped. Believing that Diem needed a strong army to maintain control over the South Vietnamese people, American officials channeled large amounts of money into military rather than civilian projects. In fact, 78 percent of all the American financial aid to South Vietnam was used for military purposes, while only 1.25 percent went into industry and mining. Diem added to the problem by importing large quantities of consumer goods rather than machinery needed for industrial development. Diem resisted American advice to reduce spending on consumer items because he feared that a lower standard of living would create social unrest and thereby endanger his regime. So while Diem received the largest share of the American foreign aid budget during these years, he did little to help South Vietnam achieve economic independence.

Although the United States supplied the Saigon government with four times more military aid than economic assistance, the South Vietnamese army still did not become a strong and effective fighting force. Diem promoted officers because they were loyal to him, even if they were incompetent on the battlefield. Hence, his officer corps was riddled with favoritism and nearly devoid of patriotism. Many senior ARVN officers had fought on the French side during the recent war, and almost none of them had participated in the anticolonial resistance movement. To make matters worse, the South Vietnamese army was corrupt to the core. Many officers regarded military service as an opportunity to enrich themselves rather than as an obligation to defend their country. Although their pay was extraordinarily high by Asian standards, ARVN officers often supplemented their regular income by embezzling funds and selling drugs. And those in the lower ranks frequently robbed the very peasants they were supposed to protect. In short, the South Vietnamese army was basically a mercenary force, primarily designed to help Diem maintain his police state.

Despite all of this, the American economic aid package did help Diem win political support in the urban areas of South Vietnam. Under the commercial import program, the Saigon government received free dollars from the United States and then sold them to local importers for South Vietnamese piasters at about half the official exchange rate. The commercial import program, subsidized by American taxpayers, provided Diem with the means to pay most of the cost of his military forces and civil servants without having to impose high taxes on the South Vietnamese middle class. The privileged merchants used their cheap dollars to import a vast array of consumer goods that were sold to urban dwellers at low prices. Besides producing an artificial prosperity in the towns and cities of South Vietnam, the commercial import program enabled the select group of merchants to reap huge profits, and those who received importing licenses from the government became staunch supporters of both Diem and his American sponsors.

At the same time, Diem sought political support from the large rice planters in the fertile Mekong Delta. Many affluent landlords had sympathized with the French during the recent war, and the Vietminh had confiscated their large holdings and distributed small plots to a great number of landless peasants. After Diem came to power in South Vietnam, however, he would not allow these peasants to keep the land that they now considered their own unless they paid high prices to compensate the former owners. Few peasants could afford to buy the land, and as a result, most of the property was returned to the original holders. Since Diem refused to implement a land reform program that would alienate the powerful rice planters, only 2.5 percent of the landholders owned 50 percent of the acreage under cultivation in the Mekong Delta. Most peasants in the area remained tenant farmers who had to pay high land rents, ranging from one-quarter to one-third of their total rice crop. Although the unequal distribution of agricultural land and the ruthless exploitation of tenant farmers generated widespread peasant discontent, Diem was able to win and retain the loyalty of the planter class that dominated the Mekong Delta.

The Diem regime, supported by the great landlords and wealthy merchants, attempted to crush all political opposition. Although the Geneva Agreements promised amnesty for everyone who had participated in the war, Diem immediately launched a campaign against the Vietminh to prevent them from organizing a political challenge to his government. He stopped at nothing in an effort to suppress the Vietminh soldiers and political cadres who had been born and raised in the south and had decided to remain there after the war ended. Peasants were dragooned into mass meetings and pressured into informing against Vietminh members and sympathizers, and before long, a large number of political dissidents were either executed or sent to concentration camps. In the spring of 1956, a South Vietnamese government official acknowledged that between 15,000 and 20,000 people had been incarcerated for the purpose of "reeducation." Diem did succeed in smashing many Vietminh cells, but his brutal treatment of former war heroes alienated large segments of the South Vietnamese population.

Although Diem posed in republican dress, his regime was a repressive dictatorship. Real power in South Vietnam remained in the hands of Diem and his three brothers who ruled the country, through the secret Can Lao Party, which was deeply entrenched in the armed forces and the civil service. Fearing that the Vietminh would win positions in local governments throughout South Vietnam, Diem decided in 1956 to abolish the traditional practice of holding elections for village councils and to appoint local officials who were loyal to him. Many of those appointed to office were Catholic refugees from the north. Some were corrupt, and most held the common people in contempt. Diem also made sure that only his supporters would be allowed to run for the national assembly, and his secret police, headed by his brother Ngo Dinh Nhu, used intimidation to assure huge electoral victories for his candidates. People who questioned his authority were imprisoned, while newspapers that criticized his government were shut down. In other words, Diem employed physical coercion rather than social reform in order to maintain political control over the South Vietnamese populace.

His repressive policies soon triggered a revolutionary upheaval within South Vietnam. Until July 1956, the Vietminh fighters and organizers who had stayed in the south following the Geneva Agreements could hope that there would be a peaceful reunification of Vietnam as a result of general elections. But after that date had passed, the Vietminh leaders in the south decided to resort to violence in order to achieve their cherished goal of national reunification. Thus, a revolt from below erupted inside South Vietnam. The insurgents were soon joined by native southerners who had remained in the north after the Geneva Accords to receive special training in the art of revolutionary warfare. These Vietminh veterans were not outside invaders with strange manners and different accents, although a few northern-born advisors accompanied them when they returned home. Together with other indigenous southerners, they engaged in an energetic campaign to recruit new members for their struggle against Diem, and during 1957, the rebel ranks swelled as more and more southern peasants joined the insurgency.

Ho Chi Minh and his colleagues in Hanoi, however, were reluctant to become involved in a military struggle to liberate South Vietnam. These leaders of the Lao Dong, or Vietnamese Workers Party (formerly the Communist Party), feared that renewed warfare would undermine their effort to promote economic development in North Vietnam. They also worried that the United States might intervene if northern soldiers were sent to help the southern rebels. In November 1956, therefore, the northern communists told their southern comrades that they should use peaceful means to grasp power. Yet many southerners, hounded by the secret police, began agitating for a policy of armed rebellion rather than peaceful resistance. Hanoi responded in November 1957 with a clear message that the time was not yet ripe for armed insurrection. But Diem became increasingly successful in his repressive measures during the next year, and as more and more insurgents were captured or killed, southern pressure for a change in northern policy grew apace. Finally, in February 1959, the Lao Dong leaders authorized the use of military force by southerners, but only in support of the political struggle against the Saigon government. Hanoi gave clear instructions that the goal should be to topple the Diem regime by a general uprising rather than through guerrilla warfare.

Meanwhile, Diem continued to implement policies that fanned the flames of insurgency in South Vietnam. During 1957, he began establishing large Vietnamese settlements in the Central Highlands at the expense of mountain tribesmen who were pushed off lands that they needed for their slash-and-burn agricultural methods. The ethnic Vietnamese from the coastal lowlands viewed the mountaineers as savages, and in late 1958, the Central Intelligence Agency reported growing tribal discontent with the Saigon government. Worse yet, in May 1959, Diem started forcing peasants to resettle in fortified agrovilles in an effort to separate them from the rebels in the surrounding countryside. The peasants resented being forced to relocate away from their ancestral burial grounds and family rice paddies. The agroville program was eventually abandoned, but not before it had spawned an enormous amount of hostility in rural areas against the Diem regime. As a result, more and more South Vietnamese peasants responded favorably to the rebel promise that better days would come after the downfall of Diem.

After resorting to violence to assure their own survival, the southern insurgents became increasingly bold in their efforts to bring down the Diem regime. In 1958, the rebels assassinated about 700 local government officials, and two years later, the number of political assassinations in South Vietnamese villages leaped to more than 100 a month. Moreover, during the last half of 1959, the insurgents shifted from hit-and-run operations to large-scale attacks against exposed units of the South Vietnamese army. They also intensified their drive to win support from the rural population of South Vietnam. Diem responded to the rising tide of revolution by launching a propaganda campaign to discredit the South Vietnamese insurgents. Although many of the old Vietminh veterans and the new recruits to the revolutionary cause were not communists, Diem claimed that anyone who opposed his government was by definition a communist. Thus, he began referring to the indigenous rebels as Vietcong (meaning Vietnamese communist) rather than as Vietminh (meaning Vietnamese nationalist). The term Vietcong (or VC, as they were also often called) soon gained widespread currency and helped justify American efforts to counter the insurgency in South Vietnam.

At the same time, the communist leaders in Hanoi felt compelled to accommodate their policies to maintain control over the revolutionary movement in South Vietnam. Although they had decided in May 1959 to construct a route through Laos (later known as the Ho Chi Minh Trail) to move men and supplies southward, they continued to warn against rash adventures in South Vietnam. The Lao Dong cautioned in March 1960 that the southern insurgents were not yet ready for a direct revolution against Diem. But the impatient southerners could not be restrained by Hanoi. In April 1960, a group of noncommunists in Saigon issued a manifesto demanding that Diem make sweeping reforms, and after consulting with Chinese officials a month later, the North Vietnamese decided to authorize political and military action aimed at overthrowing the Diem regime. In December 1960, with the approval of Hanoi, the southern rebels formed the National Liberation Front (NLF) to rally their compatriots behind a program calling for a coalition government in Saigon and the gradual reunification of Vietnam through peaceful negotiations. The new organization, like the old Vietminh, included a large number of noncommunists who were willing to take their instructions from northern communists in order to achieve their nationalist goals.

American leaders had by then become apprehensive about the situation in South Vietnam. Disappointed with the performance of the South Vietnamese army, they decided in May 1959 to begin sending American advisers on military missions with ARVN units. Although Ambassador Elbridge Durbrow argued that Diem needed to make reforms in order to gain enough popular support to defeat the insurrection in South Vietnam, most American military advisers continued to view the problem in battlefield terms. Despite their narrow perspective, however, American military authorities began to lose their sense of complacency about the armed forces buttressing the Saigon government. They also began to realize that the immediate danger to the Diem regime came from the revolution in South Vietnam and not from a massive invasion by North Vietnam. In the summer of 1960, therefore, the United States belatedly shifted the emphasis of its military training program away from conventional warfare and toward counterinsurgency. American military planners quite logically concluded that the way to defeat an insurgency was to engage in counterinsurgency. But while the United States was finally beginning to apply appropriate military measures to fight the Vietcong, it was not doing much in the political arena to deal with the underlying social and economic causes of the revolution in South Vietnam.

Despite the change in military orientation, political conditions in South Vietnam remained chaotic. A State Department intelligence report warned in August 1960 that South Vietnamese army officers were becoming increasingly discontent about the promotion of incompetent commanders and the influence of the Can Lao Party on military affairs. The report also noted that criticism of the Diem regime had mounted among government officials who were upset about the activities of Ngo Dinh Nhu and his wife. "Should a coup materialize," the report concluded, "the immediate and principal objective would probably be to oust the Nhus and their entourage and then leave Diem with the alternative of either continuing in office with reduced power or resigning." Ambassador Durbrow promptly encouraged Diem to take steps to reduce the prospects for a coup. He advised Diem to remove the unpopular Nhu from his position of power in the government and to alter the nature of the Can Lao Party. But Diem refused to diminish the authority of his brother or to change the character of the principal instrument that the Ngo family used to rule South Vietnam.

When it became clear that Diem would not make any meaningful reforms, the disgruntled military officers decided to stage a coup against his regime. The rebels struck in November 1960, but fundamental disagreements over their ultimate objectives helped foil their effort to grasp power. While some of the conspirators aimed to get rid of Diem along with Nhu, others wanted to keep Diem as a figurehead in a new government after eliminating his brother. The American embassy in Saigon, hoping to prevent bloodshed, urged both Diem and the coup leaders to settle their differences through negotiations. With rebel troops surrounding his palace, Diem maneuvered to buy time by promising to make far-reaching concessions. The rebel officers took the bait and agreed to enter into discussions. Diem then took advantage of the opportunity to order loyal troops to Saigon to quell the rebellion. But the coup attempt had almost succeeded, and the event seriously damaged the relationship between the Ngo brothers and their patrons in Washington. Believing that some American officials had encouraged the rebels, Diem and Nhu became ever more suspicious and distrustful of the United States.

DOCUMENT 3-1

The Final Declaration on Indochina of the Geneva Conference Promulgated on July 21, 1954

Final Declaration, dated the 21st July, 1954, of the Geneva Conference on the problem of restoring peace in Indo-China, in which the representatives of Cambodia, the Democratic Republic of Viet-Nam, France, Laos, the People's Republic of China, the State of Viet-Nam, the Union of Soviet Socialist Republics, the United Kingdom, and the United States of America took part.

1. The Conference takes note of the agreements ending hostilities in Cambodia, Laos and Viet-Nam and organizing international control and the supervision of the execution of the provisions of these agreements.

2. The Conference expresses satisfaction at the ending of hostilities in Cambodia, Laos and Viet-Nam; the Conference expresses its conviction that the execution of the provisions set out in the present declaration and in the agreements on the cessation of hostilities will permit Cambodia, Laos and Viet-Nam henceforth to play their part, in full independence and sovereignty, in the peaceful community of nations.

3. The Conference takes note of the declaration made by the Governments of Cambodia and Laos of their intention to adopt measures permitting all citizens to take their place in the national community, in particular by participating in the next general elections, which, in conformity with the constitution of each of these countries, shall take place in the course of the year 1955, by secret ballot and in conditions of respect for fundamental freedoms.

4. The Conference takes note of the clauses in the agreement on the cessation of hostilities in Viet-Nam prohibiting the introduction into Viet-Nam of foreign troops and military personnel as well as of all kinds of arms and munitions. The Conference also takes note of the declarations made by the Governments of Cambodia and Laos of their resolution not to request foreign aid, whether in war material, in personnel or in instructors except for the purpose of the effective defense of their territory and, in the case of Laos, to the extent defined by the agreements on the cessation of hostilities in Laos.

5. The Conference takes note of the clauses in the agreement on the cessation of hostilities in Viet-Nam to the effect that no military base under the control of a foreign State may be established in the regrouping zones of the two parties, the latter having the obligation to see that the zones allotted to them shall not constitute part of any military alliance and shall not be utilized for the resumption of hostilities or in the service of an aggressive policy. The Conference also takes note of the declarations of the Governments of Cambodia and Laos to the effect that they will not join in any agreement with other States if this agreement includes the obligation to participate in a military alliance not in conformity with the principles of the Charter of the United Nations or, in the case of Laos, with the principles of the agreement on the cessation of hostilities in Laos or, so long as their security is not threatened, the obligation to establish bases on Cambodian or Laotian territory for the military forces of foreign Powers.

6. The Conference recognizes that the essential purpose of the agreement relating to Viet-Nam is to settle military questions with a view to ending hostilities and that the military demarcation line is provisional and should not in any way be interpreted as constituting a political or territorial boundary. The Conference expresses its conviction that the execution of the provisions set out in the present declaration and in the agreement on the cessation of hostilities creates the necessary basis for the achievement in the near future of a political settlement in Viet-Nam.

7. The Conference declares that, so far as Viet-Nam is concerned, the settlement of political problems, effected on the basis of respect for the principles of independence, unity and territorial integrity, shall permit the Viet-Namese people to enjoy the fundamental freedoms, guaranteed by democratic institutions established as a result of free general elections by secret ballot. In order to ensure that sufficient

(continued)

DOCUMENT 3-1 Continued

progress in the restoration of peace has been made, and that all the necessary conditions obtain for free expression of the national will, general elections shall be held in July 1956, under the supervision of an international commission composed of representatives of the Member States of the International Supervisory Commission, referred to in the agreement on the cessation of hostilities. Consultations will be held on this subject between the competent representative authorities of the two zones from 20 July 1955 onwards.

8. The provisions of the agreements on the cessation of hostilities intended to ensure the protection of individuals and of property must be most strictly applied and must, in particular, allow everyone in Viet-Nam to decide freely in which zone he wishes to live.

9. The competent representative authorities of the Northern and Southern zones of Viet-Nam, as well as the authorities of Laos and Cambodia, must not permit any individual of collective reprisals against persons who have collaborated in any way with one of the parties during the war, or against members of such persons' families.

10. The Conference takes note of the declaration of the Government of the French Republic to the effect that it is ready to withdraw its troops from the territory of Cambodia, Laos and Viet-Nam, at the request of the governments concerned and within periods which shall be fixed by agreement between the parties except in the cases where, by agreement between the two parties, a certain number of French troops shall remain at specified points and for a specified time.

11. The Conference takes note of the declaration of the French Government to the effect that for the settlement of all the problems connected with the re-establishment and consolidation of peace in Cambodia, Laos and Viet-Nam, the French Government will proceed from the principle of respect for the independence and sovereignty, unity and territorial integrity of Cambodia, Laos and Viet-Nam.

12. In their relations with Cambodia, Laos and Viet-Nam, each member of the Geneva Conference undertakes to respect the sovereignty, the independence, the unity and territorial integrity of the above-mentioned states, and to refrain from any interference in their internal affairs.

13. The members of the Conference agree to consult one another on any question which may be referred to them by the International Supervisory Commission, in order to study such measures as may prove necessary to ensure that the agreements on the cessation of hostilities in Cambodia, Laos and Viet-Nam are respected.

Source: Department of State, *Foreign Relations of the United States,* 1952–1954, vol. XVI, 1540–1542.

DOCUMENT 3-2

Report on the Covert Operations Conducted by the Saigon Military Mission in 1954 and 1955

I. Foreward

...This is the condensed account of one year in the operations of a "cold war'" combat team, written by the team itself in the field, little by little in moments taken as the members could. The team is known as the Saigon Military Mission. The field is Vietnam....

The Geneva Agreements signed on 21 July 1954 imposed restrictive rules upon all official Americans, including the Saigon Military Mission.... We worked to help stabilize the government [in the south] and to beat the Geneva time-table of the Communist takeover in the north....

DOCUMENT 3-2 Continued

II. Mission

The Saigon Military Mission (SMM) was born in a Washington policy meeting early in 1954, when Dien Bien Phu was still holding out against the encircling Vietminh. The SMM was to enter into Vietnam quietly and assist the Vietnamese, rather than the French....

The broad mission for the team was to undertake paramilitary operations against the enemy and to wage political-psychological warfare....

III. Highlights of the Year

a. Early Days

The Saigon Military Mission (SMM) started on 1 June 1954, when its Chief, Colonel Edward G. Lansdale, USAF, arrived in Saigon....Lt-General John O'Daniel and Embassy Charge Rob McClinton had arranged for his appointment as Assistant Air Attache.... Secret communications with Washington were provided through the Saigon station of CIA.

There was a deepening gloom in Vietnam. Dien Bien Phu had fallen. The French were capitulating to the Vietminh at Geneva....

Working in close cooperation with George Hellyer, USIS Chief, a new psychological warfare campaign was devised for the Vietnamese Army and for the government in Hanoi....

The first rumor campaign was to be a carefully planted story of a Chinese Communist regiment in Tonkin taking reprisals against a Vietminh village whose girls the Chinese had raped, recalling Chinese Nationalist troop behavior in 1945 and confirming Vietnamese fears of Chinese occupation under Vietminh rule; the story was to be planted by soldiers of the Vietnamese Armed Psywar company in Hanoi dressed in civilian clothes....

On 1 July, Major Lucien Conein arrived, as the second member of the team. He is a paramilitary specialist.... He was assigned to MAAG for cover purposes....

Ngo Dinh Diem arrived on 7 July, and within hours was in despair as the French forces withdrew from the Catholic provinces of Phat Diem and Nam Dinh in Tonkin....On 21 July, the Geneva Agreement was signed. Tonkin was given to the Communists.

Anti-Communists turned to SMM for help in establishing a resistance movement and several tentative initial arrangements were made....

b. August 1954

...Major Conein was given responsibility for developing a paramilitary organization in the north, to be in position when the Vietminh took over....The team had headquarters in Hanoi, with a branch in Haiphong....

A second paramilitary team was formed to explore possibilities of organizing resistance against the Vietminh from bases in the south....

c. September 1954

Highly-placed officials from Washington visited Saigon and, in private conversations, indicated that current estimates led to the conclusion that Vietnam probably would have to be written off as a loss. We admitted that prospects were gloomy, but were positive that there was still a fighting chance....

[The arrest of some Vietnamese Army officers] brought into the open a plot by the Army Chief of Staff, General Hinh, to overthrow the government.....

While various U.S. officials...participated in U.S. attempts to heal the split between the President and his Army, Ambassador Heath asked us to make a major effort to end the controversy. This effort strained relations with Diem and never was successful, but did dampen Army enthusiasm for the plot. At one moment, when there was the likelihood of an attack by armored vehicles on the Presidential Palace, SMM told Hinh bluntly that U.S. support most probably would stop in such an event....

As a result of the Hinh trouble, Diem started looking around for troops upon whom he could count.... Diem made an agreement with general Trinh Minh The, the leader of some 3,000 Cao Dai dissidents in the vicinity of Tayninh, to give General The some needed financial support; The was to give armed support to the government if necessary and to provide a safe haven for the government if it had to flee.... At Ambassador Heath's request, the U.S. secretly furnished Diem with funds for The, through the SMM....

(continued)

DOCUMENT 3-2 Continued

The northern SMM team under Conein had organized a paramilitary group, (which we will disguise by the Vietnamese name of Binh)....Thirteen Binhs were quietly exfiltrated through the port of Haiphong, under the direction of Lt Andrews, and taken on the first stage of the journey to their training area by a U.S. Navy ship....

Another paramilitary group for Tonkin operations was being developed in Saigon....The project was given to Major Allen. (We shall give this group the Vietnamese name of Hao)....

Towards the end of the month, it was learned that the largest printing establishment in the north intended to remain in Hanoi and do business with the Vietminh. An attempt was made by SMM to destroy the modern presses, but Vietminh security agents already had moved into the plant and frustrated the attempt....

d. October 1954

Hanoi was evacuated on 9 October. The northern SMM team left with the last French troops....

The northern team had spent the last days of Hanoi in contaminating the oil supply of the bus company for a gradual wreckage of engines in the buses, in taking the first actions for delayed sabotage of the railroad (which required teamwork with a CIA special technical team in Japan who performed their part brilliantly), and in writing detailed notes of potential targets for future paramilitary operations (U.S. adherence to the Geneva Agreement prevented SMM from carrying out the active sabotage it desired to do against the power plant, water facilities, harbor, and, bridge)....

e. November 1954

General Lawton Collins arrived as Ambassador on 8 November....

Collins, in his first press conference, made it plain that the U.S. was supporting President Diem. The new Ambassador applied pressure on General Hinh and on 29 November Hinh left for Paris. His other key conspirators followed.

Part of the SMM team became involved in staff work to back up the campaign to save Vietnam which General Collins pushed forward. Some SMM members were scattered around the Pacific, accompanying Vietnamese for secret training, obtaining and shipping supplies to be smuggled into north Vietnam and hidden there....

On 23 November, twenty-one selected Vietnamese agents and two cooks from our Hao paramilitary group were put aboard a Navy ship in the Saigon River, in daylight. They appeared as coolies, joined the coolie and refugee throng moving on and off the ship, and disappeared one by one....The ship took the Hao agents to an overseas point, the first stage in a movement to a secret training area.

f. December 1954

...There was still much disquiet in Vietnam, particularly among anti-Communist political groups who were not included in the government. SMM officers were contacted by a number of such groups who felt that they "would have to commit suicide in 1956" (the 1956 plebiscite promised in the 1954 Geneva agreement), when the Vietminh would surely take over against so weak a government....A number of these groups asked SMM for help in training personnel for eventual guerrilla warfare if the Vietminh won....Plans were made with Major Bowman and Mr. John C. Wachtel in the Philippines for a solution of this problem; the United states backed the development, through them, of a small Freedom Company training camp in a hidden valley on the Clark AFB reservation.

g. January 1955

The Vietminh long ago had adopted the Chinese Communist thought that the people are the water and the army is the fish. Vietminh relations with the mass of the population during the fighting had been exemplary, with a few exceptions; in contrast, the Vietnamese National Army had been like too many Asian armies, adept at cowing a population into feeding them, providing them with girls. SMM had been working on this problem from the beginning....

The patriot we've named Trieu Dinh had been working on an almanac for popular sale, particularly in the northern cities and towns we could still reach. Noted Vietnamese astrologers were hired to write predictions about coming disasters to certain Vietminh leaders and undertakings, and to predict unity in the south. The work was carried out under the direction of Lt Phillips, based on our concept of the use of astrology for psywar in

DOCUMENT 3-2 Continued

Southeast Asia. Copies of the almanac were shipped by air to Haiphong and then smuggled into Vietnamese territory....

Arms and equipment for the Binh paramilitary team were being cached in the north in areas still free from the Vietminh....

Major Conein had briefed the members of the Binh paramilitary team and started them infiltrating into the north as individuals. The infiltration was carried out in careful stages over a 30 day period, a successful operation. The Binhs became normal citizens, carrying out every day civil pursuits, on the surface.

We had smuggled into Vietnam about eight and a half tons of supplies for the Hao paramilitary group. They included fourteen agent radios, 300 carbines, 90,000 rounds of carbine ammunition, 50 pistols, 10,000 rounds of pistol ammunition, and 300 pounds of explosives. Two and a half tons were delivered to the Hoa agents in Tonkin, while the remainder was cached along the Red River by SMM, with the help of the Navy....

h. April 1955

...The Hao paramilitary team had finished its training at the secret training site and been flown by the Air Force to a holding site in the Philippines, where Major Allen and his officers briefed the paramilitary team. In mid-April, they were taken by the Navy to Haiphong, where they were gradually slipped ashore. Meanwhile, arms and other equipment including explosives were being flown into Saigon via our smuggling route, being readied for shipment north by the Navy task force handling refugees....

Haiphong was taken over by the Vietminh on 16 May. Our Binh and northern Hao teams were in place, completely equipped. It had taken a tremendous amount of hard work to beat the Geneva deadline, to locate, select, exfiltrate, train, infiltrate, equip the men of these two teams and have them in place, ready for actions required against the enemy. It would be a hard task to do openly, but this had to be kept secret from the Vietminh, the International Commission with its suspicious French, Poles and Indians, and even friendly Vietnamese. Movement of personnel and supplies had had to be over thousands of miles....

Source: *The Pentagon Papers: Senator Gravel Edition* (Boston: Beacon Press, 1971), vol. I, 573–583.

DOCUMENT 3-3

John Foster Dulles, Report on Meeting with Chiefs of American Missions, March 2, 1955

Following the formal signing of the SEATO pact in Manila, Secretary of State John Foster Dulles reported on his meeting with the Chiefs of American Missions in Asia during a background press conference on March 2, 1955.

I gave a two-hour presentation this morning at which I tried to make clear to our people from these different posts the broad outlines of our policy for this area and to make clear the connection of what we do in one country with the interests of another. This is an extremely difficult thing to get across through the normal exchange of diplomatic cables and instructions. We fall into the habit of dealing with each Chief of Mission in relation to the problems of his country, and we don't often adequately, I am afraid, explain, for instance, to our Ambassador in Australia the meaning to Australia of what we may be doing in Korea or Japan. This gave me an opportunity to outline our basic philosophy and to point out that in this part of the world, at least, the United States does occupy a position of central power and influence and that we have an overall strategy which [relates] to each of these countries, but does not, necessarily, try to solve the problems in terms of that country alone. I pointed

(continued)

DOCUMENT 3-3 Continued

out the broad strategy which underlies our desire to maintain at least a potential of three fronts against the Chinese Communists if they should commit open aggression—the one in Korea, the one in Formosa, and the one in Indochina—and the fact that we have those three fronts is far more protective of everybody than if, for example, we concentrated on an effort in any one of these fronts. I outlined the military strategy which dictates a mobility of power rather than a segregation of power by dividing it up between different areas. There is a capacity to move rapidly into whatever area we chose as circumstances indicate desirable, and that it is much better to have all our power available for that purpose than to have it split up into fractions no one of which might be adequate to do the job. I reviewed the economic policies which lead us to try to develop the economic health of the area as a whole and not just concentrate on one country or even a group of countries represented at the Manila Pact; and I particularly emphasized the economic problem with Japan. That, incidentally, is the problem certain aspects of which meet us right away in Indochina, as was, I guess, remarked at the time we had our Saigon meeting. As Indochina becomes independent and has dollars directly available to it, there exists a competitive situation and there is a good chance of Japanese textile goods, for instance, moving into Indochina. The French are somewhat concerned about that, and I don't blame the French for being concerned about it but I don't think you can go on indefinitely having a protected preferential market for the French if Indochina..., particularly Vietnam, is to be an independent country and have its own source of dollars. You see, in the past we have given the dollars to the French and the French have in turn given French francs to Vietnam so that the purchases of Vietnam almost had to be made in the franc area. Now with us giving the dollars direct they will have the currency which is good for use anywhere and the situation becomes competitive....

Q: Do you anticipate, Mr. Secretary, that in addition to Japanese textiles other goods will likely be brought in increasing numbers from Japan by the Vietnamese once their dollars become available?

A: We have always felt that a major market for Japanese goods would be and, in fact, should be the Southeast Asia area including not only Indochina but Indonesia, Thailand, Burma, and also perhaps South Asia, India and Pakistan. The Japanese make the type of goods which find a ready market. It's a cheaper type of good than is desired really in our own markets and is within the capacity of people to buy. Also, they should be able to contribute some heavy industry goods in the way of machinery and things of that sort, so that we have always looked forward to a development of the Japanese market in that area and I think what is taking place there is a logical and almost inevitable development. And if you take the French situation—if you take the overall picture—I don't have the figures in mind, but by and large the French trade that may be dislocated will not seriously affect the French economy. The French economy is getting along very well despite political crises and governmental crises....I do not think the increasing independence, both political and economic, of Indochina will have a serious effect on the French economy as a whole. It may not be pleasant for some individual concerns in France, but by and large the impact on the French economy will not be serious. As I said to you in Saigon, there is no desire on the part of the United States to try to displace French influence in that area. A certain displacement is, I think, inevitable.

Q: You mentioned the French fears of this thing. Have you run into any indication of similar apprehension on the part of the British?

A: No. I discussed this somewhat with (British Foreign Secretary Anthony) Eden when we were there and I think that he recognized that British interests had to be prepared to accept a certain competition

DOCUMENT 3-3 Continued

of Japanese goods in that area and that it would probably be better to meet the competition there than to try to meet it by having Japanese goods going directly into the United Kingdom.

If the reciprocal trade agreements act is extended, and I hope it will be, and when we carry through our negotiations under that act, and when we have got operating our

more complete economic program, for Southeast Asia and South Asia, which will be geared to promoting trade with Japan to that area, I think the combination of those things will really pretty well take care of the Japanese economic problem. That, of course, assumes that the Southeast Asia and South Asia area does not go Communist.

Source: John Foster Dulles Papers, Princeton University.

Chronological List of Main Events

July 1953	The Korean War armistice
March 1954	The beginning of the Battle of Dien Bien Phu
May 1954	The opening of the Indochina phase of the Geneva Conference
June 1954	The establishment of the Saigon Military Mission
September 1954	The formation of the South East Asia Treaty Organization
October 1955	The election of Ngo Dinh Diem as the President of South Vietnam
July 1956	The beginning of the revolution in South Vietnam
May 1959	The establishment of the agroville program
December 1960	The organization of the National Liberation Front

Study Questions

1. What was the Navarre Plan?
2. What was Operation Vulture?
3. Why did the Eisenhower administration oppose general elections in 1956 to reunify Vietnam?

4. Would Diem have been able to win broad popular support if he had implemented as extensive land reform program in South Vietnam?

4

The Summons of the Trumpet

What I am concerned about is that Americans will get impatient and say, because they don't like events in Southeast Asia or they don't like the Government in Saigon, that we should withdraw. That only makes it easier for the Communists. I think we should stay. We should use our influence in as effective a way as we can, but we should not withdraw.

PRESIDENT JOHN F. KENNEDY, 1963

THE GLOBAL DOMINO THEORY

President John F. Kennedy, a Democrat from the east coast, was determined to defeat the growing communist challenge to the liberal capitalist world system. In his inaugural address delivered in January 1961, Kennedy set the tone for the beginning of a bold American foreign policy designed to promote economic freedom and political liberty around the globe. His manner was vigorous and energetic; his words were militant and defiant: "We shall pay any price, bear any burden, meet any hardship, support any friend, oppose any foe to assure the survival and success of liberty." Just two weeks earlier, Premier Nikita S. Khrushchev had belligerently pledged that the Soviet Union would support wars of national liberation. And Radio Hanoi, in a broadcast coinciding with the bellicose statement from Moscow, announced the formation of the National Liberation Front to direct the forces of revolt against the Ngo Dinh Diem regime in Saigon. In his response to these ominous developments, Kennedy called on the American people to join with him in launching a New Frontier. "Now," the youthful Democratic president exhorted, "the trumpet summons us."

The Kennedy administration confronted a wave of social revolutions that threatened to destroy the institution of private property and the principle of free trade throughout large parts of Asia, Africa, and Latin America. While Patrice Lumumba was leading a struggle in the Congo against the old order of colonialism, Fidel Castro was engaged in a campaign to transform Cuba into a showcase for communism in the heart of the Caribbean basin. Kennedy and his advisers feared that radicals would gain control of revolutionary movements elsewhere in the Third World, adopt a communist model for economic development, and place severe restrictions on international commercial and financial transactions. In an effort to encourage leaders in underdeveloped countries to follow a capitalist recipe for material accumulation, Professor Walt W. Rostow of the Massachusetts Institute of Technology wrote a book entitled *The Stages of Economic Growth: A Non-Communist Manifesto*. Kennedy agreed with Rostow's prescription for the Third World, and shortly after winning the presidential election in November 1960, he selected Rostow to serve as a top national security aide.

Kennedy and his advisers planned to employ a dual diplomacy in an attempt to keep Third World countries functioning within the framework of the liberal capitalist international order. On the positive side, they intended to offer the economic carrot to eradicate the conditions of poverty that provided seedbeds for the growth of communism in underdeveloped areas. Programs of financial and technical assistance were devised to induce political leaders in the Third World to maintain their allegiance to capitalism. On the negative side, Kennedy and his aides aimed to use the military stick to defeat revolutionary movements that threatened to bring communist regimes to power. Counterinsurgency programs were organized to teach American soldiers effective methods for combating guerrilla forces operating in tropical regions. In short, if the Peace Corps failed to do the job, the Green Berets stood ready for action.

Growing apprehensions about revolutionary upheavals in the Third World had produced a significant metamorphosis in the domino theory by the time Kennedy entered the White House. During the 1950s, American policymakers had feared that the fall of Indochina to communism would lead to the loss of the rest of Southeast Asia as a market for Japan. But by the 1960s, they also worried that the fall of Indochina to communism would lead to the loss of Africa and Latin America as markets for the United States and its European trading partners. Thus, the old regional formula, "so goes Vietnam, so goes Malaya and Indonesia," became the new global refrain, "so goes Vietnam, so goes Guatemala and the Congo." And as the domino theory assumed world-wide dimensions, South Vietnam loomed large as the testing ground for wars of national liberation. The communist leaders in North Vietnam hoped to receive ample military supplies from China, where Mao Zedong was busy portraying the United States as a paper tiger. "South Vietnam is the model of the national liberation movement of our time," General Vo Nguyen Giap declared. "If the special warfare that the United States imperialists are testing in South Vietnam is overcome, then it can be defeated anywhere in the world."

Determined to protect American economic and strategic interests around the world, Kennedy and the New Frontiersmen made preparations to combat the communist menace in Southeast Asia. They intended to refute Mao by demonstrating that the United States had not just the ability but also the resolve to prevent Giap from directing a successful war of national liberation. If the United States appeared weak and hesitant in the face of the communist challenge in South Vietnam, American leaders feared that rebel groups throughout the Third World would be emboldened. Thus, they felt compelled to maintain the prestige and credibility of the United States as a vital part of their commitment to perpetuate the Pax Americana. Domestic political considerations reinforced these global concerns. Recalling that the Republicans had blamed Truman for the loss of China to Mao and his comrades, Kennedy feared that he would become the target of similar criticism if South Vietnam fell into communist hands.

During his last months in the White House, however, President Dwight D. Eisenhower had regarded Laos rather than South Vietnam as the most dangerous trouble spot in Indochina. The United States had been supporting a right-wing regime in that country, but in 1960, Laotian neutralists joined hands with the Pathet Lao communist rebels in an effort to oust the American-sponsored government. By the end of the year, North Vietnam and the Soviet Union were giving substantial aid to the anti-American forces, and Eisenhower was seriously considering the option of military intervention. On the eve of his retirement in January 1961, Eisenhower briefed president-elect Kennedy about the menacing situation. The fall of Laos would endanger Thailand, Cambodia, and South Vietnam, he warned, and if the United States did not draw the line there, all of Southeast Asia might be lost to communism. Having thus defined Laos as the key domino in the whole region, Eisenhower advised Kennedy that the United States should attempt to persuade its SEATO allies to undertake multilateral action. But if they refused to comply with American wishes, Eisenhower concluded, the United States might have to resort to unilateral intervention as a last, desperate effort to save Laos.

After taking the oath of office on the next day, Kennedy gave serious thought to the question of whether or not the United States should dispatch combat troops to Laos. But the new president was given pause when he learned that a large American task force could not be deployed in that country unless the United States withdrew troops from Europe, where a crisis concerning Berlin was becoming increasingly acute. Kennedy realized that the American strategic reserve would be inadequate to meet other contingencies that might occur anywhere around the world if the United States became involved in a big military operation in Laos. Therefore, he decided to send American diplomats to Geneva to participate in an international peace conference. The Soviet delegation sought a permanent settlement in Laos to help pave the way for a relaxation in tensions with the United States. But the representatives from China and North Vietnam only wanted an agreement that would forestall a major American military intervention in Laos and buy time for the Pathet Lao to build up their armed forces in preparation for an eventual communist takeover of the country. The Geneva Treaty, concluded in July 1962 after a year of negotiations, stipulated that Laos would be a neutral nation with a coalition government representing communist as well as moderate and conservative elements.

Nevertheless, even if this compromise temporarily ended the turmoil in Laos, the situation in South Vietnam remained very serious. A few days after his inauguration in January 1961, President Kennedy read an alarming report prepared by General Edward G. Lansdale about the steady growth of the insurgency in South Vietnam and the increasing problems of the shaky Ngo Dinh Diem regime in Saigon. Lansdale predicted a large-scale Vietcong offensive before the end of the year. And he warned that if the communists won in South Vietnam, they would have easy pickings in the remainder of Southeast Asia because the toughest anticommunist forces in the region would be gone. The loss of South Vietnam, he asserted, would be "a major blow to U.S. prestige and influence, not only in Asia but throughout the world." Lansdale made two important policy recommendations. First, he advocated a major American effort to defeat the Vietcong drive to gain control of South Vietnam. Second, he argued that Ambassador Elbridge Durbrow should be transferred from his post in Saigon because Diem believed that he had sympathized strongly with the leaders of the recently aborted coup.

President Kennedy was impressed by the Lansdale memorandum, and he quickly demonstrated his readiness to take steps to prevent the South Vietnam domino from toppling. Following a meeting with a small group of his closest advisers on January 28, Kennedy approved an additional $42 million in American aid to fund an expansion of the Army of the Republic of Vietnam. The president also decided to replace Ambassador Durbrow with Frederick E. Nolting, who was sent to Saigon to carry out the difficult assignment of improving relations with Diem. Three months later, on April 27, an interagency work group warned that South Vietnam was nearing a decisive phase in its battle for survival as an independent, noncommunist nation. Kennedy quickly responded to this report by dispatching another 100 American military advisers to South Vietnam along with 400 Special Forces troops to teach ARVN units counterinsurgency techniques. Besides authorizing an increase in American military personnel in South Vietnam, Kennedy decided to sponsor a new program of covert operations against North Vietnam. The United States soon began to infiltrate undercover teams of South Vietnamese across the seventeenth parallel to sabotage North Vietnamese installations and to agitate against the communist government in Hanoi. At the same time, the United States initiated a secret war in Laos by arming and training Hmong or Meo tribesmen for attacks against the Ho Chi Minh Trail.

Yet many American military leaders thought that the United States would have to take even more forceful actions to prevent South Vietnam from falling into the hands of the National Liberation Front. The Joint Chiefs of Staff did not believe that the dispatch of Green Berets and the expansion of the Military Assistance Advisory Group would be sufficient to subdue the Vietcong, and in May 1961, they formally recommended that the United States immediately deploy regular military forces in South Vietnam. Kennedy quickly instructed Vice President Lyndon B. Johnson to raise the question in Saigon, but Diem indicated that he did not want American combat troops except in the case of overt aggression from North Vietnam. Critics were already referring to the Saigon government as the "American-Diem" regime, and Johnson reported that the introduction of a large number of troops from the United States would intensify anticolonial emotions in South Vietnam. Endeavoring to reassure Diem that he could count on American support, Johnson publicly described him as "the Winston Churchill of Southeast Asia." But the vice president was less enthusiastic when a reporter later asked in private if he really meant what he had said. "Shit," Johnson drawled, "Diem's the only boy we got out there."

Not long after Johnson left Saigon, alarming reports reached Washington about sharply escalating Vietcong attacks in the Mekong Delta. The insurgents mounted three assaults in units of more than 1,000 men during September 1961, and on one occasion, they briefly occupied a provincial capital just fifty-five miles from Saigon. In an intelligence estimate made on October 5, the Central Intelligence Agency calculated that the rebel forces had grown from about 4,000 to around 16,000 during the past year and a half. The CIA noted that 80 to 90 percent of the Vietcong soldiers were local recruits and that 10 to 20 percent were southerners who had gone north for training before returning home via mountain trails through Laos. Unable to find evidence of any communist-bloc military equipment in South Vietnam, the CIA concluded that the guerrillas obtained their arms from small, local arsenals and by capturing them from South Vietnamese army units.

THE SECOND INDOCHINA WAR

During a Lao Dong party conference, convened by the Central Office for South Vietnam in the autumn of 1961, communist leaders reviewed the progress of their revolutionary movement. The Central Committee of the party observed that forms of limited guerrilla warfare and partial uprisings had set the stage for the beginning of a period of prolonged political crisis in South Vietnam. "The revolutionary forces will be rapidly built and developed and forms of revolutionary government will appear in localities everywhere," it predicted, "and a general offensive and general uprising of the people will break out, overthrow the U.S.-Diem regime and liberate the South." To hasten that process, the Central Committee outlined a plan of action for the National Liberation Front: Political struggle was to remain primary in the cities, but in the plains region, political and military struggle were to be placed on the same level, and in the mountainous areas, military struggle was to become primary. The Central Committee concluded that the revolutionary forces should be prepared not only to take advantage of future coup attempts against the Saigon government but also to cope with "the possibility of armed intervention by bringing troops of U.S. imperialism and its lackeys into the South."

Already thinking along such lines, President Kennedy decided to send a mission, headed by Walt Rostow and his personal military adviser, General Maxwell D. Taylor, to assess the situation in South Vietnam. Kennedy made it clear during a meeting in early October 1961 that the group should weigh the need for the deployment of American combat troops to deal with the Vietcong. Upon their arrival in Saigon a week later, Taylor and Rostow found that South Vietnam was suffering from a double crisis in confidence: doubt that the United States was determined to save Southeast Asia and doubt that Diem could defeat the communists with the defensive tactics he was employing. After completing their two-week tour of the country, Taylor and Rostow recommended a series of specific measures that the United States should take to prevent a further deterioration of the situation in South Vietnam. They advocated the training and equipping of the Civil Guard and the Self-Defense Corps to relieve the regular South Vietnamese army of static assignments, together with the provision of considerably more American helicopters and light aviation to increase the mobility of ARVN units for offensive operations. They also urged the expansion of the Military Assistance Advisory Group and the introduction of American military personnel to perform difficult tasks such as air reconnaissance and special intelligence that were beyond the capacity of the South Vietnamese forces.

Further, although Diem still opposed the introduction of American combat troops, Taylor and Rostow proposed the dispatch of an 8,000-man military task force to South Vietnam. The ostensible purpose of the unit would be to assist in repairing the extensive damage caused by flooding in the Mekong Delta. But under the cloak provided by the humanitarian activity of engineers and medics, American infantrymen would conduct combat operations against the Vietcong. Taylor and Rostow argued that the presence of American soldiers would raise morale in South Vietnam and demonstrate the resolve of the United States to resist communism in Southeast Asia. They concluded that the task force would not only furnish an emergency reserve to back up the ARVN in the case of a heightened military crisis in South Vietnam but also serve as an advance party if more American ground troops were needed to stem the tide in the future.

Secretary of Defense Robert S. McNamara and the Joint Chiefs of Staff, however, thought that the United States should go well beyond these recommendations. In a memorandum sent to President Kennedy in early November 1961, they warned that the introduction of only 8,000 American soldiers in the context of flood relief would neither convince the communist leaders in Hanoi that the United States meant business nor tip the scales decisively against the Vietcong guerrillas. Thus, they reasoned that the initial dispatch of American troops should be accompanied by a definite commitment to prevent the fall of South Vietnam to communism and by a warning to Ho Chi Minh that the United States would retaliate against North Vietnam if he continued to support the Vietcong rebels. While not quite sure how many American troops would be needed to put the ARVN on the road to victory, McNamara and the JCS assured Kennedy that no more than about 205,000 American ground forces would be required even in the event that both North Vietnam and Red China intervened overtly in South Vietnam. They therefore supported the Taylor-Rostow recommendations, but only as the first steps toward the fulfillment of American objectives.

Taking a contrary stand, the State Department opposed sending any American combat troops to South Vietnam. Secretary of State Dean Rusk doubted that the deployment of a small American task force would have a decisive influence if Diem remained unwilling to make essential political and military reforms. While attaching great importance to checking the spread of communism in Southeast Asia, Rusk was reluctant to make a major commitment of "American prestige to a losing horse." Under Secretary of State Chester Bowles and ambassador-at-large W. Averell Harriman likewise questioned the viability of the Saigon government, and their skepticism about the Diem regime led them to advocate a diplomatic rather than a military solution. In a memorandum to Kennedy delivered on November 11, Harriman proposed a peace settlement based on national elections, as envisaged in the 1954 Geneva Accords. But he warned that if Diem continued to be "repressive, dictatorial and unpopular," South Vietnam would not in any case long remain an independent, noncommunist country.

Beset by divided counsel, Kennedy was in a quandary about what should be done. Yet it soon became clear that he was firmly opposed to a negotiated settlement. In a brief presented to Rusk and McNamara on November 14, Kennedy asserted that the basic issue was not whether Diem was a good ruler but whether the United States would remain passive while North Vietnam continued supporting the guerrillas in South Vietnam. "If we postpone action in Vietnam to engage in talks with the Communists," he concluded, "we can surely count on a major crisis of nerve in Vietnam and throughout Southeast Asia." But while he wanted to show the strength and determination of the United States, the president balked at committing American ground forces and embarking on what might become an unending program of military escalation. "The troops will march in, the bands will play, the crowds will cheer," he grumbled, "and in four days everyone will have forgotten. Then we will be told we have to send in more troops. It's like taking a drink. The effect wears off, and you have to take another."

Thus rejecting the alternatives of either negotiating a peace settlement or deploying a task force, Kennedy decided to take a middle course. At a National Security Council meeting on November 15, the president explained that he would approve a substantial increase in American military aid for South Vietnam but that he wanted to defer the combat option for future consideration. The State Department immediately notified Ambassador Nolting that the United States would not at the present time introduce combat troops into South Vietnam. But he was also informed about contingency plans for the dispatch of American ground forces should North Vietnam pursue a policy of direct military intervention below the seventeenth parallel. A week later, on November 22, the State Department instructed Nolting to tell Diem that in an effort to arrest the military and political deterioration in South Vietnam, the United States proposed to do the following: (1) send more military advisers, and assume greater control over combat operations; (2) provide more helicopters and light aircraft, along with pilots to fly them; and (3) supply additional equipment and personnel to gather intelligence and to execute bombing and strafing missions.

Nolting ran into a stone wall, however, when he indicated that the United States expected Diem to reciprocate both by broadening the base of his government to win popular support and by overhauling the command structure of his army to create an effective military organization. Diem replied that the quid pro quo aspects of the American proposals "played right into the hands of the communists" by making his regime appear subservient to a foreign country. Arguing that the United States was "putting the cart before the horse" by demanding that he implement political reforms, Diem stressed that first he would have to provide military security for the South Vietnamese people in order to regain their allegiance. Nolting immediately backed away from a confrontation with Diem. In a cable to Washington, he suggested that the United States emphasize the need for governmental efficiency rather than political reform in negotiations with Saigon. Kennedy quickly came to the same conclusion. And convinced that he could not find another South Vietnamese leader as capable as Diem, the president decided to furnish the additional military assistance without insisting on basic reforms in return.

Kennedy also agreed with Nolting regarding the issue of how American military escalation should be justified before the bar of world opinion. The ambassador had already anticipated the eventual need to increase the number of U.S. military advisers in South Vietnam far beyond the limits established in 1954 at Geneva. Thus, he had recommended that the American government announce it could no longer be bound by those restrictions because of the failure of international controls to prevent North Vietnam from violating them. Kennedy ultimately directed the State Department to prepare a White Paper that would rationalize whatever breach in the Geneva Accords he might make by charging that North Vietnam was already disregarding the agreements with impunity. Released in December 1961, the official State Department brief was entitled *A Threat to the Peace: North Vietnam's Efforts to Conquer South Vietnam.*

So advertised as a response to North Vietnamese aggression, the American military buildup in South Vietnam proceeded apace. The United States began shipping a vast array of equipment and supplies in an effort to enhance the combat effectiveness of the South Vietnamese army. Before long, a steady stream of helicopters, fixed-wing aircraft, trucks, armored personnel carriers, howitzers, mortars, machine guns, petroleum, napalm, herbicides, and other items were flowing across the Pacific and pouring into South Vietnam. Waves of American military specialists also splashed ashore in order to train South Vietnamese soldiers and show them how to use the weapons arriving from the United States. The number of American military advisers stationed in South Vietnam jumped from less than 700 in January 1961 when Kennedy became president to more than 3,000 by the end of his first year in office. The swift military expansion prompted the United States to replace the Military Assistance Advisory Group in February 1962 with a new organization called the Military Assistance Command, Vietnam (MACV). Under the supervision of General Paul A. Harkins, who ran the MACV from his headquarters in Saigon, the number of American military specialists in South Vietnam continued to grow by leaps and bounds, reaching 9,000 in January 1963 and exceeding 16,000 by the end of that year.

This massive infusion of men and weapons from the United States provided an immediate boost to the morale and effectiveness of the South Vietnamese army. The helicopters quickly gave the ARVN the upper hand in the fight against the guerrillas. "Roaring in over the treetops, they were a terrifying sight to the superstitious Viet Cong peasants," a State Department official later recalled. "In those first few months, the Viet Cong simply turned and ran—and, flushed from their foxholes and hiding places, and running in the open, they were easy targets." At the same time, in the flat stretches of the Mekong Delta, armored personnel carriers were chasing down fleeing guerrillas like hounds pursuing rabbits in an open prairie. The speed and mobility of the new American equipment enabled the South Vietnamese army to take the offensive, and during the spring of 1962, it appeared that the ARVN had gained the edge. But it would soon become evident that the tide of the battle had only temporarily turned against the rebels.

For even if the ARVN had assumed the initiative against the guerrillas, the revolution against the Diem regime continued to gain momentum in the South Vietnamese countryside. The situation in Long An province, which occupies a strategic position separating Saigon from the rice fields of the Mekong Delta, provides a case in point. Between 1961 and 1963, as more and more peasants decided to defy the government's authority, land tax collections declined from 50.6 to 40.3 percent in Long An. Large numbers of peasants in the province also refused to report for induction into the South Vietnamese army. Many parents preferred an illegal status for their sons rather than conscription for military service in some distant part of the country, and many young men and boys who wished to avoid the draft turned to the insurgents for protection from the government and ultimately joined the Vietcong. As a result, between 1962 and 1963, both the number of armed rebels in Long An and the size of the area that they controlled in the province increased by more than 10 percent.

One reason for the growing peasant alienation in Long An and other provinces was the widespread corruption of the Diem regime. More concerned about their own wealth than the welfare of the South Vietnamese people, Ngo Dinh Nhu and his wife exerted an increasing influence in the government as the ruling clique in Saigon kept shrinking. Finally, only members of the Ngo family held power. And the Nhus set a bad example of nepotism and corruption for the political and military pawns of the Ngo family oligarchy. Although Diem personally may have found the resulting waste and graft distasteful, he never did anything to root out the corruption and brutality that surrounded him. Diem realized that the survival of his regime depended on the secret police that Nhu used as an instrument to control the people of South Vietnam. Diem also understood that he could not punish or dismiss lazy and corrupt officials without destroying his own base of support.

So, while tolerating corruption within his government as a means of retaining power, Diem stubbornly resisted American suggestions that he should clean house. American leaders had hoped that their huge military assistance program would give them leverage to induce Diem to make essential reforms. But they soon learned that while Diem wanted American military aid, he did not want political advice from the United States. Confident that he was indispensable to his American patrons, he rejected their pleas to broaden his government as he relied more and more on Nhu for guidance. Diem also acted contrary to American recommendations by tightening rather than relaxing government controls in South Vietnam. Besides prohibiting all types of public gatherings unless they were approved in advance, the Saigon regime imposed a rigorous censorship on all material written in the country. The veteran *Newsweek* correspondent François Sully, for example, was expelled from Saigon because he made critical remarks about Madame Nhu.

Like a giant octopus, the Diem regime had long tentacles extending out from the palace in Saigon and reaching down to the villages and hamlets in the most remote areas of South Vietnam. The centrally appointed province and district chiefs selected local notables to serve as hamlet chiefs and members of the village councils, and these subordinate officials at the lowest levels of government dutifully carried out the policies established in Saigon. Although theoretically impartial bodies, the village councils under Diem were actually controlled by the landlords and used to collect taxes and exploit the peasants. Local officials often embezzled government funds and extorted money from peasants, and efforts by honest administrators to promote clean government were usually frustrated by central authorities. "Naturally, I would try to salvage as many corrupt officials as I could," one province chief recalled. "Hopeless cases I would send back to Saigon with the reasons why I refused to have such an individual in my province. But frequently the very reason these people were in the government was that they had relatives or friends back in Saigon, who would just 'lose' my reports, and the individual would end up getting a better assignment than he had in the first place. It often happened that in the place of a corrupt official I would receive a corrupt official who had been thrown out of another province and then assigned to me."

THE GROWTH OF THE VIETCONG

The roots of the revolution in the rice paddies of South Vietnam ran a great deal deeper than mere complaints about official corruption. The land issue remained the single most important factor in turning the rural population against the Saigon government. During the war against the French and their client Bao Dai, the Vietminh had destroyed the status quo in liberated areas of the countryside when they instituted a land reform program. The peasants had seen the landlords flee and their large holdings then divided into small plots and distributed to the landless. After the United States helped Diem consolidate his power in Saigon, however, the status quo was restored in rural South Vietnam. The landlords returned to repossess their property in areas secured by government troops. But as the Vietcong extended their control over the countryside, they launched another land reform program. Once again, the landlords were chased away and their holdings given to the landless, and it was a lesson that the communists would not allow the peasants to forget.

Communist cadres told the peasants in South Vietnam that the revolution was directed against feudalism as well as imperialism. Because the local landlords were sponsored by the U.S.-Diem regime, they lectured, the peasants needed to support the struggle against the American imperialists and their lackeys in Saigon in order to obtain land or keep the plots that had been taken from the old owners and given to them. The communists warned that if the imperialists won the war, the big landlords would come back and the peasants would return to their former condition of servitude. Only by sending their sons into the National Liberation Front army and paying taxes to support the rebel forces, the cadres concluded, could the peasants assure the defeat of the imperialists and thereby win the right to become or remain landowners. Buttressed by recent developments in South Vietnam, their arguments prompted more and more peasants to contribute to the Vietcong cause. In fact, many Vietcong soldiers who became war prisoners told American interrogators that they had joined the revolution against the Saigon government to satisfy their hunger for land.

The economic assistance programs financed by the United States did little to dissuade many peasants in South Vietnam from cooperating with the revolutionary movement. Maintaining its conservative disposition, the Diem regime used American funds to promote economic development rather than to redistribute property ownership among different social classes. The construction of roads and canals added to the productive capacity of the country as a whole, but these developmental projects did nothing to shift the allocation of wealth and power within South Vietnam. And while the communist insurgents sponsored a program of progressive taxation and land redistribution, the Saigon government imposed a regressive tax structure and a reactionary land policy. The contrast was clear even to the least sophisticated peasants. Committed to preserving the traditional social order in South Vietnam, Diem was unable to win the hearts and minds of the small farmers and sharecroppers.

Nor could the American-sponsored strategic hamlet program win the war at the rice-roots level. Like the earlier agroville arrangement, the strategic hamlet program brought peasants from scattered villages together into fortified settlements surrounded by moats and barbed-wire fences. The proponents of the plan had two purposes. First, by separating the peasants from the guerrillas, they aimed to cut the rebels off from their source of food, intelligence, and manpower. Second, by providing schools, fertilizer, and medical care in compensation for the burdens of forced relocation, they hoped to persuade the peasants that the Saigon government offered better living conditions than the Vietcong. But much of the money furnished by the United States for social and economic services ended up in the pockets of corrupt officials. And the displaced peasants resented having to build new homes away from their long-time rice fields and ancestral graves. Disenchanted peasants often welcomed rebel agents into the strategic hamlets at night, and eventually, the Vietcong overran many of the settlements. While failing to prevent the guerrillas from living off the rural population, the strategic hamlet program added to the mounting discontent in the countryside.

Actions by the South Vietnamese army compounded the problem. Operating in the confusing conditions engendered by a bitter civil war, ARVN soldiers did not always successfully distinguish between armed insurgents and innocent civilians. The widespread use of napalm and defoliants, sanctioned by the United States, likewise failed to discriminate between friend and foe. Besides doing extensive ecological damage, these lethal chemicals sometimes injured or killed women and children as well as crops and animals. But beyond unintended civilian deaths, peasants suspected of sympathizing with the Vietcong were frequently shot, and villages suspected of harboring guerrillas were often strafed and bombed. At the same time, it was customary for the forces of the Saigon government to torture prisoners held for questioning about possible rebel connections. These military measures proved counterproductive as they made it easier for the Vietcong to mobilize the masses.

The armed forces of the National Liberation Front and the Republic of Vietnam presented sharply contrasting images in the eyes of the South Vietnamese peasants. On the one hand, the troops serving under Diem acted a lot like those who had fought for the French. They routinely patrolled hamlets during the day, grabbed a few chickens for lunch, and then disappeared before dark. Despite American efforts to get them to treat civilians with respect, ARVN soldiers continued to plunder the people they were sent to protect. "Up to the very end," General Lansdale lamented after the war, "the army was still stealing from the population." On the other hand, the NLF guerrillas resembled those who had fought against the French. The Vietcong, like the Vietminh, dressed in lightweight black clothes, used hit-and-run tactics, and set up their own governments, which not only collected taxes and recruited young men to fight against Diem but also provided the peasants with educational services and medical care. Having watched their fathers expel the French and Bao Dai from the northern half of Vietnam, they dedicated themselves to liberating the rest of their country from the yoke of the American-Diem dictatorship. Thus, the Vietcong guerrillas, unlike the ARVN regulars, were ready and willing to die for their cause.

During the autumn of 1962, the tide of the battle began to turn against the South Vietnamese army. The fighting had become increasingly bloody as ARVN battalions, following American advice, tried to close in on and kill the National Liberation Front forces. In classic textbook fashion, the Saigon government troops would sweep into an area, establish blocking positions, and then attempt to encircle and liquidate the Vietcong. But these aggressive search-and-destroy operations led to heavy losses for ARVN as well as NLF units. Apparently worried that high casualty rates would result in intensified political agitation against his regime, Diem hastily ordered his military commanders to limit their losses on the battlefield. They responded by employing search-and-avoid maneuvers designed to leave an escape route for the Vietcong. Moreover, while ARVN officers were becoming increasingly cautious, the insurgents were rapidly overcoming their fear of the noisy American helicopters hovering overhead. The rebels learned to remain camouflaged in their hiding places and to hold their fire until the helicopters landed to discharge ground forces. More and more of the slow aircraft were shot down with small arms, and their landing parties were frequently mauled during the ensuing ambush. And as the Vietcong guerrillas became increasingly bold, they quickly regained the initiative against their opponents.

One battle in particular epitomized the fundamental shift in the fortunes of the war. In early January 1963, a large ARVN force of 2,500 soldiers attacked a small group of 200 guerrillas near the village of Ap Bac, located in the Mekong Delta only fifty miles from Saigon. The troops fighting for Diem not only were equipped with amphibious personnel carriers and artillery but also were supported by American bombers and helicopters. Yet the Vietcong battalion managed to kill sixty-one attackers and wound over 100 more, to shoot down five helicopters and damage nine others, and then to escape almost intact through a big hole that the Saigon government troops had intentionally left open. Despite having the advantages of superior numbers and firepower, the ARVN force had blown the opportunity to corner and crush the rebels. The failure revealed all of the deficiencies of the South Vietnamese army: its lack of aggressiveness, its hesitancy about taking casualties, its lack of battlefield leadership, and its almost nonexistent chain of command. The American military advisers who had taken part in the fighting were disgusted by the poor performance of their ARVN pupils. The Battle of Ap Bac, more than any other setback, convinced them that Diem was not willing to buy victory with blood.

The official American response to this deteriorating military situation sowed the seeds for a widening chasm between rhetoric and reality, or what later came to be called the "credibility gap." Believing that no other South Vietnamese leader was capable of filling Diem's shoes, both Ambassador Nolting and General Harkins made repeated pronouncements claiming that the ARVN forces were winning the war. Harkins even went so far as to describe the Battle of Ap Bac as a victory for the Saigon government. But while the American embassy and the MACV continued to exude great optimism about the progress of counterinsurgency, the American press corps in Saigon, after talking with John Paul Vann, the senior American military adviser who had observed the ARVN shortcomings at Ap Bac, began to challenge the official line. Correspondents such as David Halberstam of the *New York Times* and Neil Sheehan of United Press International, while denouncing the Diem regime as corrupt and repressive, argued that the ARVN was losing the war. Diem reacted angrily. Some American reporters were forced to leave South Vietnam, and others had their phones tapped and their writings censored. When Halberstam refused to mute his criticism, President Kennedy tried unsuccessfully to get the *New York Times* to recall him. Kennedy also attempted to deceive the American people during press conferences when he denied that the military advisers he had sent to South Vietnam were involved in combat.

Despite their public posture of complacency, however, American officials worried privately about their relations with the Diem regime. The rapid arrival of American civilian and military advisers and their growing assertiveness in South Vietnam soon began to alarm Diem. And tension between Washington and Saigon mounted in April 1963, when Ambassador Nolting reported that Diem opposed plans for an expanded and deepened American advisory effort. Nolting admitted that the proliferation and zeal of the American advisers were creating the impression that South Vietnam had become a "protectorate" of the United States. Warning that Diem might demand a reduction in the number of Americans stationed in his country, Nolting proposed that the United States should threaten to cut military aid to Diem in order to convince him that "we mean business." Diem ultimately withdrew his objection to American plans to send more personnel to South Vietnam, but not before policymakers in Washington had become increasingly concerned about the pliability of their protégé in Saigon.

American apprehensions about conditions in South Vietnam were greatly heightened when the long-smoldering issue of religious discrimination suddenly burst into flames. From the very outset of his rule in Saigon, Diem had regarded the Catholic refugees from North Vietnam as the core of his constituency. Believing that these anticommunist Catholics could be trusted, Diem appointed them to high positions in the government and military in return for their personal loyalty. Many ambitious South Vietnamese natives got the message, and in the hope of securing better jobs, they conveniently converted to Catholicism. As a result, most district and province chiefs were Catholics who often exercised authority over a completely Buddhist populace. And the Buddhists increasingly complained that Diem was discriminating against them. Constituting a large majority of the population of South Vietnam, they charged that the Catholics, who made up only 10 percent of the population, held a disproportionate share of political and military offices. In brief, the Buddhists resented the fact that they had become second-class citizens while Catholics had become a privileged minority in South Vietnam.

Finally, in the spring of 1963, an act of religious discrimination provoked a political crisis that shook the very foundations of the Diem regime. The trouble began on May 8, when thousands of Buddhists assembled in Hué to celebrate the 2,527th birthday of the founder of their religion. The Catholic deputy province chief sought to restrain them by enforcing an old decree that prohibited the flying of religious flags. A week earlier, however, he had allowed Catholics in the same city to display papal banners to commemorate the twenty-fifth anniversary of the ordination of Diem's brother, Archbishop Ngo Dinh Thuc. The blatant inconsistency dismayed the

Buddhists of Hué, and several thousand of them gathered peacefully in protest. After failing to disperse the demonstrators, the Catholic deputy province chief ordered his troops to fire into the crowd. Nine people were killed on the spot. Buddhists throughout South Vietnam protested and demanded that the officials responsible for the massacre at Hué be punished. But Diem ignored their demands. And adding insult to injury, he made the preposterous claim that a Vietcong bomb had caused the deaths even though thousands of people had witnessed the government troops firing on the crowd.

Reacting with remarkable speed and skill, the Buddhist leaders proceeded to organize a massive protest movement. They agitated among relatives, sponsored numerous rallies, and distributed leaflets denouncing religious persecution. On May 30, while hundreds of Buddhist monks staged a demonstration in Saigon, thousands of their colleagues began a fast in the pagodas at Hué. The United States promptly urged Diem to conciliate the Buddhists, but he merely created an innocuous committee to investigate their complaints. Then, the Buddhists exploded a bombshell. On June 11, at a busy intersection in Saigon, an elderly monk sat down on the street and crossed his legs, and while he pressed his hands together in prayer, his companions doused him with gasoline and set him ablaze. An Associated Press correspondent who had been tipped off in advance by Buddhist militants arrived with a camera in time to photograph the martyr just as a sheet of flames enveloped his body. On the next day, a ghastly picture of the burning monk appeared on the front page of newspapers and on television screens around the world. The American people were horrified. Having been told that the United States was defending democracy in South Vietnam, they wondered what the Saigon government had done to drive the venerable religious leader to sacrifice his life.

President Kennedy, a Catholic himself, became increasingly embarrassed and disturbed about the treatment of the Buddhists in South Vietnam. While Diem continued to do nothing to mollify the distressed Buddhists, several more monks burned themselves to death. Madame Nhu, the beautiful and haughty Dragon Lady, publicly ridiculed the immolation of the monks. "Let them burn," she jeered, "and we shall clap our hands." Her husband was equally scornful. "If the Buddhists want to have another barbecue," he declared, "I will be glad to supply the gasoline." American policymakers began thinking in private that Nhu and his wife should be removed from positions of influence, and on June 27, Kennedy announced that Henry Cabot Lodge, Jr., would replace Nolting as the American ambassador in Saigon. But before Nolting left his post, thousands of students took to the streets of Saigon to denounce the Diem regime. Nolting therefore decided to make one last effort to reason with Diem, and during his farewell visit on August 14, Diem assured him that no further repressive actions would be taken against the Buddhists.

This promise was broken a week later when Nhu unleashed his Special Forces against the Buddhists. Striking without warning shortly after midnight on August 21, Nhu's men raided and ransacked the pagodas in Saigon, Hué, and other cities throughout South Vietnam. Several monks were killed, many others were injured, and more than 1,000 were arrested. The brutal assaults outraged people from all walks of life. The South Vietnamese ambassador in Washington resigned in protest, and the foreign minister in Saigon quit his post and shaved his head in the fashion of a Buddhist monk. The sons and daughters of middle-class families were equally outspoken in their criticism of the government. Students at the University of Saigon began a massive demonstration against the Diem regime on August 24, and more than 4,000 of the protesters were carted off to jail before the rally could be subdued. As the unrest spread, the Buddhist movement grew stronger and became more political. Soon, the most militant Buddhist leaders even began to harbor dark thoughts about overthrowing Diem.

Thich Quang Duc, an elderly Buddhist monk, immolating himself on a busy street in Saigon on June 11, 1963. From AP Photos.

THE PLOT TO TOPPLE DIEM

Even before the pagodas in Saigon were viciously attacked, dissident South Vietnamese army officers had already begun plotting a coup against Diem. And on the Fourth of July 1963, General Tran Van Don met with Lieutenant Colonel Lucien Conein, a top CIA operative in South Vietnam. General Don hinted that a coup was in the making, and he asked Conein how the United States would react if the conspirators attempted to depose Diem. But the disgruntled army officers remained hesitant until the brutal August crackdown against the Buddhists provided them with both an opportunity and an excuse to move against the government. When news of the pagoda raids reached Washington, the State Department immediately ordered Henry Cabot Lodge to hurry to South Vietnam to appraise the situation. Ambassador Lodge arrived in Saigon on August 22 and promptly confirmed reports that certain army officers had inquired if the United States would support a coup. But Lodge cautioned that the military opposition to the government lacked cohesion. On the next day, Conein reported to Washington that General Don did not seem to think that there was enough support among the officer corps to overthrow Diem. The CIA agent concluded that Don appeared "not to know what to do next."

On August 24, President Kennedy hastily authorized the dispatch of a cable, which had been drafted in the State Department, informing Ambassador Lodge that the American government could not tolerate the fact that Nhu had maneuvered himself into a commanding position in Saigon. The cable instructed Lodge to give Diem a chance "to rid himself of Nhu and his coterie" and to replace them with the best military and political personalities available. If Diem remained obdurate, the cable explained, "we must face the possibility that Diem himself cannot be preserved." The ambassador was also instructed to tell key military leaders that the United States would find it impossible to continue supporting the South Vietnamese government unless immediate steps were taken to release the arrested Buddhist monks. Moreover, after informing the appropriate military commanders that the United States was prepared to abandon Diem if he refused to remove Nhu, Lodge was to assure them of direct American support during any interim period of breakdown in the central government. Finally, the State Department message indicated that Lodge and his colleagues should "urgently examine all possible alternative leadership and make detailed plans as to how we might bring about Diem's replacement if this should become necessary."

Lodge quickly carried out his instructions. But when he met Diem for the first time on August 26, the ambassador could hardly believe his eyes. "I could see a cloud pass across his face," Lodge recalled years later, "when I suggested that he get rid of Nhu and improve his government." Immediately after his frigid encounter with Diem, the ambassador asked Conein to contact the coup leaders. But General Duong Van Minh told the CIA agent that the rebel generals would remain cautious until they had visible evidence that the United States would not betray them. General Minh urged a severance of economic aid to the Diem government as a sign of American determination to support the coup group. Hoping to encourage the waffling South Vietnamese generals, Lodge appealed to Washington on August 29 for permission to give them the green light that Minh had requested. "We are launched on a course," he cabled, "from which there is no respectable turning back: the overthrow of the Diem government." Stressing that the chance of bringing off a coup "depends at least as much on us" as on the generals, Lodge urged that the United States should make an "all-out effort" to get the insurgents to "move promptly."

President Kennedy and his State Department advisers responded positively to these recommendations. In a cable on August 29, the State Department instructed Lodge to have General Harkins reassure the South Vietnamese army officers that the United States would support a coup that appeared to have a good chance of success. But while establishing liaison with the coup planners, Harkins was to explain that American military forces would not assist them in toppling the Diem regime. The State Department also authorized Lodge to announce, at the proper time, a suspension of American aid to the Saigon government. Lodge was to use his own discretion in giving the plotting generals the signal that they were waiting to receive from Washington. And in a strictly private message later on the same day, the president pledged his support for Lodge but advised him to disengage if he thought the coup would fail. "We will do all that we can," Kennedy promised, "to help you conclude this operation successfully."

When fears that Nhu had gotten wind of their plans led some of the conspirators to waver, however, General Minh and his key supporters abruptly called off the coup. Lodge then reasoned that the United States should attempt to work out an accommodation with Diem. In a cable on August 31, the ambassador proposed an arrangement calling for Madame Nhu and Archbishop Thuc to leave the country and for Nhu to limit his role in the government. Secretary of State Dean Rusk agreed that these steps should be taken to improve the situation in South Vietnam.

Chairing a meeting of top American policymakers to consider the suggestions received from Lodge earlier in the day, Rusk asked "if anyone present had any doubt but that the coup was off." Only Paul Kattenburg, a junior State Department officer, thought that American officials might still be able to engineer a coup against Diem. Warning that the United States would be thrown out of South Vietnam within a year if Washington attempted to live with the repressive Saigon regime, Kattenburg stated that "at this juncture it would be better for us to make the decision to get out honorably." But Rusk promptly dismissed such thoughts and concluded that the basis of American policy should be "that we will not pull out of Vietnam until the war is won, and that we will not run a coup."

American military leaders were relieved that the political maneuvering in Saigon had come to naught and that they could now get back to the job of helping the ARVN defeat the Vietcong. General Harkins, while overseeing military operations from his headquarters at the MACV, had always maintained a cautious attitude toward the idea of a coup. And although Harkins had come to favor ousting Nhu, he remained opposed to the removal of Diem from his seat of power. Harkins feared that the downfall of Diem would create a political vacuum in Saigon and thereby undermine the war effort against the Vietcong. His superiors in Washington shared these apprehensions. Both Secretary of Defense McNamara and General Taylor, currently the chairman of the Joint Chiefs of Staff, worried that a coup against Diem would work to the advantage of the Vietcong by causing political chaos in Saigon. Doubtful that the plotting generals could provide adequate political leadership for South Vietnam, McNamara and Taylor hoped that the United States could reestablish friendly relations with Diem and return to the task of winning the war.

President Kennedy concurred. Although the vicious persecution of the Buddhists during the summer of 1963 had presented him with a golden opportunity to withdraw from South Vietnam without losing face, Kennedy chose merely to make a temporary retreat to his earlier policy of urging Diem to mend his ways. He clarified his position on September 2 in a widely publicized television interview with Walter Cronkite of CBS. Asserting that the South Vietnamese government had gotten out of touch with the people and that the repression of the Buddhists was very unwise, the president stated that he did not think the ARVN could win the war unless Diem made a greater effort to obtain popular support. "With changes in policy and perhaps with personnel," he suggested, the Saigon regime would be able to regain the support of the people. Kennedy admitted that more than forty Americans had already been killed in combat with the Vietcong. "But I don't agree with those who say we should withdraw," he emphasized. "That would be a great mistake."

The president reiterated his views on September 9 in a television interview with Chet Huntley and David Brinkley of NBC. After referring to the difficulties with the Buddhists, he explained that the United States was attempting to persuade the Saigon government to take steps to win back popular support. But Kennedy said that he did not think that it would be helpful at the present time to reduce American aid to South Vietnam. Nor did he believe that there was any reason to doubt the validity of the domino theory. If South Vietnam fell, Kennedy declared, it would "give the impression that the wave of the future in Southeast Asia was China and the Communists." He therefore insisted that the United States must not disengage from South Vietnam: "What I am concerned about is that Americans will get impatient and say, because they don't like events in Southeast Asia or they don't like the Government in Saigon, that we should withdraw. That only makes it easier for the Communists. I think we should stay. We should use our influence in as effective a way as we can, but we should not withdraw."

President Kennedy, however, soon had reason to fear that the United States might be asked to leave by the South Vietnamese government itself. Although Diem agreed that Madame

Nhu and Archbishop Thuc should make extensive trips abroad, he refused to remove Nhu from his position of authority. Ambassador Lodge therefore concluded on September 11 that an accommodation with Diem was now out of the question. And widespread reports that Nhu was seriously negotiating with the North Vietnamese convinced many in Washington that Lodge was right. Roger Hilsman, the assistant secretary of state for Far Eastern affairs, summarized their arguments in a memorandum presented to Secretary of State Rusk on September 16. In that memo, Hilsman asserted that it would be futile to pursue a policy of reconciliation toward the Saigon regime because Nhu had already decided to approach Hanoi. He reasoned that the minimum goal of Nhu would be to reduce sharply American influence in South Vietnam and to avoid any meaningful concessions that would go against his mandarin outlook. "The maximum goal," Hilsman warned, "would be a deal with North Vietnam for a truce in the war, a complete removal of the U.S. presence, and a 'neutralist' or 'Titoist' but still separate South Vietnam."

Meanwhile, as American officials were becoming increasingly worried about the possibility of a rapprochement between Saigon and Hanoi, the South Vietnamese generals were reviving their plans for a coup against the Diem regime. General Minh informed Conein on October 5 that the conspirators needed assurances that the United States would not thwart their effort to overthrow the government. Although he and the other generals did not expect any American support for their coup, Minh explained, they would need American military and economic aid after they seized power. Kennedy immediately decided to give the generals the assurances they sought. "While we do not wish to stimulate a coup," Lodge was instructed on October 6, "we also do not wish to leave impression that the U.S. would thwart a change of government or deny economic and military assistance to a new regime if it appeared capable of increasing effectiveness of military effort, ensuring popular support to win war and improving relations with U.S." A few days later, Conein conveyed the message to Minh. The generals received further encouragement during the following weeks when the United States not only announced that economic aid to the Diem regime would be suspended but also threatened that funds for the Special Forces of the South Vietnamese government would be cut unless they were taken away from Nhu and transferred to the field.

After flashing the green light to the generals, however, Kennedy began to have second thoughts. The White House was still haunted by memories of the American-sponsored assault at the Bay of Pigs and the subsequent failure to bring down Castro and reintegrate Cuba into the liberal capitalist world system. Kennedy feared that an American-backed coup attempt against Diem would likewise end in disaster and that he would be held responsible for another embarrassing fiasco. "We are particularly concerned about the hazard that an unsuccessful coup, however carefully we avoid direct engagement, will be laid at our door by public opinion almost everywhere," National Security Adviser McGeorge Bundy cabled Lodge on October 25. "Therefore, while sharing your view that we should not be in a position of thwarting a coup, we would like to have the option of judging and warning on any plan with poor prospects of success." Cabling Lodge again on October 30, Bundy expressed fears that the balance of forces in Saigon were approximately equal and that defeat, or even just prolonged fighting, could be disastrous for American interests. Bundy concluded that if the coup leaders could not show that their prospects for a quick success were good, "we should discourage them from proceeding since a miscalculation could result in jeopardizing U.S. position in Southeast Asia."

Ambassador Lodge and General Harkins were working at cross-purposes in Saigon during the autumn of 1963. Analyzing the problem in South Vietnam primarily in military terms,

Harkins had recently tried to dissuade the rebel generals from implementing their coup plans. Harkins cabled Washington on October 30 that in his opinion, there were "no generals qualified to take over" if Diem were dumped. Thus, he recommended that the United States should try to "win the military effort as quickly as possible" and then let the South Vietnamese "make any and all changes they want." Defining the problem in South Vietnam fundamentally as a political matter, however, Lodge had not abandoned his doubts that the war could be won under a government headed by Diem. He therefore cabled Washington on October 30 that rather than discouraging the coup leaders, the United States should provide them with funds to buy off any potential opposition. "My general view is that the United States is trying to bring this medieval country into the twentieth century," Lodge explained with characteristic American arrogance. "We have made considerable progress in military and economic ways, but to gain victory we must also bring them into the twentieth century politically, and that can only be done by either a thoroughgoing change in the behavior of the present government or by another government."

Kennedy remained content to have Lodge decide whether or not he should make a last-minute effort to stop or delay the coup. In a second cable to the ambassador on October 30, Bundy indicated that Lodge should base his decision on his own judgment regarding the likelihood of success or failure. "If you should conclude that there is not clearly a high prospect of success," he instructed, "you should communicate this doubt to generals in a way calculated to persuade them to desist at least until chances are better." "But once a coup under responsible leadership has begun," Bundy explained, "it is in the interest of the U.S. Government that it should succeed." It was a foregone conclusion that Lodge would do nothing to discourage the coup leaders, and on November 1, they struck. As the coup got under way, the rebel generals asked Conein to come to their headquarters and maintain telephone contact with the CIA office in Saigon. Conein brought a bag of money with him in case the insurgents needed any funds to accomplish their objective. With the balance of forces overwhelmingly against him, Diem offered to negotiate, but rather than falling into that trap again, the generals brutally murdered both Diem and Nhu.

News of the slaying of the Ngo brothers produced great jubilation throughout South Vietnam. In Saigon, elated crowds danced in the streets, destroyed statues of Diem, and decorated victorious soldiers with garlands of flowers. The celebration spread rapidly into the countryside as well, where happy peasants released their pent-up hostility by demolishing the hated strategic hamlets. Ambassador Lodge was especially delighted when he heard about the death of the dictators. A day after the coup, the Brahmin from Boston invited the triumphant generals to his office in Saigon to congratulate them for ending the rule of the Vietnamese mandarin who had refused to remake himself in the image of his American patrons. Lodge assured the new leaders of South Vietnam that their government would immediately receive economic assistance and diplomatic recognition from the United States. In a cable he sent to Washington a few days later, Lodge optimistically predicted that the overthrow of Diem would shorten the war against the Vietcong.

With the strings of his puppet in Saigon severed, President Kennedy was also hopeful about the prospects for a more effective war effort in South Vietnam. On November 6, he cabled his appreciation to Lodge for a job well done. "Your own leadership in pulling together and directing the whole American operation in South Vietnam in recent months has been of the greatest importance," Kennedy praised. "As you say, while this was a Vietnamese effort, our actions made it clear that we wanted improvements, and when these were not forthcoming from the Diem Government, we necessarily faced and accepted the possibility that our position might encourage a change of government." But the youthful president did not live to see the fate of South Vietnam following the death of Diem. A few weeks later, Kennedy himself was assassinated while traveling down the streets of Dallas in an open car. Vice President Johnson was suddenly elevated to the pinnacle of power in Washington, and now it would be his turn to answer the summons of the trumpet.

DOCUMENT 4-1

State Department Cable to Ambassador Henry Cabot Lodge, Jr., in Saigon on August 24, 1963

It is now clear that whether military proposed martial law or whether Nhu tricked them into it, Nhu took advantage of its imposition to smash pagodas with police and Tung's Special Forces loyal to him, thus placing onus on military in eyes of world and Vietnamese people. Also clear that Nhu has maneuvered himself into commanding position.

U.S. Government cannot tolerate situation in which power lies in Nhu's hands. Diem must be given chance to rid himself of Nhu and his coterie and replace them with best military and political personalities available.

If, in spite of all your efforts, Diem remains obdurate and refuses, then we must face the possibility that Diem himself cannot be preserved.

We now believe immediate action must be taken to prevent Nhu from consolidating his position further. Therefore, unless you in conversation with [General Paul A.] Harkins [head of MACV in Saigon] perceive overriding objections you are authorized to proceed along following lines:

1. First we must press on appropriate levels of GVN [Government of Vietnam] following line:

   a. USG [U.S. Government] cannot accept actions against Buddhists taken by Nhu and his collaborators under cover of martial law.
   b. Prompt dramatic actions redress situation must be taken, including repeal of decree 10, release of arrested monks, nuns, etc.

2. We must at same time also tell key military leaders that U.S. would find it impossible to continue support GVN militarily and economically unless above steps are taken immediately which we recognize requires removal of Nhus from the scene. We wish give Diem reasonable opportunity to remove Nhus, but if he remains obdurate, then we are prepared to accept the obvious implications that we can no longer support Diem. You may also tell appropriate military commanders we will give them direct support in any interim period of breakdown central government mechanism.

3. We recognize the necessity of removing taint on military for pagoda raids and placing blame squarely on Nhu. You are authorized to have such statements made in Saigon as you consider desirable to achieve this objective. We are prepared to take same line here and to have Voice of America make statements along lines contained in next numbered telegram whenever you give the word, preferably as soon as possible.

Concurrently, with above, Ambassador and country team should urgently examine all possible alternative leadership and make detailed plans as to how we might bring about Diem's replacement if this should become necessary.

Assume you will consult with General Harkins re any precautions necessary to protect American personnel during this crisis period.

You will understand that we cannot from Washington give you detailed instructions as to how this operation should proceed, but you will also know we will back you to hilt on actions you take to achieve our objectives.

Needless to say we have held knowledge of this telegram to minimum essential people and assume you will take similar precautions to prevent premature leaks.

Source: *The Pentagon Papers: Senator Gravel Edition* (Boston: Beacon Press, 1971), vol. II, 734–735.

DOCUMENT 4-2
Ambassador Lodge Cable to the State Department on October 5, 1963

1. [CIA operative] Lt. Col. [Lucien] Conein met with Gen. Doung Van Minh at Gen. Minh's Headquarters on Le Van Duyet for one hour and ten minutes morning of 5 Oct 63. This meeting was at the initiative of Gen. Minh and has been specifically cleared in advance by Ambassador Lodge. No other persons were present. The conversation was conducted in French.

2. Gen. Minh stated that he must know American Government's position with respect to a change in the Government of Vietnam within the very near future. Gen. Minh added the Generals were aware the situation is deteriorating rapidly and that action to change the Government must be taken or the war will be lost to the Viet Cong because the Government no longer has the support of the people. Gen. Minh identified among the other Generals participating with him in this plan:

   Maj. Gen. Tran Van Don

   Brig. Gen. Tran Thien Khiem

   Maj. Gen. Tran Van Kim

3. Gen. Minh made it clear that he did not expect any specific American support for an effort on the part of himself and his colleagues to change the Government but he states he does need American assurances that USG [U.S. Government] will not RPT not attempt to thwart this plan.

4. Gen. Minh also stated that he himself has no political ambitions nor do any of the other General Officers except perhaps, he said laughingly, Gen. Ton That Dinh. Minh insisted that his only purpose is to win the war. He added emphatically that to do this continuation of American Military and Economic Aid at the present level (He said one and one half million dollars per day) is necessary.

5. Gen Minh outlined three possible plans for the accomplishment of the change of Government:

   a. Assassination of Ngo Dinh Nhu and Ngo Dinh Can keeping President Diem in Office. Gen. Minh said this was easiest plan to accomplish.

   b. The encirclement of Saigon by various military units particularly the unit at Ben Cat. (Comment: Fifth Division elements commanded by Gen. Dinh).

   c. Direct confrontation between military units involved in the coup and loyalist military units in Saigon. In effect, dividing the city of Saigon into sectors and cleaning it out pocket by pocket. Gen. Minh claims under the circumstances Diem and Nhu could count on the loyalty of 5,500 troops within the city of Saigon.

6. Conein replied to Gen. Minh that he could not answer specific questions as to USG non-interference nor could he give any advice with respect to tactical planning. He added that he could not advise concerning the best of the three plans.

7. ...Minh stated that [Ngo Tran] Hieu was formally a Communist and still has Communist sympathies. When Col. Conein remarked that he had considered Col. Tung as one of the more dangerous individuals, Gen. Minh stated "if I get rid of Nhu, Can and Hieu, Col. Tung will be on his knees before me."

8. Gen. Minh also stated that he was worried as to the role of Gen. Tran Thien Khiem since Khiem may have played a double role in August. Gen. Minh asked that copies of the documents previously passed to Gen. Khiem (plan of Camp Long Thanh and munitions inventory at that camp) be passed to Gen. Minh personally for comparison with papers passed by Khiem to Minh purportedly from CAS [Classified American Source referring to the Central Intelligence Agency].

9. Minh further stated that one of the reasons they are having to act quickly was the fact that many regimental, battalion and company commanders are working on coup plans of their own which could be abortive and a "catastrophe."

10. Minh appeared to understand Conein's position of being unable to comment at the

DOCUMENT 4-2 Continued

present moment but asked that Conein again meet with Gen. Minh to discuss the specific plan of operations which Gen. Minh hopes to put into action. No specific date was given for the next meeting. Conein was again noncommittal in his reply. Gen. Minh once again indicated his understanding and

stated that he would arrange to contact Conein in the near future and hoped that Conein would be able to meet with him and give the assurances outlined above.

Source: *The Pentagon Papers: Senator Gravel Edition* (Boston: Beacon Press, 1971), vol. II, 767–768

DOCUMENT 4-3

National Security Adviser McGeorge Bundy Cable to Ambassador Lodge on October 30, 1963

1. Our reading of your thoughtful [cable numbered] 2063 leads us to believe a significant difference of shading may exist on one crucial point (see next para.) and on one or two lesser matters easily clarified.

2. We do not accept as a basis for U.S. policy that we have no power to delay or discourage a coup. In your paragraph 12 you say that if you were convinced that the coup was going to fail you would of course do everything you could to stop it. We believe that on this same basis you should take action to persuade coup leaders to stop or delay any operation which, in your best judgment, does not clearly give high prospect of success. We have not considered any betrayal of generals to Diem, and our [cable numbered] 79109 explicitly rejects that course. We recognize the danger of appearing hostile to generals, but we believe that our own position should be on as firm ground as possible, hence we cannot limit ourselves to proposition implied in your message that only conviction of certain failure justifies intervention. We believe that your standard for intervention should be that stated above.

3. Therefore, if you should conclude that there is not clearly a high prospect for success, you should communicate this doubt to generals in a way calculated to persuade them to desist at least until chances are better. In such a communication you should use the weight

of U.S. best advice and explicitly reject any implication that we oppose the effort of the generals because of preference for present regime. We recognize need to bear in mind generals' interpretation of U.S. role in 1960 coup attempt, and your agent should maintain clear distinction between strong and honest advice given as a friend and any opposition to their objectives.

4. We continue to be deeply interested in up-to-the-minute assessment of prospects and are sending this before reply to our CAS 79126 [National Security Council cable transmitted by the Central Intelligence Agency]. We want continuous exchange latest assessments on this topic....

5. This paragraph contains our present standing instructions for U.S. posture in the event of a coup.

   a. U.S. authorities will reject appeals for direct intervention from either side, and U.S.-controlled aircraft and other resources will not be committed between battle lines or in support of either side, without authorization from Washington.

   b. In event of indecisive contest, U.S. authorities may in their discretion agree to perform any acts agreeable to both sides, such as removal of key personalities or relay of information. In such actions, however, U.S. authorities will strenuously

(continued)

DOCUMENT 4-3 Continued

avoid appearance of pressure on either side. It is not in the interest of USG [U.S. Government] to be or appear to be either instrument of existing government or instrument of coup.

c. In event of imminent failure or actual failure of coup, U.S. authorities may afford asylum in their discretion to those to whom there is any express of implied obligation of this sort. We believe however that in such a case it would be in our interest and probably in interest of those seeking asylum that they seek protection in other Embassies in addition to our own. This point should be made strongly if need arises.

d. But once a coup under responsible leadership has begun, and within these restrictions, it is in the interest of the U.S. Government that it should succeed.

6. We have your message about return to Washington and we suggest that all public comment be kept as low-key and quiet as possible, and we also urge that if possible you keep open the exact time of your departure. We are strongly sensitive to great disadvantage of having you out of Saigon if this should turn out to be a week of decision, and if it can be avoided we would prefer not to see you pinned to a fixed hour of departure now.

Source: *The Pentagon Papers: Senator Gravel Edition* (Boston: Beacon Press, 1971), vol. II, 792–793.

Chronological List of Main Events

January 1961	The decision to increase American military aid to South Vietnam	**May 1963**	The beginning of the Buddhist protest movement in Hué
December 1961	The publication of a State Department White Paper on Vietnam	**June 1963**	The self-immolation of a Buddhist monk in Saigon
February 1962	The establishment of the Military Assistance Command, Vietnam	**July 1963**	The beginning of a military plot to topple the South Vietnamese government
July 1962	The agreement to form a coalition government in Laos	**November 1963**	The assassination of Ngo Dinh Diem
January 1963	The Battle of Ap Bac		

Study Questions

1. What was the Ho Chi Minh Trail?
2. What was the strategic hamlet program?
3. Why did Buddhist leaders in South Vietnam become increasingly hostile to the Diem regime in Saigon?

4. Would it have been easier to defeat the Vietcong insurgents if the South Vietnamese generals had not overthrown the Saigon government?

5

The Master of Deceit

So just for the moment I have not thought we were ready for American boys to do the fighting for Asian boys....We are not going north and drop bombs at this stage of the game.

PRESIDENT LYNDON B. JOHNSON, 1964

POLITICAL DISORDER IN SOUTH VIETNAM

When Lyndon B. Johnson, a Democrat from Texas, became president following the assassination of John F. Kennedy in November 1963, he pledged to continue the policies of his fallen predecessor. Johnson demonstrated his intentions by retaining Kennedy's top foreign affairs counselors: Dean Rusk as secretary of state, Robert McNamara as secretary of defense, and McGeorge Bundy as national security adviser. These men shared the same basic assumptions and general outlook that had guided the diplomacy of the Kennedy administration. They all believed that foreign markets were needed to absorb surplus American products so that high levels of employment could be maintained in the United States. They all feared that revolutionary upheavals in underdeveloped countries would undermine the liberal capitalist world system and retard the flow of international commerce. They all subscribed to a global version of the domino theory, which held that indigenous revolutions in Southeast Asia could spread by example into Africa and Latin America. And they all viewed the defense of South Vietnam as a test of their resolve to sustain the Pax Americana.

From the very outset of his administration, President Johnson made it clear that he was determined to draw the line against the spread of communism into South Vietnam. "I am not going to lose Vietnam," he asserted within hours after taking the oath of office on November 22. "I am not going to be the President who saw Southeast Asia go the way China went." Two days later, after listening to Henry Cabot Lodge, Jr., describe the situation in South Vietnam, Johnson instructed the ambassador to return to Saigon and tell the generals who had replaced Diem that the United States would make good on its promise to provide them with monetary and military assistance. Johnson was concerned not only about the domestic political ramifications but even more about the global economic and strategic effects if South Vietnam went communist. The president, like his principal advisers, believed that the way the United States responded to the communist challenge in Southeast Asia would have profound consequences all around the world. A few months after he entered the White House, Johnson even went so far as to tell a veteran

American diplomat that a firm stand against communism in South Vietnam would ensure international order and stability by demonstrating that the United States would resist violent changes in the status quo.

Despite his determination to defend the New Frontier throughout the Third World, however, Johnson confronted a rapidly deteriorating situation in South Vietnam. State Department officials had hoped that the removal of Diem and Nhu would restore political harmony, but as American military leaders had feared, Saigon soon plunged into the throes of political instability. Shortly after the death of the Ngo brothers, the coup leaders established a twelve-member Military Revolutionary Council headed by General Duong Van Minh. But rather than organizing an effective war effort against the Vietcong, the members of the military junta bickered endlessly among themselves. The ruling generals were unable to bring the Buddhists and Catholics together into a strong anticommunist coalition. Nor were they able to build a solid base of support in the countryside, where the strategic hamlet program lay in shambles. In early December 1963, the senior American representative in Long An reported that since the summer, three-quarters of the 200 strategic hamlets in the province had been destroyed either by the Vietcong or by their own occupants. "The only progress made in Long An province," he concluded, "has been by the Vietcong."

Ho Chi Minh and his comrades in Hanoi hoped to take advantage of the political disorder in Saigon following the overthrow of Diem and his family. Meeting in December 1963, the Central Committee of the Lao Dong party decided to promote a military buildup in South Vietnam to tip the balance of forces in favor of the Vietcong. "We must strive to attain victory step by step," the Central Committee resolved, "and gradually push back the enemy before reaching the General Offensive and Uprising to win complete victory." The communist leaders in Hanoi not only authorized the infiltration of more men and weapons into South Vietnam, they also directed the National Liberation Front to launch a political campaign to weaken the new government in Saigon. Therefore, while the members of the Military Revolutionary Council were struggling to consolidate their power, the NLF put forth a conciliatory manifesto calling for a cease-fire, general elections, and the formation of a coalition government representing "all forces, parties, tendencies and strata of the South Vietnamese people." The NLF advocated the establishment of an independent South Vietnam that would pursue a neutralist policy until reunification with North Vietnam could eventually be carried out "step by step on a voluntary basis."

Although President Johnson and his advisers assumed that the military junta in Saigon would remain firmly opposed to communism, they feared that the growing antiwar sentiment in South Vietnam might impel the feuding generals to make an accommodation with the National Liberation Front. American leaders contemplated an alarming scenario: Negotiations between the contending political groups in Saigon might lead to a halt in the fighting and the emergence of a coalition government; and the new regime might bend to popular pressure in favor of neutralism and demand the withdrawal of American military personnel from South Vietnam. "Neutralism," Ambassador Lodge cabled the State Department in early December 1963, "is always present in varying degrees here in South Vietnam." Lodge and his colleagues in Washington became increasingly worried that the ultimate consequences of a movement toward neutralism would be a complete collapse of the anticommunist forces in South Vietnam, a reunification with North Vietnam, and the triumph of communism in the rest of Southeast Asia and elsewhere in the Third World.

After a brief visit to South Vietnam, Secretary of Defense McNamara reported to President Johnson on December 21 that conditions had deteriorated to a far greater extent than American officials realized. "The situation is very disturbing," he warned. "Current trends, unless reversed in the next two to three months, will lead to neutralization at best and more likely to a Communist-controlled state." McNamara pointed out that the Vietcong had made substantial progress since the coup against Diem. "The Vietcong now control very high proportions of the people in certain key provinces, particularly those directly south and west of Saigon," he noted. "In these key provinces, the Vietcong have destroyed almost all major roads, and are collecting taxes at will." But McNamara thought that the new government in Saigon was the greatest source of concern. He observed that the military junta "is indecisive and drifting" and that military operations "are not being effectively directed because the generals are so preoccupied with essentially political affairs." McNamara ended his gloomy assessment on an ominous note. "We should watch the situation very carefully, running scared, hoping for the best, but preparing for more forceful moves if the situation does not show early signs of improvement."

The Joint Chiefs of Staff shared his anxiety about conditions in South Vietnam and his readiness to unleash American military power to subdue the Vietcong insurgents. In a memorandum prepared for McNamara in January 1964, they pressed for bolder actions to accomplish American objectives in Southeast Asia. The JCS regarded the conflict in South Vietnam as "the first real test of our determination to defeat the communist wars of national liberation formula." Believing that South Vietnam occupied a pivotal position in the worldwide confrontation between capitalism and communism, they warned that a Vietcong victory would damage American prestige and credibility throughout Asia and have "a corresponding unfavorable effect upon our image in Africa and Latin America." The JCS complained that the United States was fighting under self-imposed restrictions by keeping the war within the boundaries of South Vietnam and by avoiding the direct use of American combat forces. They thought that the time was fast approaching when Uncle Sam would have to take off his gloves and strike his enemy with a combination of punches.

Determined to score a victory in South Vietnam, the Joint Chiefs of Staff recommended that the United States be ready to take the following actions: (1) give the head of the MACV responsibility for the total American program in South Vietnam, (2) induce the Saigon government to turn over the tactical direction of the war to the American military commander, (3) persuade the rulers of South Vietnam to conduct overt ground operations in Laos to impede the flow of men and material from North Vietnam, (4) arm and aid South Vietnamese forces in the aerial bombing of critical targets in North Vietnam and in the mining of sea approaches to that country, (5) advise and support South Vietnamese units in conducting large-scale commando raids inside North Vietnam, and (6) if necessary, commit additional American forces in support of combat action within South Vietnam. "It is our conviction," the JCS concluded, "that any or all of the foregoing actions may be required to enhance our position in Southeast Asia."

A week later, on January 30, a group of young officers headed by General Nguyen Khanh overthrew the divided and ineffective military junta in Saigon. Some of the rebel officers had supported the ouster of Diem but now felt insufficiently rewarded under the Minh regime, while others who had been close to Diem feared that they would lose their positions if Minh and his cohorts remained in power. General Khanh himself was also motivated by personal ambition, but he justified his actions by claiming that the leading members of the Military Revolutionary Council were preparing to make an agreement with the National Liberation Front. While the coup against Minh was in progress, Khanh informed Ambassador Lodge that he was eager to turn to the United States for political advice. "It is safe to say," the Central Intelligence Agency promptly reported from Saigon, "that Khanh's group will be essentially pro-American, anti-communist and anti-neutralist in general orientation." President Johnson welcomed the news, and on February 2, he sent Khanh a warm note promising that the United States would support his government.

Khanh quickly demonstrated his desire to cooperate fully with the United States. After revamping the Military Revolutionary Council and promoting several young officers to key positions in his new regime, he yielded to American wishes and retained Minh in a figurehead capacity to make it appear that no basic change in the government had taken place. Khanh then proceeded to work closely with the United States in carrying out military operations against the Vietcong, and in early February 1964, he began participating in an enlarged, American-directed program of covert action against North Vietnam. This scheme, code-named Operation Plan 34 Alpha (OPLAN 34 A), involved intelligence overflights, the dropping of propaganda leaflets, and commando raids. While some American-trained South Vietnamese units parachuted into North Vietnam on sabotage missions, others attacked facilities along the North Vietnamese coast from patrol boats provided by the United States. The OPLAN 34 A program also included electronic espionage missions conducted by American destroyers in the Gulf of Tonkin to pinpoint the location of radar stations and antiaircraft networks in North Vietnam. These maritime surveillance operations, code-named De Soto patrols, were initiated in anticipation of future air and naval attacks against North Vietnam.

In a long memorandum prepared for President Johnson on the first day of March 1964, Assistant Secretary of Defense William P. Bundy recommended that the United States also begin taking overt military actions against North Vietnam. After discussing the situation with his brother McGeorge, William Bundy argued that American forces should first blockade the port of Haiphong and then bomb roads and railroads, power stations and industrial plants, and military training camps in North Vietnam. Bundy explained that one purpose of the blockade and bombing campaign would be to get North Vietnam to stop, or at least cut down, the shipment of supplies to the Vietcong. He also hoped that such a demonstration of American determination to prevent the spread of communism in Southeast Asia would stiffen the Khanh government and "discourage moves toward neutralism in South Vietnam." Although he admitted that the proposed military measures would normally require a declaration of war, Bundy warned that an attempt to induce Congress to do so might spark a major political controversy in the United States. He therefore suggested that President Johnson circumvent the constitutional requirement for a legislative declaration of war by obtaining a congressional resolution freeing him to take punitive action against North Vietnam.

As pressure for overt military action against North Vietnam increased, Secretary of Defense McNamara made another trip to Saigon to assess the situation. McNamara found that conditions in South Vietnam had grown much worse since his last visit, and on March 16, he reported to President Johnson that about 40 percent of the countryside was under Vietcong control or predominant influence. McNamara pointed out that while ARVN desertion rates were high and increasing, the Vietcong were recruiting energetically and effectively. He also noted that the North Vietnamese were supplying the Vietcong with a growing assortment of Chinese weapons, including recoilless rifles, machine guns, rocket launchers, and mortars. Despite the enhanced military capability of the Vietcong, however, McNamara still believed that the greatest problem in South Vietnam was the uncertain viability of the Saigon government. "Large groups of the population are now showing signs of apathy and indifference," he warned. "There is a constant threat of assassination or of another coup, which would drop morale and organization nearly to zero."

McNamara urged that the United States do everything possible to help Khanh build up his base of support and root out the Vietcong. He recommended that American officials at all levels "continue to make it clear that we fully support the Khanh government and are totally opposed to any further coups." McNamara also recommended that the United States provide funds for a substantial increase in the size of the South Vietnamese armed forces. If the Khanh regime

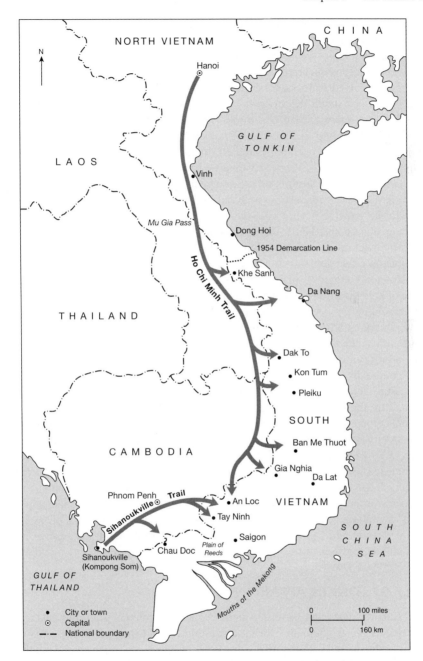

Supply routes for North Vietnamese and Vietcong soldiers fighting in South Vietnam.

succeeded in taking hold during the next few months, he added, the United States might want to exert graduated military pressure against North Vietnam to undermine the confidence of the Vietcong and to bolster the morale of the ruling clique in Saigon. But McNamara advised against bombing North Vietnam at the present time. "Unless and until the Khanh government has established its position, and preferably is making significant progress in the South," he argued, "an overt extension of operations in the North carries the risk of being mounted from an extremely weak base which might at any moment collapse and leave the posture of political confrontation worsened rather than improved."

President Johnson concurred. After approving a mobilization plan to put South Vietnam on a war footing, he cabled Ambassador Lodge on March 17 that the United States believed that ARVN ground troops should begin cross-border penetrations into Laos to impede the flow of military equipment down the Ho Chi Minh Trail. But the president indicated that he would reserve judgment regarding the question of launching overt American military attacks against North Vietnam. Three days later, on March 20, Johnson cabled Lodge that for the moment, any overt measures against North Vietnam would be premature. Johnson explained that "our planning for action against the North is on a contingency basis" and that the immediate task in the South "is to develop the strongest possible military and political base for possible later action." He pointed to the growing hostility between Moscow and Beijing and noted that an American bombing campaign against North Vietnam would be more practicable after a complete breakdown in Sino-Soviet relations. Worried that in the meantime the South Vietnamese government might negotiate a peace settlement calling for the withdrawal of American military personnel, Johnson instructed Lodge to explain to authorities in Saigon that his mission was "precisely for the purpose of knocking down the idea of neutralization wherever it rears its ugly head."

While holding the decision to bomb North Vietnam in abeyance, President Johnson and his top foreign policy advisers were eager to do everything they could to shore up the Khanh regime in South Vietnam. "In our efforts to help the Vietnamese to help themselves, we must not let any arbitrary limits on budget, or manpower, or procedures stand in our way," Johnson cabled Lodge on April 28. "You must have whatever you need to help the Vietnamese do the job, and I assure you that I will act at once to eliminate obstacles or restraints wherever they may appear." But the military junta in Saigon did not make much progress in building a solid base of popular support or in gaining the initiative against the Vietcong. In a cable to Lodge on May 21, Secretary of State Rusk revealed his growing exasperation with Khanh and his cohorts. "Is there any way we can shake the main body of leadership by the scruff of the neck and insist that they put aside all bickering and lesser differences in order to concentrate upon the defeat of the Viet Cong?" Rusk asked. "Can we find some way by which General Khanh can convince larger segments of the people that they have a stake in the success of his leadership against the Viet Cong?" Searching for an answer, Rusk concluded: "Somehow we must change the pace at which people move, and I suspect that this can only be done with a pervasive intrusion of Americans into their affairs."

THE GULF OF TONKIN AFFAIR

Unlike Secretary of State Rusk, several American leaders wanted to go further and employ military force against North Vietnam. During a conference held in Honolulu in early June 1964, Ambassador Lodge joined with the Joint Chiefs of Staff in advocating the aerial bombardment of North Vietnam. Specialists in the Pentagon drew up a list of ninety-four targets for potential air strikes, and a small group of civilian officials in Washington prepared a rough draft of a congressional resolution empowering the president to commit American military forces anywhere in Southeast Asia. William P. Bundy, then the assistant secretary of state for Far Eastern affairs, outlined the arguments in favor of such a resolution. "The situation in South Viet-Nam," he reasoned on June 12, "could deteriorate to the point where we [would have] to consider at least beginning stronger actions to the north in order to put greater pressure on Hanoi and lift morale in South Viet-Nam." Bundy concluded that the proposed resolution would demonstrate American firmness and provide "complete flexibility in the hands of the Executive in the coming political months."

Not wanting to look like a warmonger on the eve of the presidential election, Johnson decided to take a different tack. He asked the Canadian government to send J. Blair Seaborn on a secret mission to persuade the communist leaders in North Vietnam to stop supporting the Vietcong insurgents. During a confidential meeting in Hanoi on June 18, Seaborn warned Prime Minister Pham Van Dong that the United States held North Vietnam directly responsible for the guerrilla war in South Vietnam. He hinted that the United States would reward the North Vietnamese with economic assistance if they agreed to confine their energy to developing their own resources. Seaborn also implied that the United States would punish the North Vietnamese with devastating attacks if they continued to support the Vietcong rebels. But Dong replied that a just solution to the war would require an American withdrawal from Indochina, the participation of the National Liberation Front in a coalition government in Saigon, and the peaceful reunification of Vietnam. And after asserting that the Vietnamese people were determined to carry on the struggle, he defiantly predicted that they would eventually achieve their goals. His confidence grew a week later when Mao Zedong promised that China would send combat troops to defend his country if American ground forces invaded North Vietnam.

Despite this failure to intimidate the rulers of North Vietnam, President Johnson was not about to abandon his efforts to assure the survival of an independent, noncommunist regime in South Vietnam. Johnson demonstrated his desire to infuse greater vigor into the counterinsurgency campaign in South Vietnam on June 20 when he promoted the resolute and energetic General William C. Westmoreland to replace the ever-optimistic General Harkins as the commander of the MACV. The number of American military advisers serving under Westmoreland was quickly increased by more than 4,000. And when Ambassador Lodge resigned his position to seek the Republican nomination for president, Johnson appointed General Maxwell D. Taylor to take charge of the American embassy in Saigon. The American economic aid package was rapidly expanded after Taylor began his new job on July 2, and before long, the United States was pouring money into South Vietnam at a rate of nearly $2 million a day.

The American-directed program of covert harassment and naval surveillance was also pressed forward with great vigor against North Vietnam. On July 31, South Vietnamese commandos carried out clandestine OPLAN 34 A raids against two islands a few miles off the coast of North Vietnam. The next day, the American destroyer *Maddox*, operating under explicit orders, conducted a De Soto mission of electronic espionage in the same general vicinity. The North Vietnamese mistakenly concluded that the *Maddox* was running cover for the South Vietnamese commandos, and on August 2, three North Vietnamese torpedo boats attacked the American destroyer. As the small craft swiftly approached his ship, Captain John J. Herrick directed his crew to commence firing while he radioed the aircraft carrier *Ticonderoga* for air support. Only one bullet struck the *Maddox* before American jets arrived overhead to help sink one of the North Vietnamese boats and cripple the other two. "The other side got a sting out of this," Secretary of State Rusk told reporters. "If they do it again, they'll get another sting."

Rather than attempting to avoid another clash with North Vietnamese patrol boats, however, American leaders continued to authorize provocative actions in the Gulf of Tonkin. Commander-in-Chief for the Pacific Admiral Ulysses Sharp ordered the *Maddox*, together with the destroyer *Turner Joy*, to resume operations and to repel any further attacks. As the two American ships zigzagged off the North Vietnamese coast on August 3, South Vietnamese commandos returned to the area and raided communication facilities along the North Vietnamese shore. Captain Herrick soon reported to his superiors in Hawaii that intercepts of communist radio messages indicated that the North Vietnamese thought the De Soto operations were tied in with the commando forays. Wanting to steer away from probable trouble, he proposed that the *Maddox* and *Turner Joy* retreat to the open sea. But Admiral Sharp ordered both destroyers to continue their maneuvers "to assert our legitimate rights in these international waters." Rusk promptly cabled Saigon to explain to Ambassador Taylor how Washington viewed the situation: "We believe that present OPLAN 34 A activities are beginning to rattle Hanoi, and MADDOX incident is directly related to their efforts to resist these activities. We have no intention of yielding to pressure."

American statesmen and seamen were fully prepared for a second incident in the Gulf of Tonkin. As the *Maddox* and *Turner Joy* proceeded cautiously in anticipation of another ambush, their crews carefully scanned sonar instruments in an effort to pick up noise from the propellers of any North Vietnamese patrol boats that might be lurking in the area. On the night of August 4, the two destroyers began getting distorted radar beams in the midst of a violent thunderstorm, and the anxious American sailors began firing wildly into the dark. After calling for air support, Captain Herrick reported to Honolulu that the *Maddox* and *Turner Joy* were engaged in battle. But he soon had second thoughts. Not a single sailor on either American ship had seen or heard any enemy gunfire, and none of the pilots from the *Ticonderoga* had been able to detect any trace of enemy boats. Herrick promptly reported that "no actual sightings" had been made and that "freak weather effects" may have caused the erratic radar blips. He therefore suggested that a "complete evaluation" of the episode be made before any further actions were taken.

Despite the lack of solid evidence for the supposed second attack in the Gulf of Tonkin, President Johnson seized the opportunity to implement contingency plans that had been temporarily shelved. Johnson appeared on television screens across the nation just before midnight on August 4 and solemnly announced that the United States was retaliating against North Vietnam for "repeated acts of violence" directed at American forces. While he was speaking, American jets flew sixty-four sorties against North Vietnamese naval bases and nearby oil storage facilities. A few days later, Johnson privately expressed his own doubts about the alleged second attack on American seamen. "Hell," he confided to one of his advisers, "those dumb, stupid sailors were just shooting at flying fish." But Johnson was not about to forego the chance to obtain bipartisan support for whatever military action he might desire to take in the future. And his aides had already broadened their earlier draft of the proposed congressional resolution to give him wide discretionary authority to deploy American military forces in Southeast Asia. Johnson wanted a resolution that would strengthen the morale of the Saigon government and authorize him to exercise unlimited American military power in Southeast Asia.

President Johnson and Secretary of State Rusk made a concerted effort to mobilize support for the resolution in the Senate. During private meetings with a select group of senators, Johnson and Rusk claimed that they sought no wider war but wanted to convince the North Vietnamese that Americans were united in their determination to safeguard South Vietnam. J. William Fulbright, the chairman of the Foreign Relations Committee, agreed to shepherd the resolution through the Senate. Fulbright, however, faced a small number of skeptical colleagues. Fearful of giving the president a blank check to take whatever action he deemed necessary, Senator Gaylord Nelson of Wisconsin began preparing an amendment to the resolution to indicate that Congress opposed any direct American military involvement in Southeast Asia. But Fulbright told Nelson that Johnson desired unanimous backing for the permissive measure simply to frighten Ho Chi Minh and his comrades in Hanoi into stopping their support for the insurgency in South Vietnam. Having been assured that the president had no intention of sending American combat troops to Vietnam, Nelson finally decided against introducing a restrictive amendment to the resolution.

Only two isolated senators continued to oppose the maneuver to grant the president the power to make war in the absence of a congressional declaration. Charging that the reported incidents in the Gulf of Tonkin were the inevitable consequence of an aggressive American policy in Southeast Asia, Ernest Gruening of Alaska pleaded with his colleagues not to authorize the president to send "American boys into combat in a war in which we have no business." So did Wayne Morse of Oregon. "I believe that history will record that we have made a great mistake in subverting and circumventing the Constitution of the United States," Morse declared. "Future generations will look with dismay and great disappointment upon a Congress which is now about to make such a historic mistake." But his warnings were cast aside. And on August 7, with the House voting 416 to 0 in favor and only Gruening and Morse dissenting in the Senate, Congress passed the Gulf of Tonkin Resolution, which authorized the president "to take all necessary measures to repel any armed attack against the forces of the United States and to prevent further aggression."

President Johnson had proved himself the master of deceit. His spokesmen had withheld critical information about the South Vietnamese commando assaults along the North Vietnamese coast, and they had described the American destroyers as the targets of deliberate communist aggression while performing routine patrols in international waters. In so doing, they had helped the president gain an almost unanimous endorsement for the unlimited exercise of executive power from a badly misled Congress. Johnson was delighted with the broad authority that the Gulf of Tonkin Resolution had given him. "Like grandma's nightshirt," he later quipped, "it covered everything." Johnson had not only obtained a free hand to pursue a militant policy in Southeast Asia, he had also prepared the way for his victory in the fast-approaching presidential election. By taking a firm but restrained stand against what were portrayed as unprovoked attacks on the high seas, the president won widespread support from the American people. Overnight, his ratings in the Harris public opinion poll skyrocketed from 42 to 72 percent. Thus, Johnson had succeeded in outmaneuvering Barry Goldwater, the hawkish Republican nominee for president, on the potentially disruptive war issue.

THE RHETORIC OF RESTRAINT

Johnson projected himself as the peace candidate for the Democratic Party as the 1964 presidential campaign got under way. And not wanting to jeopardize his strong position in the polls, he proceeded with caution immediately after the Gulf of Tonkin affair. Johnson temporarily suspended both the De Soto patrols and the American-sponsored clandestine attacks along the North Vietnamese coast. But while he assumed the posture of a dove in an effort to maintain the support of moderate voters across the country, Goldwater cast himself as a hawk who wanted to go all out to achieve a quick victory against the forces of communism in Southeast Asia. Taking advantage of the militant rhetoric of his Republican adversary, Johnson shrewdly implied that Goldwater was an irresponsible fool. "Some others are eager to enlarge the conflict," Johnson declared in a campaign speech on August 12. "They call upon us to supply American boys to do the job that Asian boys should do. They ask us to take reckless action which might risk the lives of millions and engulf much of Asia and certainly threaten the peace of the entire world." He warned that "such action would offer no solution at all to the real problems of Vietnam."

Renewed political turmoil in South Vietnam gave President Johnson additional reason to remain cautious. As the apprehension grew that North Vietnam might retaliate for the Tonkin Gulf air strikes, General Khanh jumped at the chance to consolidate his power in Saigon. Khanh hastily declared a state of emergency, severely limited civil liberties, and sharply restricted the press. On

August 16, he moved to oust Minh as chief of state by introducing a new constitution that eliminated the position of his principal rival. Simultaneously, Khanh announced that he would assume the new post of president while remaining chairman of the Military Revolutionary Council. These abrupt moves sparked an explosive reaction in Saigon. Streaming into the streets, Buddhist militants and their student allies led massive demonstrations against Khanh. The angry Buddhists demanded that he establish a civilian government, assure religious freedom, and schedule elections for the coming year. Retreating in the face of the mounting protest movement, Khanh announced that he would revise the new constitution and relax government controls. But these modest concessions failed to satisfy the Buddhists, and they continued to press for major reforms.

Americans on the scene were alarmed about the political uproar in Saigon. As the Buddhists became increasingly assertive in their confrontations with Khanh, American observers feared the emergence of a coalition government that would seek neutralist goals. "War weariness and a desire for a quick solution to the long struggle against the Viet Cong may be an important factor underlying the current agitation," the Central Intelligence Agency warned on August 25. "The confused situation is extremely vulnerable to exploitation by the Communists and by the proponents of a negotiated settlement." American officials became even more anxious when they learned that malcontents within the armed forces were plotting a coup against Khanh. Ambassador Taylor worked hard to discourage the conspiring officers and to help Khanh solidify his position. But machinations within the officer corps continued, and Taylor remained pessimistic about the future. "We should not delude ourselves," he cabled from Saigon on September 2, "that we can put together any combination of personalities that will add up to a really effective government."

President Johnson promptly ordered Ambassador Taylor to return to Washington to participate in a full review of American policy. During a conference at the White House on September 7, the president and his top advisers considered the option of embarking on an accelerated program of military action against North Vietnam. General Earle Wheeler, the chairman of the Joint Chiefs of Staff, argued that the United States should launch a bombing campaign against North Vietnam as soon as possible. He and his colleagues believed that only significant military pressure on North Vietnam could provide the psychological boost necessary to attain political stability in South Vietnam. Taylor, however, wanted to postpone the bombardment of North Vietnam until Khanh had time to strengthen his military position against the Vietcong. Fearing the development of a popular front that would demand the withdrawal of American forces from South Vietnam, Taylor concluded that beginning around December 1, the United States would have to commence bombing North Vietnam. "If we leave Vietnam with our tail between our legs," he warned, "the consequences of this defeat in the rest of Asia, Africa and Latin America would be disastrous."

Two days later, on September 9, Johnson met once again with his top advisers to discuss what actions the United States should take to assure the survival of an independent, noncommunist South Vietnam. Secretary of Defense McNamara reported that there was an important division among the Joint Chiefs of Staff. The Air Force and Marine Corps representatives believed that the situation in South Vietnam would continue to deteriorate unless immediate air strikes were launched against North Vietnam. But General Wheeler, together with the Army and Navy representatives, now agreed with Ambassador Taylor that it was important not to overstrain the currently weakened Saigon government by drastic action in the immediate future. While acknowledging that this was his own view, Taylor also emphasized that sooner or later, the United States would indeed have to act more forcefully against North Vietnam. John McCone, the director of the Central Intelligence Agency, likewise argued that a sustained air attack against North Vietnam would be dangerous at present because of the weakness of the South Vietnamese government. While agreeing that the decision to bombard North Vietnam should be delayed, Secretary of State Rusk suggested that by December, the deepening Sino-Soviet split might make the Chinese communists more reluctant to respond aggressively to bolder American moves in Southeast Asia.

The president and his advisers were preoccupied with the problem of political disorder in South Vietnam. When Johnson asked whether the United States could stop the internal feuding in Saigon, Taylor replied that it would be difficult to accomplish much with "a group of men who turned off their hearing aids in the face of appeals to the public weal." He explained that the present rulers of South Vietnam "regularly estimated matters in terms of their own personal gains and losses." When Johnson asked him to compare Khanh and Diem in regard to popular support, Taylor responded that the South Vietnamese people did not care for either one. McNamara was equally concerned about the internal discord in South Vietnam. He emphasized the importance of funneling American economic aid into the urban areas to lower the level of student and Buddhist pressure and to increase the political base of support for the government. Endorsing this judgment, McCone stated that the Central Intelligence Agency was "disturbed by the prospect that the internal movement toward negotiations might be increasing and that there was some sign also of anti-American feeling in South Vietnam."

President Johnson asked if anyone present doubted whether South Vietnam was worth all the effort that would be necessary to achieve American objectives in Southeast Asia. "We could not afford to let Hanoi win," Ambassador Taylor replied, "in terms of our overall position in the area and in the world." General Wheeler reported that the Joint Chiefs of Staff were in unanimous agreement with that assessment. "If we should lose in South Vietnam, we would lose Southeast Asia," he declared with considerable force. "Country after country on the periphery would give way and look toward Communist China as the rising power of the area." McCone and Rusk concurred that the United States must not allow the South Vietnam domino to fall into the clutches of communism. Then, after watching his aides reach a consensus, Johnson said that in his opinion, the United States should not take extensive action against North Vietnam until the government in South Vietnam could be strengthened. "With a weak and wobbly situation," he reasoned, "it would be unwise to attack until we could stabilize our base." Johnson ended the September 9 meeting by asking Wheeler to explain to his colleagues on the JCS that "we would be ready to do more when we had a base."

The political structure in South Vietnam continued to rest on shaky foundations, however. On September 13, a group of disgruntled officers led their forces into Saigon in an effort to wrest control from General Khanh. And when Khanh requested help, American officials raced to the rescue. The Voice of America announced that the United States backed Khanh, and General Westmoreland persuaded some of the rebel officers to remove their troops from Saigon. Although the coup attempt quickly collapsed, Khanh concluded that he would have to broaden his base of support to gain leverage against his military rivals. He realized that the Buddhist monks were the only noncommunist leaders with a large following in South Vietnam, so in an attempt to win their favor, Khanh yielded to their demands for a civilian government. On September 26, he created the High National Council composed of seventeen elderly civilians and charged them with the task of selecting a chief of state. The council of elders proceeded to set up a civilian administration, but Khanh retained real power in his hands. Although American officials feared that the Buddhists might ultimately push Khanh toward neutralism, they saw no alternative except to continue supporting him.

Meanwhile, during the final phase of his campaign for reelection in the autumn of 1964, President Johnson continued telling the American people what he thought they wanted to hear.

Johnson assured his audiences on numerous occasions that he sought no wider war in Southeast Asia. Yet his campaign speeches often contained escape clauses tailored to keep his options open. While addressing a crowd in New Hampshire on September 28, for example, Johnson stated that he would consider attacking North Vietnam "only as a last resort" in order to prevent a communist takeover in South Vietnam. "We are not going north and drop bombs," he proclaimed, adding the qualifying phrase, "at this stage of the game." Johnson also indicated that he wanted to be very careful with regard to the situation in the south. "So just for the moment," he hedged, "I have not thought we were ready for American boys to do the fighting for Asian boys." The American people registered their approval of this rhetoric of restraint on November 3 when they cast their votes. As a result, Johnson crushed Goldwater by a larger vote margin than any previous candidate had scored in a presidential election in the United States. The spectacular Democratic landslide kept Johnson in the White House and gave his party huge majorities in both chambers of Congress.

Under Secretary of State George W. Ball was the only high American official who took a private position that corresponded with the public posture of the president. In October 1964, Ball prepared a long memorandum that argued forcefully in favor of negotiation rather than escalation. He not only challenged the contention that an American air offensive against North Vietnam would improve morale in South Vietnam, he also questioned whether a bombing campaign would compel Hanoi to stop supporting the insurgency against the Saigon government. Ball warned that North Vietnam might retaliate by pouring a large number of combat troops into South Vietnam. If the United States responded in kind, he reasoned, China might intervene with unlimited manpower. And this spreading military conflict, Ball cautioned, might lead to a nuclear holocaust. "Once on the tiger's back," he wrote, "we cannot be sure of picking the place to dismount." Not wanting to see the United States entangled in a process of mutual escalation, he advocated a political solution to the military struggle. Ball suggested that the United States should encourage the organization of a neutralist South Vietnamese government that would negotiate a settlement with the National Liberation Front. If the likely communist takeover of South Vietnam were postponed for a substantial period of time, he concluded, the damage to the global prestige of the United States would be minimized.

Shortly after his smashing victory over Goldwater on November 3, Johnson created a National Security Council Working Group to study American options in Southeast Asia. The members of the Working Group, chaired by William Bundy, held frequent sessions before they formulated a range of possibilities for the president to consider. The representative for the Joint Chiefs of Staff advocated an all-out air offensive against North Vietnam to impede the flow of military supplies into South Vietnam and to compel Hanoi to stop supporting the Vietcong insurgents. But though they were ready to begin taking aggressive steps, many civilians on the committee feared that a sudden and massive bombing campaign might provoke North Vietnam to send combat units into South Vietnam and spur China to intervene in the war. On November 21, the Working Group prepared a position paper that outlined three broad courses of action for the United States to take in Southeast Asia. Option A called for reprisal actions against North Vietnam for any spectacular attack by the Vietcong within South Vietnam. Option B required a systematic program of rapidly increasing military pressures against North Vietnam. Option C demanded slowly graduated military moves, first against infiltration routes in Laos and then against targets in North Vietnam. In short, rather than urging a negotiated settlement along the lines advocated by George Ball, the Working Group presented three formulas for military escalation.

Before returning to Washington to help shape the final recommendations for the president, Ambassador Taylor set forth his views in a comprehensive memorandum. In it, Taylor emphasized the lack of an adequate political base in South Vietnam. "It is impossible to foresee a stable and effective government under any name in anything like the near future," he observed. "We sense a mounting feeling of war weariness and hopelessness that pervade South Vietnam." In contrast, Taylor marveled at the continued strength of the Vietcong guerrillas. "Not only do the Vietcong units have the recuperative power of the phoenix, but they have an amazing ability to maintain morale." Taylor argued that the United States should make a concerted effort to change the situation before it was too late. To raise morale in Saigon, he reasoned, the United States should be ready to bomb selected targets in North Vietnam in retaliation for any outrageous Vietcong attack in South Vietnam. And if a satisfactory government could be established in Saigon, he concluded, Washington should be prepared to embark on "a methodical program of mounting air attacks" in order to induce Hanoi not only to stop aiding the guerrillas but also to pressure them into ending the revolution in South Vietnam.

President Johnson met with his top foreign policy advisers on December 1, 1964, to discuss what actions the United States should take in Southeast Asia. His senior advisers advocated an air offensive to be implemented in two stages. Phase I called for bombing raids on the Ho Chi Minh Trail in Laos plus reprisal strikes on targets in North Vietnam in response to any dramatic Vietcong actions in South Vietnam. Phase II provided for a program of gradually extended air attacks against North Vietnam. But the president refused to authorize provocative actions against Hanoi until the government in Saigon demonstrated more stability. Reluctant to hit North Vietnam unless South Vietnam was able to take a punch in return, Johnson said he did not want "to send a widow woman to slap Jack Dempsey." He stressed that the South Vietnamese must put their house in order before the United States provoked the North Vietnamese dragon. Johnson agreed that Operation Barrel Roll, a secret bombing campaign against infiltration trails in Laos, should begin promptly. But he was not yet ready to approve the implementation of either Phase I or Phase II plans for the bombing of North Vietnam.

Two days later, on December 3, President Johnson spelled out his position in instructions to Ambassador Taylor. "There are certain minimum criteria of performance in South Vietnam which must be met," he explained, "before new measures against North Vietnam would be either justified or practical." Johnson insisted that South Vietnamese leaders should be capable of maintaining law and order in the principal centers of population and be able to carry out effective counterinsurgency operations in the countryside. He also demanded that the Saigon government "must have the means to cope with the enemy reactions which must be expected to result from any change in the pattern of our operations." While American air strikes against North Vietnam could contribute to the campaign against the Vietcong, the president argued, they could not in and of themselves end the guerrilla war in South Vietnam. Even if Hanoi stopped aiding the Vietcong, he reasoned, it would be necessary to have a stable and effective government in Saigon to defeat the revolutionary forces in South Vietnam. Johnson therefore instructed Taylor to inform the political and military leaders in Saigon that continued American support for South Vietnam depended on the establishment of governmental stability and national unity. Taylor was authorized to promise an increase in American military aid if they demonstrated political cohesion and improvement in fighting the Vietcong.

Ambassador Taylor, however, was unable to foster harmony among the various civilian and military factions in South Vietnam. Shortly after he returned to his post in Saigon, the Buddhists began staging demonstrations against Prime Minister Tran Van Huong and his recently installed civilian government. General Khanh and a group of young officers known as the Young Turks, who were headed by Air Vice Marshal Nguyen Cao Ky, feared that the political disturbances might provide an opening for General Minh to worm his way back into power. They promptly began plotting to protect their position. Alarmed by rumors of an impending coup, Taylor invited General Nguyen Van Thieu, Air Vice Marshal Ky, and a few other young officers to dinner on December 8 and warned them that chronic disorder in Saigon might discourage Congress from increasing aid to South Vietnam. Despite his threats, the Young Turks soon demanded that the High National Council pass a law requiring the immediate retirement of Minh and eight other Old Guard generals accused of fomenting unrest. But the civilian leaders refused to yield, and on December 20, Khanh and his cohorts on the Military Revolutionary Council abolished the High National Council. While allowing Huong to remain as the prime minister, they set up a new Armed Forces Council as the real authority in Saigon.

Taylor was furious. He promptly summoned Ky and Thieu along with two other young officers to the American embassy and gave them a humiliating lecture. Taylor reminded the officers that he had recently told them over dinner that their American patrons were tired of coups. "Apparently I wasted my words," he scolded. "Now you have made a real mess. We cannot carry you forever if you do things like this." But once again, his threats fell on deaf ears. Taylor lost all patience when shortly after the meeting and against his wishes Khanh announced to the press that the Armed Forces Council had dissolved the High National Council. The angry ambassador told Khanh that he should resign and leave the country. But Khanh was not about to quit, and he publicly denounced Taylor for meddling in the internal affairs of South Vietnam. Despite their reliance on American aid, Khanh and his colleagues remained convinced that the United States needed them as pawns in the struggle to prevent the spread of communism in Southeast Asia. Thus, Taylor learned, as Lodge had before him, that Americans lacked leverage in dealing with their weak Asian clients.

A stunning Vietcong attack on Americans stationed in South Vietnam, however, soon raised the question of whether or not the United States should launch Phase I reprisal air strikes against North Vietnam. On Christmas Eve 1964, Vietcong agents planted a bomb in the Brinks Hotel, which housed American officers on duty in Saigon. The resulting explosion killed two Americans and injured thirty-eight others. And on December 30, Taylor urged President Johnson to authorize retaliatory bombing raids against North Vietnam. The president, however, refused to sanction any action that might provoke a strong communist reaction. South Vietnam had yet to demonstrate greater political stability or military capability, and Johnson remained skeptical about the effectiveness of American air power. "I have never felt that this war will be won from the air," he replied to Taylor on December 30, "and it seems to me that what is much more needed and would be more effective is a larger and stronger use of rangers and special forces and marines, or other appropriate military strength on the ground and on the scene." Johnson indicated that he was now prepared to permit American troops to do more fighting in South Vietnam. "Although I know that it may involve the acceptance of larger American sacrifices," he emphasized, "I myself am ready to substantially increase the number of Americans in Vietnam if it is necessary to provide this kind of fighting force against the Viet Cong."

THE DECISION TO BOMB NORTH VIETNAM

A major military setback for the Saigon government during the first week of 1965 suggested the need for the United States to do something fast to stave off a complete collapse in South Vietnam. On January 2, two crack companies of ARVN rangers walked into a Vietcong ambush inside a rubber plantation near the village of Binh Gia, located about forty-five miles northeast of Saigon. The South Vietnamese field commanders threw two of their best battalions into the engagement. But even though the ARVN units and their American advisers were supported by tanks, artillery, and helicopters, they suffered a devastating defeat. General Wheeler reported in a secret memorandum on January 5 that there had been 445 ARVN and 16 American casualties, compared with just 132 Vietcong losses, during the Battle of Binh Gia. Despite the relative superiority of the ARVN in force size, firepower, and air mobility, Wheeler warned, the Vietcong might now feel strong enough to compete in a conventional war because of their better sources of intelligence, more intimate knowledge of the terrain, and greater control over the local population.

On January 6, only four days after the Binh Gia disaster, Ambassador Taylor sent the president a somber assessment of current political and military conditions in South Vietnam. The ambassador pointed out that he was confronted with a seriously deteriorating situation characterized by continued political turmoil, lethargy in the counterinsurgency program, and the loss of morale throughout the country. "Unless these conditions are somehow changed and trends reversed," he warned, "we are likely to face a number of unpleasant developments ranging from anti-American demonstrations, further civil disorders, and even political assassinations to the ultimate installation of a hostile government which will ask us to leave while it seeks accommodation with the National Liberation Front and Hanoi." Opposed to the introduction of American combat troops into South Vietnam, Taylor advocated a program of graduated air attacks to sap the will of the enemy in North Vietnam. "With regard to your feeling that this guerrilla war cannot be won from the air," he wrote, "I am in entire agreement, if we are thinking in terms of the physical destruction of the enemy." But Taylor assumed that a sustained bombing campaign would have a profound psychological impact on the communist leaders in Hanoi. "As practical men," he concluded, "they cannot wish to see the fruits of ten years of labor destroyed by slowly escalating air attacks."

Taylor then advocated implementing a two-stage bombing program against North Vietnam to help turn the situation around in South Vietnam. He argued that the president should be prepared to approve Phase I reprisal air strikes against North Vietnam to lift morale in South Vietnam. To give an added boost to South Vietnamese spirits, Taylor continued, American representatives should indicate their intention of joining with Saigon officials in planning for Phase II bombing operations designed to deter Hanoi. Taylor wanted to make a conditional commitment: If the South Vietnamese government attained a certain level of performance, the United States would initiate a gradually escalating air war against North Vietnam. "Hopefully," he explained, "by such action we could improve the government, unify the armed forces to some degree, and thereupon move into the Phase II program without which we see little chance of breaking out of the present downward spiral." Therefore, Taylor asked for permission to begin joint planning with authorities in Saigon and to give a conditional pledge to carry out a sustained bombing campaign against North Vietnam.

President Johnson agreed to meet Taylor halfway. In a message cabled to the ambassador on January 7, Johnson indicated that he was now inclined to adopt a policy of prompt and clear reprisal against North Vietnam in response to any spectacular Vietcong attacks in South Vietnam. He also gave Taylor permission to start joint planning for sustained air operations in the future. But the ambassador was not to make any commitment with regard to the timing or scale of Phase II bombing. In planning for this contingency with Saigon officials, Taylor was to make it very clear that American decisions concerning a gradually escalating air campaign against North Vietnam would depend on South Vietnamese progress in achieving political stability. "My decisions on Phase II," Johnson emphasized, "will necessarily be affected by performance in earlier activities." In short, while he was now ready to launch retaliatory Phase I bombing strikes, the president was still not prepared to embark on a graduated program of air attacks against North Vietnam.

Taylor worked hard during the next week to promote a stable political base in Saigon. By threatening to withhold American funds earmarked for a major expansion of the South Vietnamese military establishment, he induced General Khanh and the Armed Forces Council to continue backing Tran Van Huong as prime minister. He subsequently prevailed on Huong to add four of the Young Turk officers to his cabinet. Then, after persuading the South Vietnamese military leaders to raise draft levels, Taylor agreed to release the American funds required to increase the size of the armed forces under their command. But these moves provoked an explosion in the major cities of South Vietnam. Beginning on January 19, the Buddhists and their student allies led huge demonstrations against the Huong government. The protestors accused Taylor of misconduct and demanded that he be recalled. They also sacked U.S. Information Service buildings in Saigon and Hué. As the demonstrations took an increasingly bitter anti-American tone, Taylor warned Washington that Khanh might arrange a marriage of convenience with the Buddhists directed toward the overthrow of Huong.

The political disorder rocking South Vietnam during the first month of 1965 prompted McGeorge Bundy and Robert McNamara to urge President Johnson to abandon his preconditions for bombing North Vietnam. On January 26, Bundy prepared a long memorandum, which he and McNamara presented to the president the next morning. "Both of us are now pretty well convinced that our current policy can only lead to disastrous defeat," Bundy explained. "What we are doing now, essentially, is to wait and hope for a stable government." But he and McNamara had come to the conclusion that there was little chance for the emergence of such a government in South Vietnam unless the United States employed military force against North Vietnam. "The underlying difficulties in Saigon arise from the spreading conviction that the future is without hope for anti-Communists," Bundy argued. "Our best friends have become somewhat discouraged by our own inactivity in the face of major attacks on our own installations." Acknowledging that Dean Rusk still sought a way to make the present wait-and-see policy work, Bundy warned that he and McNamara believed this passive course could "only lead to eventual defeat and an invitation to get out in humiliating circumstances."

President Johnson received an additional prod on January 27, when he heard that another coup had occurred in Saigon. With Buddhist support, General Khanh had ousted Prime Minister Huong and taken charge of the government on behalf of the Armed Forces Council. "The most sinister aspect of this affair," Ambassador Taylor immediately warned the president, "is the obvious danger that the Buddhist victory may be an important step toward the formation of a government which will eventually lead the country into negotiations with Hanoi and the National Liberation Front." Johnson was inclined to judge the situation in the same way. "I am determined," he quickly replied, "to make it clear to all the world that the U.S. will spare no effort and no sacrifice in doing its full part to turn back the communists in Vietnam." Five days later, on February 2, 1965, Taylor advised the president that the United States should no longer demand the establishment of a stable government in South Vietnam as a prerequisite for bombing North Vietnam. Taylor concluded that only the initiation of sustained air operations against North Vietnam offered the slightest hope of preventing the eventual appearance in Saigon of a neutralist government that would seek a negotiated settlement and ask the United States to withdraw from South Vietnam.

The opportunity to begin Phase I reprisal air raids came shortly after Taylor had summarized the argument for bombing North Vietnam. On February 7, Vietcong soldiers attacked an American army barracks and helicopter base near the South Vietnamese market town of Pleiku, located in the Central Highlands. Eight Americans were killed, more than 100 others were wounded, and ten aircraft were destroyed. President Johnson hastily convened the National Security Council, and after a brief discussion, he announced that the United States would strike back against North Vietnam. Johnson had finally overcome his reluctance to take bold action. Using the Vietcong assault at Pleiku as a pretext, he ordered the immediate implementation of Operation Flaming Dart, a tit-for-tat retaliatory bombing of a previously selected target in North Vietnam. Three American aircraft carriers, poised to strike from the Gulf of Tonkin, launched forty-nine jets to bomb a North Vietnamese army camp.

In a long memorandum presented to the president on February 7, McGeorge Bundy urged that the United States move beyond Phase I retaliatory bombing raids and step toward a Phase II program of gradually escalating air operations. "The situation in Vietnam is deteriorating, and without new U.S. action defeat appears inevitable," he warned. "We believe that the best available way of increasing our chance of success in Vietnam is the development and execution of a policy of sustained reprisal against North Vietnam." Bundy suggested that at the outset, American officials might wish to relate their air attacks to highly visible Vietcong acts, such as the Pleiku incident. But he thought that once the bombing program was clearly underway, it should not be necessary to connect each specific act against North Vietnam to a particular event in South Vietnam. Bundy stressed that the United States should cite the whole Vietcong campaign of violence in the south to justify air action against the north. "We are convinced that the political values of reprisal require a continuous operation," he explained. "Episodic responses geared on a one-for-one basis to 'spectacular' outrages would lack the persuasive force of sustained pressure."

Bundy argued that the main reason for bombing North Vietnam was to influence the course of the struggle in South Vietnam. He predicted that a sustained reprisal policy would produce a sharp increase in optimism among noncommunist groups throughout South Vietnam and thereby provide the United States with an opportunity to exert greater influence in pressing for a more effective government in Saigon. Bundy also speculated that such a demonstration of American determination might have a substantially depressing effect on the morale of Vietcong cadres in South Vietnam. "We emphasize that our primary target in advocating a reprisal policy is the improvement of the situation in South Vietnam," he stated. "The immediate and critical targets are in the South—in the minds of the South Vietnamese and in the minds of the Viet Cong cadres." Bundy admitted, however, that a policy of sustained reprisal bombing might not succeed in changing the course of the contest. But he concluded: "What we can say is that even if it fails, the policy will be worth it. A reprisal policy—to the extent that it demonstrates U.S. willingness to employ this new norm in counterinsurgency—will set a higher price for the future upon all adventures of guerrilla warfare, and it should therefore somewhat increase our ability to deter such adventures."

During the morning of February 8, President Johnson called a meeting of the National Security Council to consider the Bundy memorandum. A few of those present expressed reservations about the wisdom of military escalation, but Johnson decided to endorse the graduated bombing program that had been outlined in early December. "It is our hope," he declared, "that current U.S. action may pull together the various forces in Saigon and thus make possible the establishment of a stable government." On that evening, Johnson cabled Ambassador Taylor that he was now ready to apply escalating pressure against North Vietnam in an effort to promote the building of a minimum government in South Vietnam. "I have today decided," he informed Taylor, "that we will carry out our December plan for continuing action against North Vietnam." Five days later, on February 13, the president formally authorized a program of sustained bombing against North Vietnam.

Taylor, however, did not believe that the Khanh regime provided an adequate political foundation in South Vietnam for the projection of American air power against North Vietnam. Fearing that Khanh would negotiate a settlement with the National Liberation Front, Taylor had already begun courting ambitious ARVN officers in an effort to promote a coup in Saigon. But

Khanh continued to exercise his authority, and on February 14, he prevailed on the Armed Forces Council to appoint Phan Huy Quat as the new prime minister of South Vietnam. But although Khanh had succeeded in installing a civilian government subject to his own domination, he did not have time to consolidate his position. On February 19, two dissident ARVN officers led their troops into Saigon in a bid to grab power. Air Vice Marshall Ky refused to support the rebels, however, and they promptly agreed to withdraw from Saigon on the condition that Khanh be removed as the head of the South Vietnamese military establishment. Air Vice Marshall Ky and General Thieu jumped at the chance to get rid of Khanh. And on February 20, they persuaded the Armed Forces Council to oust Khanh and to maintain Quat as a figurehead prime minister. Thus, the veneer of a civilian government remained in South Vietnam, and Taylor now felt that the political ground had been prepared for sustained American air operations against North Vietnam.

American leaders immediately launched a propaganda campaign designed to win public support for a policy of military escalation. At a press conference held on February 25, Secretary of State Rusk told reporters that there could be no peace talks until the communist regime in Hanoi agreed to respect the political independence and territorial integrity of South Vietnam. His aides had already begun gathering evidence to convince the American people that North Vietnam was carrying out a carefully conceived plan of aggression against South Vietnam. To help the State Department officials prove their case, the Central Intelligence Agency took more than 100 tons of communist bloc weapons from its warehouses, loaded them on a boat, sunk the vessel just off the coast of South Vietnam, and then invited reporters to inspect what was described as a cargo of arms lost by a North Vietnamese ship during a firefight. The State Department incorporated this phony evidence in a White Paper drafted to justify the continuous bombardment of North Vietnam. Published on February 27, the document was entitled *Aggression from the North: The Record of North Viet-Nam's Campaign to Conquer South Viet-Nam.*

Three days later, on March 2, the United States launched Operation Rolling Thunder, which started with a soft rumble and slowly grew into a deafening roar. The Joint Chiefs of Staff had advocated a "fast squeeze" bombing campaign intended to deliver a knockout blow before the North Vietnamese had time to develop an effective air defense system. But President Johnson and his civilian advisers, fearing that an all-out air assault might provoke Chinese or Russian intervention, decided to implement a "slow squeeze" bombing program designed to inflict more and more pain until the North Vietnamese reached the breaking point. Johnson gradually expanded the list and the location of targets: Starting with infiltration routes just above the demilitarized zone, the bombing expanded first to military bases, transportation facilities, and supply depots further north; and then to oil pumping equipment in Haiphong and petroleum storage tanks near Hanoi; and finally to electrical plants, steel factories, and even targets close to the Chinese border. As the pace of Rolling Thunder steadily accelerated, a violent cascade of American explosives rained down on North Vietnam. Indeed, the tonage of American bombs dropped on North Vietnam between March 1965 and January 1973 was three times greater than the amount that had been dropped on Europe, Asia, and Africa during the entire course of World War II.

As Rolling Thunder got under way in the spring of 1965, the Johnson administration encountered growing pressure for a negotiated settlement. United Nations Secretary General U Thant proposed a preliminary conference to lay the foundation for a peace treaty, and seventeen nonaligned nations issued an urgent plea for immediate negotiations. Even England and Canada, two of the staunchest allies of the United States, joined in the drive to promote a peaceful solution to the military struggle in Vietnam. At the same time, the massive aerial attack against North Vietnam provoked the beginning of an antiwar movement in the United States. Professors at some major American universities conducted "teach-ins" to provide information about the nature of the

The Ho Chi Minh Trail showing the effects of American bombardment. Bettmann/Corbis.

Vietnam conflict, and students on various college campuses held small demonstrations to protest against the bombardment of North Vietnam. But the burgeoning peace movement was not confined to the academic community. Prominent Democratic Senators such as Frank Church, Mike Mansfield, and George McGovern called on the president to search for a negotiated settlement, and a few influential newspapers and political columnists joined the crusade against the war.

President Johnson moved quickly to counter his domestic and foreign critics. His public relations campaign began on March 25, when he announced that the United States would strive to achieve a just settlement to the Vietnam conflict. "I am ready," he declared, "to go anywhere at any time, and meet with anyone whenever there is promise of progress towards an honorable peace." Two weeks later, in a speech at Johns Hopkins University, he told his audience that the United States was prepared to enter into "unconditional discussions" in an effort to achieve peace in Vietnam. Johnson also said that he would be willing to ask Congress for $1 billion to help promote the economic development of Southeast Asia. But the president affirmed that the United States would do everything necessary to prevent North Vietnam from conquering South Vietnam. "Our objective," he stressed, "is the independence of South Viet-Nam." Shortly after his address at Johns Hopkins, his White House aides began sending apologists to speak at other universities in an attempt to check the spread of antiwar sentiment among student groups.

Contrary to the rhetoric emanating from the White House, however, President Johnson had no desire to begin serious peace talks until he could strengthen his bargaining position. The president remained firmly committed to maintaining a separate, noncommunist South Vietnam, and he had no intention of compromising with North Vietnam on this fundamental issue. Johnson did not even bother to respond when Hanoi advanced a four-point program on April 13 to serve as the basis for negotiations with the United States. The peace plan called for the withdrawal of American military personnel from South Vietnam, the termination of hostile actions against North Vietnam, the formation of a coalition government in Saigon with National Liberation Front participation, and the peaceful reunification of Vietnam without any foreign interference. Johnson and his senior advisers feared that if Washington accepted these proposals, the result would be a united Vietnam under communist domination. Thus, they concluded that the United States would have to take stronger military measures before opening a dialogue with North Vietnam.

President Johnson thereupon made a concerted effort to build domestic support for a program of military escalation. On May 4, he asked Congress for an additional $700 million to sustain the struggle against communism in South Vietnam. Johnson made it clear that he would regard a vote for the appropriation as an endorsement of his policies in Southeast Asia. Not wanting to be charged with refusing to support American troops already in the field, Congress approved the request by an overwhelming margin, which provided Johnson with a basis for claiming that he had widespread backing for his actions. The president then took one more step to clear the way for the further application of American military power to save South Vietnam. To silence the advocates of a negotiated settlement, Johnson approved a five-day suspension in the bombardment of North Vietnam. The bombing pause, which began on May 12, was timed to coincide with Buddha's birthday in order to achieve the maximum effect on public opinion. But while Johnson hoped to convince his critics that he desired negotiations, Hanoi perceptively denounced his peace gesture as a "deceitful maneuver to pave the way for American escalation."

DOCUMENT 5-1
The Gulf of Tonkin Resolution, August 7, 1964

The Gulf of Tonkin Resolution passed by the Senate and House of Representatives on August 7, 1964.

To Promote the Maintenance of International Peace and Security in Southeast Asia

Whereas naval units of the Communist regime in Vietnam, in violation of the principles of the Charter of the United Nations and of international law, have deliberately and repeatedly attacked United States naval vessels lawfully present in international waters, and have thereby created a serious threat to international peace; and

Whereas these attacks are part of a deliberate and systematic campaign of aggression that the Communist regime in North Vietnam has been waging against its neighbors and the nations joined with them in the collective defense of their freedom; and

Whereas the United States is assisting the peoples of southeast Asia to protect their freedom and has no territorial, military or political ambitions in that area, but desires only that these peoples should be left in peace to work out their own destinies in their own way: Now, therefore, be it

Resolved by the Senate and House of Representatives of the United States of America in Congress assembled.

That the Congress approves and supports the determination of the President, as Commander in Chief, to take all necessary measures to repeal any armed attack against the forces of the United States and to prevent further aggression.

SEC. 2. The United States regards as vital to its national interest and to world peace the maintenance of international peace and security in southeast Asia. Consonant with the Constitution of the United States and the Charter of the United Nations and in accordance with its obligations under the Southeast Asia Collective Defense Treaty, the United States is, therefore, prepared, as the President determines, to take all necessary steps, including the use of armed force, to assist any member or protocol state of the Southeast Asia Collective Defense Treaty requesting assistance in defense of its freedom.

SEC. 3. This resolution shall expire when the President shall determine that the peace and security of the area is reasonably assured by international conditions created by action of the United Nations or otherwise, except that it may be terminated earlier by concurrent resolution of the Congress.

Source: *Department of State Bulletin, 51* (August 24, 1964).

DOCUMENT 5-2

Discussion on When to Begin Bombing North Vietnam, September 8, 1964

President Lyndon B. Johnson discussed bombing North Vietnam with his top foreign policy advisers, including Secretary of Defense Robert McNamara, Director of the Central Intelligence Agency John McCone, Chairman of the Joint Chiefs of Staff Earl Wheeler, Ambassador to South Vietnam Maxwell Taylor, and Secretary of State Dean Rusk.

The meeting began with the president's review of a memorandum, "Courses of Action for South Vietnam," dated September 8, 1964. Initial attention was concentrated on the four specific recommendations in this paper. The Secretary of Defense reported that these recommendations, with minor adjustments, had the approval of the Joint Chiefs, but he reported also that there was an important division among the Chiefs, in that the Chief of Staff of the Air Force and the Commandant of the Marine Corps believed that it was now necessary in addition to execute extensive U.S. air strikes against North Vietnam. General Wheeler explained that these two officers now felt that the situation would continue to deteriorate unless such drastic action was taken now. He said that he and the other two colleagues were persuaded by the argument of Ambassador Taylor—the man on the spot—that it was important not to overstrain the currently weakened GVN [Government of Vietnam] by drastic action in the immediate future. General Taylor repeated that this was indeed his view, but he emphasized that he also believed that in the long run the current in-country program would not be sufficient. He had held this view for many months, but it had been reinforced by recent events in the field....

The President asked Director McCone for his opinion and the director replied that in the judgment of his Agency the four recommended actions were appropriate, and that a sustained air attack at present would be dangerous because of the weakness of the GVN. Such an attack might also trigger major increases in Chinese communist participation. The Agency remained very gravely concerned by the internal situation in South Vietnam, which

the director estimated a shade more pessimistically than Ambassador Taylor.

The President asked the ambassador whether we could stop the internal feuding. The ambassador replied that it was very difficult with a group of men who turned off their hearing aids in the face of appeals to the public weal. These people simply did not have the sense of responsibility for the public interest to which we were accustomed, and regularly estimated matters in terms of their own personal gains and losses. The President then asked the Secretary of State for his judgment. Mr. Rusk said that a major decision to go North could be taken at any time—"at 5-minutes' notice." He did not recommend such decision now. He thought we should take the four recommended actions and play for breaks. The split in the Communist bloc was deepening and would probably be sharpened by the forthcoming December meeting. As the split grew more severe, there might be real inhibitions upon adventures by Peking and Hanoi in Southeast Asia....

The President said that in his judgment the proper answer to those advocating immediate and extensive action against the North was that we should not do this until our side could defend itself in the streets of Saigon. We obviously wanted to strengthen the GVN. We believed it could be strengthened. But what specifically were we going to do in this direction?

Ambassador Taylor replied that we needed to move on in meshing our team with the GVN. This had been well started before the unrest of August. The problem was not in planning but in execution, and in the quality of the individuals in the GVN. Nevertheless we should continue to seek better individuals and continue to strengthen our cooperative effort with them.

The President accepted this as a first purpose and then asked whether we needed additional equipment as well. Ambassador Taylor said that while additional U.S. advisers would be helpful, there was currently no equipment need beyond that which was being supplied.

Secretary McNamara emphasized the importance of politico-economic action in urban the

(continued)

DOCUMENT 5-2 Continued

areas...to lower the level of student and Buddhist pressure and increase the political base of support for the GVN. Mr. McCone endorsed this judgment. He further expressed his opinion that Hanoi and Peking now believed that that were doing very well and that they were not having second thoughts about their basic policy (an implied disagreement with the Secretary of State). The Agency was also disturbed by the prospect that internal movement toward negotiations might be increasing, and that there was some sign also of anti-American feeling in South Vietnam. It could happen that the President would find that the purposes originally set forth in Eisenhower's 1954 letter were no longer supported by the people of Vietnam themselves....

The President asked whether the situation was better or worse than when Ambassador Taylor went out. Ambassador Taylor said that he thought it was somewhat worse, but made it clear in response to a further question that this weakening was political, not military. Ambassador Taylor also emphasized his belief that sooner or later we would indeed have to act more forcefully against the North. He simply did not think now was the best time.

The President asked if anyone doubted whether it was worth all this effort. Ambassador Taylor replied that we could not afford to let Hanoi win, in terms of our overall position in the area and in the world. General Wheeler supported him most forcefully, reporting the unanimous view of the Joint Chiefs that if we should lose in South Vietnam, we would lose Southeast Asia. Country after country on the periphery would give way and look toward Communist China as the rising power of the area. Mr. McCone expressed his concurrence and so did the Secretary of State, with considerable force.

The President indicated that the reason for waiting, then, must be simply that with a weak and wobbly situation it would be unwise to attack until we could stabilize our base. Secretary McNamara added that the price of waiting was low, and the promise of gain substantial....

The President asked Ambassador Taylor to compare Khanh and Diem in the people's affections. The Ambassador replied that the people did not care for either one.

Source: Memorandum for the Record, September 14, Lyndon B. Johnson Library.

DOCUMENT 5-3

Memorandum from McGeorge Bundy to President Lyndon Johnson, February 7, 1965

National Security Adviser McGeorge Bundy urged that the United States should begin a sustained bombing campaign against North Vietnam in a memorandum for President Lyndon Johnson on February 7, 1965.

A Policy of Sustained Reprisal

I. Introductory

We believe that the best available way of increasing our chance of success in Vietnam is the development and execution of a policy of *sustained reprisal* against North Vietnam—a policy in which air and naval action against the North is justified by and related to the whole Viet Cong campaign of violence and terror in the South.

While we believe that the risks of such a policy are acceptable, we emphasize that its costs are real. It implies significant U.S. air losses even if no full air war is joined, and it seems likely that it would eventually require an extensive and costly effort against the whole air defense system of North Vietnam. U.S. casualties would be higher—and more visible to American feelings—than those sustained in the struggle in South Vietnam.

Yet measured against the costs of defeat in Vietnam, this program seems cheap. And even if it

DOCUMENT 5-3 Continued

fails to turn the tide—as it may—the value of the effort seems to us to exceed its costs.

II. Outline of the Policy

1. In partnership with the Government of Vietnam, we should develop and exercise the option to retaliate against *any* VC [Vietcong] act of violence to persons or property.

2. In practice, we may wish at the outset to relate our reprisals to those acts of relatively high visibility such as the Pleiku incident. Later, we might retaliate against the assassination of a province chief, but not necessarily the murder of a hamlet official; we might retaliate against a grenade thrown into a crowded cafe in Saigon, but not necessarily to a shot fired into a small shop in the countryside.

3. Once a program of reprisals is clearly under way, it should not be necessary to connect each specific act against North Vietnam to a particular outrage in the South. It should be possible, for example, to publish weekly lists of outrages in the South and to have it clearly understood that these outrages are the cause of such action against the North as may be occurring in the current period. Such a more generalized pattern of reprisal would remove much of the difficulty involved in finding precisely matching targets in response to specific atrocities. Even in such a more general pattern, however, it would be important to insure that the general level of reprisal action remained in close correspondence with the level of outrages in the South. We must keep it clear at every stage both to Hanoi and to the world, that our reprisals will be reduced or stopped when outrages in the South are reduced or stopped—and that we are *not* attempting to destroy or conquer North Vietnam.

4. In the early stages of such a course, we should take the appropriate occasion to make clear our firm intent to undertake reprisals on any further acts, major or minor, that appear to us and the GVN [Government

of Vietnam] as indicating Hanoi's support. We would announce that that our two governments have been patient and forbearing in the hope that Hanoi would come to its senses without the necessity of our having to take further action; but the outrages continue and now we must react against those who are responsible; we will not provoke; we will not use our force indiscriminately; but we can no longer sit by in the face of repeated acts of terror and violence for which the DVR is responsible.

5. Having once made this announcement, we should execute our reprisal policy with as low a level of public noise as possible. It is to our interest that our acts should be seen—but we do not wish to boast about them in ways that make it hard for Hanoi to shift its ground. We should instead direct maximum attention to the continuing acts of violence which are the cause of our continuing reprisals.

6. This reprisal policy should begin at a low level. Its level of force and pressure should be increased only gradually—and as indicated above it should be decreased if VC terror visibly decreases. The object would not be to "win" an air war against Hanoi, but rather to influence the course of the struggle in the South.

7. At the same time it should be recognized that in order to maintain the power of reprisal without risk of excessive loss, an "air war" may in fact be necessary. We should therefore be ready to develop a separate justification for energetic flak suppression and if necessary for the destruction of Communist air power. The essence of such an explanation should be that those actions are intended solely to insure the effectiveness of a policy of reprisal, and in no sense represent any intent to wage offensive war against the North. These distinctions should not be difficult to develop.

8. It remains quite possible, however, that this reprisal policy would get us quickly into the level of military activity contemplated in the so-called Phase II of our December planning. It may even

(continued)

DOCUMENT 5-3   Continued

get us beyond this level with both Hanoi and Peking, if there is Communist counter-action. We and the GVN should also be prepared for a spurt of VC terrorism, especially in urban areas, that would dwarf anything yet experienced. These are the risks of any action. They should be carefully reviewed—but we believe them to be acceptable.

9. We are convinced that the political values of reprisal require a *continuous* operation. Episodic responses geared on a one-for-one basis to "spectacular" outrages would lack the persuasive force of sustained pressure. More important still, they would leave it open to the Communists to avoid reprisals entirely by giving up only a small element of their own program. The Gulf of Tonkin affair produced a sharp upturn in morale in South Vietnam. When it remained an isolated episode, however, there was a severe relapse. It is the great merit of the proposed scheme that to stop it the Communists would have to stop enough of their activity in the South to permit the probable success of a determined pacification effort.

III. Expected Effect of Sustained Reprisal Policy

1. We emphasize that our primary target in advocating a reprisal policy is the improvement of the situation in *South* Vietnam. Action against the North is usually urged as a means of affecting the will of Hanoi to direct and support the VC. We consider this an important but longer-range purpose. The immediate and critical targets are in the South—in the minds of the South Vietnamese and in the minds of the Viet Cong cadres.

2. Predictions of the effect of any given course of action upon the states of mind of people are difficult. It seems very clear that if the United States and the Government of Vietnam join in a policy of reprisal, there will be a sharp and immediate increase in optimism in the South, among nearly all articulate groups. The Mission believes—and our own conversations confirm—that in all sectors of Vietnamese opinion there is a strong belief

that the United States could do much more if it would, and they are suspicious of our failure to use more of our obviously enormous power. At least in the short run, the reaction to reprisal policy would be very favorable.

3. This favorable reaction should offer opportunity for increased American influence in pressing for a more effective government—at least in the short run. Joint reprisals would imply military planning in which the American role would necessarily be controlling, and this new relation should add to our bargaining power in other military efforts—and conceivably on a wider plane as well if a more stable government is formed. We have the whip hand in reprisals as we do not in other fields.

4. The Vietnamese increase in hope could well increase the readiness of Vietnamese factions themselves to join together in forming a more effective government.

5. We think it plausible that effective and sustained reprisals, even in a low key, would have a substantial depressing effect upon the morale of the Viet Cong cadres in South Vietnam. This is the strong opinion of CIA Saigon. It is based upon reliable reports of the initial Viet Cong reaction to the Gulf of Tonkin episode, and also upon the solid general assessment that the determination of Hanoi and the apparent timidity of the mighty United States are both major items in Viet Cong confidence.

6. The long-run effect of reprisals in the South is far less clear. It may be that like other stimulants, the value of this one would decline over time. Indeed the risk of this result is large enough so that we ourselves believe that a very major effort all along the line should be made in South Vietnam to take full advantage of the immediate stimulus of reprisal policy in its early stages. Our object should be to use this new policy to effect a visible upward turn in pacification, in governmental effectiveness, in operations against the Viet Cong, and in the whole U.S./GVN relationship. It is changes in these areas that can have enduring long-term effects.

DOCUMENT 5-3 Continued

7. While emphasizing the importance of reprisals in the South, we do not exclude the impact on Hanoi. We believe, indeed, that it is of great importance that the level of reprisal be adjusted rapidly and visibly to both upward and downward shifts in the level of Viet Cong offenses. We want to keep before Hanoi the carrot of our desisting as well as the stick of continued pressure. We also need to conduct the application of the force so that there is always a prospect of worse to come.

8. We cannot assert that a policy of sustained reprisal will succeed in changing the course of the contest in Vietnam. It may fail, and we cannot estimate the odds of success with any accuracy—they may be somewhere between 25% and 75%. What we can say is that even if it fails, the policy will be worth it. At a minimum it will damp down the charge that we did not do all that we could have done, and this charge will be important in many countries, including our own. Beyond that, a reprisal policy—to the extent that it demonstrates U.S. willingness to employ this new norm in counter-insurgency—will set a higher price for the future upon all adventures of guerrilla warfare, and it should therefore somewhat increase our ability to deter such adventures. We must recognize, however, that that ability will be greatly weakened if there is failure for any reason in Vietnam.

IV. Present Action Recommendations

1. This general recommendation was developed in intensive discussions in the days just before the attacks on Pleiku. These attacks and our reaction to them have created an ideal opportunity for the prompt development and execution of sustained reprisals. Conversely, if no such policy is now developed, we face the grave danger that Pleiku, like the Gulf of Tonkin, may be a short-run stimulant and a long-term depressant. We therefore recommend that the necessary preparations be made for continuing reprisals. The major steps to be taken appear to us to be the following:

(1) We should complete the evacuation of dependents.

(2) We should quietly start the necessary westward deployments of back-up contingency forces.

(3) We should develop and refine a running catalogue of Viet Cong offenses which can be published regularly and related clearly to our own reprisals. Such a catalogue should perhaps build on the foundation of an initial White Paper.

(4) We should initiate joint planning with the GVN on both the civil and military level. Specifically, we should give a clear and strong signal to those now forming a government that we will be ready for this policy when they are.

(5) We should develop the necessary public and diplomatic statements to accompany the initiation and continuation of this program.

(6) We should insure that a reprisal program is matched by renewed public commitment to our family of programs in the South, so that the central importance of the southern struggle may never be neglected.

(7) We should plan quiet diplomatic communication of the precise meaning of what we are and are not doing, to Hanoi, to Peking and to Moscow.

(8) We should be prepared to defend and to justify this new policy by concentrating attention in every forum upon its cause—the aggression in the South.

(9) We should accept discussion on these terms in any forum, but we should *not* now accept the idea of negotiations of any sort except on the basis of a stand down of Viet Cong violence. A program of sustained reprisal, with its direct link to Hanoi's continuing aggressive actions in the South, will not involve us in nearly the level of international recrimination which would be precipitated by a go-North program which was not so connected. For this reason the international pressures for negotiation should be quite manageable.

Source: *The Pentagon Papers: Senator Gravel Edition* (Boston: Beacon Press, 1971), vol. III, 687–691.

Chronological List of Main Events

November 1963   The commitment to continue
American support for South Vietnam

December 1963   The North Vietnamese decision to
increase aid to the Vietcong

February 1964   The implementation of Operation
Plan 34 Alpha

August 1964   The Gulf of Tonkin affair

November 1964   The reelection of President
Johnson as a peace candidate

December 1964   The decision to bomb the Ho Chi
Minh Trail in Laos

January 1965   The Battle of Binh Gia

February 1965   The publication of a State
Department White Paper on
Vietnam

March 1965   The beginning of Operation
Rolling Thunder

Study Questions

1. What were the De Soto patrols?
2. What was the Gulf of Tonkin Resolution?
3. Why were President Johnson and most of his senior advisers determined to prevent a communist akeover in South Vietnam?

4. Would President Johnson have been reelected in November 1964 if the American people had known that he was making plans to bomb North Vietnam?

6

The Escalating
Military Stalemate

*If the Communist world finds out we will not pursue our commitments
to the end, I don't know where they will stay their hand.*

SECRETARY OF STATE DEAN RUSK, 1965

THE DISPATCH OF AMERICAN GROUND TROOPS

President Johnson and his principal foreign policy advisers decided to wage only a limited war in Southeast Asia. Their basic objective was to maintain South Vietnam as an independent, noncommunist nation and thereby to discourage revolutionary movements elsewhere in the Third World. They were not willing to launch an all-out military crusade against North Vietnam in an effort to roll back the forces of communism to the Chinese border. The president and his civilian advisers feared that Red China would intervene, if necessary, to prevent the complete defeat of North Vietnam. The White House was still haunted by memories of Chinese troops fighting American soldiers to a stalemate in Korea, and Johnson did not want the United States to become engaged once again in a ground war against the immense armies of communist China. Nor did he want to sacrifice his domestic welfare program by authorizing unlimited military operations in Southeast Asia. Consequently, although his military advisers often urged bold moves, the president would not approve either an American invasion of North Vietnam or an unrestricted bombing campaign against Hanoi and the rest of the Red River basin.

President Johnson had good cause to worry about China. Viewing the United States as the main threat to Chinese security in the mid-1960s, Mao Zedong launched a massive construction project designed to provide China with a self-sustaining industrial complex in the remote western provinces so that factory production could continue in the event of American air attacks on urban centers along the eastern seaboard. Mao simultaneously provided extensive military and economic aid to North Vietnam for both geopolitical and ideological reasons: His primary goal was to safeguard China by weakening American influence in Southeast Asia; his secondary aim was to outflank his communist rivals in the Soviet Union by demonstrating his commitment to support wars of national liberation throughout the Third World. So as the tempo of the American air campaign against North Vietnam accelerated in June 1965, Mao began sending Chinese soldiers across the border into Tonkin to help build, repair, and protect roads, bridges, and railroads. The number of Chinese support troops stationed in North Vietnam ballooned to 170,000 in 1967, and these soldiers wore regular military uniforms because Mao wanted to signal the United States that he would use Chinese forces to rebuff an American invasion of North Vietnam.

While carefully orchestrated to avoid a confrontation with China, the initiation of the air war against North Vietnam paved the way for the introduction of American ground troops into South Vietnam. General William C. Westmoreland and his subordinates at the MACV anticipated Vietcong attacks against American airfields in retaliation for the bombardment of North Vietnam, and in late February 1965, Westmoreland asked for two marine battalions to protect the vulnerable air base at Danang. But his proposal was opposed by the American embassy in Saigon. In a cable to the White House, Ambassador Maxwell D. Taylor warned that once the United States committed combat units in South Vietnam, it would be very difficult to hold the line against future troop deployments. "Intervention with ground forces would at best buy time," he predicted, "and would lead to ever increasing commitments until, like the French, we would be occupying an essentially hostile foreign country." President Johnson, however, approved Westmoreland's request despite Taylor's reservations, and on March 8, a contingent of 3,500 marines dressed in full battle regalia splashed ashore near Danang. Welcomed by pretty South Vietnamese girls passing out leis of flowers, the two marine battalions were the first American combat troops deployed on the Asian mainland since the Korean War.

The dispatch of these foot soldiers marked a crucial change in the role of the United States in the Vietnam War. Although the initial marine mission was limited to the static defense of the air base at Danang, pressure quickly mounted for the deployment of additional American combat forces and for the commencement of offensive operations against the Vietcong. General Harold K. Johnson, the army chief of staff, hurried to Saigon to find out what more could be done to improve the military situation in South Vietnam. Upon his return to Washington on March 14, General Johnson urged the deployment of a full American army division to reinforce ARVN units in the field. But Ambassador Taylor expressed grave concern about the proposal to increase the involvement of the United States in counterinsurgency operations. Cabling the president on March 17, Taylor warned that the introduction of large numbers of American ground troops might encourage the South Vietnamese to lie down on the job and pass the military burden to the United States. He also cautioned that the arrival of an American infantry division in South Vietnam would make it look like the United States was assuming "the old French role of alien colonizer and conqueror."

While in Washington for consultations in late March 1965, however, Taylor was dismayed to find that the president and most of his top advisers were on the verge of sending more American combat troops to South Vietnam. General Westmoreland had asked for the immediate commitment of two American army divisions and for permission to use them in offensive operations in the Central Highlands. Besides endorsing this request, the Joint Chiefs of Staff pressed for the dispatch of one South Korean division to help pursue the Vietcong. Although Taylor was against these proposals, he realized that those advocating the deployment of additional ground forces were in the saddle. Thus, Taylor argued that if American soldiers were to be committed to combat, they should be restricted to enclaves along the coast of South Vietnam. Rather than employing U.S. troops in search-and-destroy operations deep in the jungles of the interior, he insisted, Westmoreland should confine them to the task of protecting American air bases and other installations near the seaboard.

Ignoring Taylor's argument, President Johnson took another significant step toward full-scale warfare at a high-level meeting held in the White House on April 1, when he decided to give General Westmoreland two more marine battalions plus an air squadron and 18,000 to

20,000 support troops. Although the marines would be stationed in enclaves around the major American air bases, they were authorized to engage in offensive actions rather than to remain in static defensive positions. Yet Johnson tried to conceal this basic change in military mission from the American people. Hoping to avoid an adverse political reaction in the United States, he ordered that the new, aggressive tactics should be employed as rapidly as possible but in ways that would minimize any appearance of a sudden change in policy. Westmoreland later criticized this lack of candor on the part of the president. "It was a masterpiece of obliquity," he charged. "To my mind the American people had a right to know forthrightly, within the actual limits of military security, what we were calling on their sons to do, and to presume that it could be concealed despite the open eyes of press and television was folly."

Though they feared media exposure, President Johnson and his senior advisers soon decided that the number of American combat forces deployed in South Vietnam should be more than doubled. And they succeeded in getting Taylor to go along with their plans. At an important conference held in Honolulu on April 20, Taylor joined with a group of top civilian and military leaders in advocating the rapid introduction of additional ground troops to fight the Vietcong. The conferees agreed that the United States could not expect to achieve a favorable settlement in South Vietnam by bombing North Vietnam. But they hoped to break the will of the North Vietnamese and the Vietcong by denying them victory in South Vietnam. Determined to hold the communists at bay while the authorities in Saigon were building up their armed strength, the conferees unanimously urged the dispatch of nine more American battalions to South Vietnam (bringing the U.S. troop level up to 82,000 men) along with one Australian and three South Korean battalions (bringing the third-country troop level up to 7,250 men). The president promptly approved their recommendations, yet he delayed announcing the troop increases for almost two months to cushion the shock of the escalation on public opinion.

Yet while American policymakers hoped to convince the communists that they could not win in South Vietnam, the tide of battle quickly turned against the forces of the Saigon government during the spring of 1965. American intelligence sources confirmed for the first time on April 21 that a regular North Vietnamese combat unit was operating in South Vietnam, and on May 11, the Vietcong began a vigorous offensive by overrunning a province capital located about fifty miles north of Saigon. During the ensuing weeks, several ARVN battalions were badly mauled in bloody engagements with aggressive Vietcong soldiers. The ineptness of the South Vietnamese army was blatantly demonstrated when two Vietcong regiments attacked a town in Phuoc Long province, and the frightened ARVN officers fled in panic. As increasing battlefield losses and desertion rates weakened the South Vietnamese army, American officials worried that it might completely collapse in the face of the Vietcong offensive.

Americans stationed in Saigon were especially alarmed about the rapidly deteriorating military situation. In a cable to Washington on June 5, Ambassador Taylor reported that the communists were scoring one victory after another on the battlefields of South Vietnam. "The apparent aims of this campaign," he observed, "are to alter the balance of military forces in favor of the Viet Cong by inflicting maximum attrition on the government forces, including specifically the piecemeal destruction of regular ARVN ground combat units." General Westmoreland feared that without substantial American reinforcements, the South Vietnamese army would not be able to stand up to the mounting communist pressure. "I see no course of action open to U.S.," he cabled Washington on June 7, "except to reinforce our efforts in SVN [South Vietnam] with additional U.S. or third country forces as rapidly as possible during the critical weeks ahead." To prevent a swift defeat in South Vietnam, Westmoreland urged the immediate dispatch of an additional 32,000 American troops and nine South Korean battalions. The Joint Chiefs of Staff not only supported his recommendations, they also advocated the deployment of ten more American battalions (bringing the U.S. troop level up to 150,000 men).

American apprehensions became even greater as the political situation in South Vietnam likewise went from bad to worse. On June 9, the Armed Forces Council decided to oust Prime Minister Phan Huy Quat and to form a new government headed by a committee of ten senior military officers. The junta installed Air Vice Marshal Nguyen Cao Ky as prime minister and General Nguyen Van Thieu as chief of state. Thus, the veneer of civilian rule in South Vietnam was completely stripped away. Disturbed by the fact that Ky and Thieu possessed little political experience, Ambassador Taylor believed that he and his colleagues would have to help them handle public affairs. Policymakers in Washington were equally concerned about the nature of the new regime in Saigon. William Bundy later recalled that the Ky-Thieu directorate "seemed to all of us the bottom of the barrel, absolutely the bottom of the barrel." But even though they realized that Ky and Thieu were political novices without popular support, American officials were relieved to learn that the new leaders in Saigon intended to continue the fight against the Vietcong.

As Ky and Thieu took the reins of power, Westmoreland reiterated his request for reinforcements to avert a catastrophe in South Vietnam. In a cable on June 14, he warned President Johnson that desertion rates for the South Vietnamese army were inordinately high and that Vietcong units were destroying ARVN battalions faster than they could be reconstituted. Westmoreland saw no likelihood for achieving a quick victory against the Vietcong, but he advocated the active commitment of additional American ground troops as "a stop-gap measure to save ARVN from defeat." In a follow-up cable to Washington on June 22, Westmoreland estimated that the deployment of forty-four more American combat battalions would be sufficient to establish a favorable balance of forces in South Vietnam by the end of the year. But if the United States were to seize the initiative from the enemy, he concluded, further increments would be required in 1966 and thereafter. Westmoreland left President Johnson with a simple choice: He could either accept a certain defeat in South Vietnam, or he could plunge the United States into a full-scale war.

At this critical point in the summer of 1965, Under Secretary of State George W. Ball was the only high-level Washington official who vigorously opposed a major increase in the number of American combat troops in South Vietnam. In a memorandum presented to the president on July 1, Ball expressed grave doubt that the United States could defeat the Vietcong. "No one," he declared, "has demonstrated that a white ground force of whatever size can win a guerrilla war—which is at the same time a civil war between Asians—in a jungle terrain in the midst of a population that refuses cooperation to the white forces (and the South Vietnamese) and thus provides a great intelligence advantage to the other side." Ball feared that an open-ended military commitment would lead to mounting American casualties and a well-nigh irreversible process of escalation. "Our involvement will be so great," he warned, "that we cannot—without national humiliation—stop short of achieving our complete objectives." Before committing American prestige to a protracted and bloody conflict of uncertain outcome, Ball concluded, policymakers in Washington should "seek a compromise settlement which achieves less than our stated objectives and thus cut our losses while we still have the freedom of maneuver to do so."

In a memorandum prepared for the president on July 20, however, Secretary of Defense Robert S. McNamara argued that no peace settlement acceptable to the United States could be negotiated until after the application of additional American military force against the Vietcong. "The situation in South Vietnam is worse than a year ago," he observed. "The government is able to provide security to fewer and fewer people in less and less territory." McNamara reported that the Vietcong were pushing hard to dismember the country and to destroy the army buttressing the unpopular regime in Saigon. And while some ARVN units had been mauled during combat and weakened by high desertion rates, he noted, the Vietcong seemed able to replace their losses and to increase their strength by drafting soldiers in areas under their control. McNamara also pointed out that the American bombardment of North Vietnam had been ineffective. "There are no signs that we have throttled the inflow of supplies for the VC or can throttle the flow while their material needs are as low as they are," he acknowledged. "Nor have our air attacks in North Vietnam produced tangible evidence of willingness on the part of Hanoi to come to the conference table in a reasonable mood."

McNamara concluded that the United States must demonstrate to the communists that the odds were against their winning the struggle in South Vietnam. He argued that a substantial increase in American military pressure against the Vietcong "would stave off defeat in the short run and offer a good chance of producing a favorable settlement in the longer run." McNamara therefore urged that the total American force level in South Vietnam be brought up to approximately 175,000 men (or 200,000 if the South Koreans refused to commit nine more battalions). But he warned that the deployment of as many as 100,000 additional American troops might be necessary in early 1966, and even more thereafter. To be prepared for future troop deployments, McNamara recommended that Congress should be asked to authorize the call-up of approximately 235,000 men in the Reserves and National Guard. He also advised expanding the draft and extending the tour of duty for men already in the service in order to increase the size of the regular armed forces of the United States by approximately 375,000 men.

President Johnson invited his senior advisers to the White House on July 21 to discuss the McNamara memorandum. When Johnson asked if anyone present opposed the course of action proposed by the secretary of defense, once again only George Ball registered a dissenting opinion. "This war will be long and protracted," he cautioned. "I truly have serious doubt that an army of westerners can successfully fight orientals in an Asian jungle." Ball argued that the best way to cut American losses in South Vietnam would be to maneuver the Saigon government into requesting that the United States leave. Although admitting that such a policy would probably lead to a communist takeover of South Vietnam, he concluded that other Asian nations would remain in the capitalist orbit. "But George," the president asked, "wouldn't all these countries say that Uncle Sam was a paper tiger, wouldn't we lose credibility breaking the word of three presidents, if we did as you have proposed?" Ball replied that a worse blow to American prestige would be to let everyone see that "the mightiest power on earth is unable to defeat a handful of guerrillas." But Secretary of State Dean Rusk clinched the argument in favor of escalation. "If the Communist world finds out we will not pursue our commitments to the end," he warned, "I don't know where they will stay their hand."

Regarding the Vietnamese conflict as a crucial test of their willingness and ability to counter wars of national liberation throughout the Third World, President Johnson and his top advisers concluded that the United States must deploy whatever force level might be required to prevent the fall of the South Vietnam domino. But Johnson wanted to Americanize the war without antagonizing Congress and thereby hindering the enactment of legislation needed to fulfill his ambitious social welfare program. Hence, he decided not to ask for authority to mobilize the Reserves or National Guard. In a nationally televised news conference on July 28, Johnson announced that the American force level in South Vietnam would be increased immediately to 125,000 men and that additional troops would be sent as requested by General Westmoreland. The president added that the number of Americans drafted into the armed services would soon be doubled as well. His announcement marked a fundamental turning point in the history of the Vietnam War. American boys would now attempt to do the job that Asian boys had failed to do.

THE PROTRACTED WAR OF ATTRITION

As American forces assumed direct responsibility for the outcome of the war in Vietnam during the autumn of 1965, the United States implemented a military strategy that involved three inter-related actions. First, American pilots carried out a steadily escalating bombing campaign against military facilities and supply lines in North Vietnam. This air offensive was launched in an effort to impede the movement of men and materiel into South Vietnam and to induce the communist regime in Hanoi to stop supporting the Vietcong insurgents. Second, American troops conducted large-scale search-and-destroy operations against Vietcong regulars and North Vietnamese forces fighting in South Vietnam. These ground maneuvers were designed to kill enemy soldiers faster than they could be replaced and thereby to convince the communists that they could not win. Third, the United States assigned ARVN the task of holding territory that had been cleared by American combat units in South Vietnam. This so-called "other war" was aimed at pacifying the countryside while the Saigon government attempted to win the hearts and minds of the South Vietnamese people.

Although American troops were able to sweep through extensive areas controlled by communist forces in South Vietnam, the results of these actions were almost always transitory. The South Vietnamese army could not provide security for pacification teams sent to build roads, schools, and hospitals in areas that had been penetrated by American soldiers. Nor could the Saigon government win popular support after the communist forces had been driven away. John Paul Vann, after serving as an adviser to the ARVN and a coordinator for the U.S. Operations Mission, put his finger on the basic problem. In a memorandum written in September 1965, Vann pointed out that despite lip service to the contrary, the military junta in Saigon had not demonstrated a sincere interest in bettering the lot of the rural population. "Many patriotic and non-Communist Vietnamese," he explained, "were literally forced to ally themselves with a Communist dominated movement in the belief that it was their only chance to secure a better government." As a consequence, communist forces usually reoccupied areas soon after American troops had completed their clearing operations and moved into other regions to begin similar maneuvers.

General Victor H. Krulak, the American marine commander in the Pacific, repeatedly argued that his forces should be used to help pacify densely populated rural areas in South Vietnam. He proposed the formation of Combined Action Platoons, made up of marine rifle squads and local South Vietnamese militia companies, that would provide security in agricultural regions along the coast. After pacification teams felt safe from guerrilla attacks, they could undertake various civil service projects designed to gain peasant support for the Saigon government. Krulak wanted to use the marines based in the northern provinces to pacify the lowlands, where 98 percent of the civilians lived. But General Westmoreland wanted the marines to pursue main force Vietcong and North Vietnamese troops in the sparsely populated highlands. He did not have enough troops to provide security in the rice paddies and also to conduct search-and-destroy operations in the jungles. Supported by the Joint Chiefs of Staff, Westmoreland used his limited resources in South Vietnam to pursue enemy soldiers in mountainous areas rather than to protect the civilian population in farming regions.

When it became apparent that pacification efforts were yielding little in terms of permanent territorial control, the United States began employing an overwhelming amount of firepower in an attempt to prevent the communists from utilizing the land and the people of South Vietnam. American artillery and B-52 bombers pounded the South Vietnamese countryside as more and more rural areas were defined as "free fire zones" subject to harassment and interdiction. American aircraft dropped more than 1 million tons of bombs on South Vietnam from 1965 to 1967, while American herbicides such as Agent Orange destroyed approximately half of the South Vietnamese timberlands. Besides disrupting communist base areas and logistical networks, the American bombs, shells, and defoliants forced a great many peasants in South Vietnam to flee from their villages and rice fields. About 4 million civilians—roughly 25 percent of the South Vietnamese population—sought safety in overcrowded cities or in refugee camps on their outskirts. Driven from their homes and farmlands by the American war machine, these displaced peasants harbored deep feelings of hostility toward the United States.

As death and destruction spread, Buddhist leaders gave vent to the rapidly growing antiwar sentiment in South Vietnam. But the monks did not openly articulate their intense desire for peace because they wanted to avoid a direct confrontation with the United States. During March 1966, the Buddhists and their student allies organized massive demonstrations in Danang, Hué, and Saigon. The protestors made immediate demands for free elections and the establishment of a civilian government to replace the military junta headed by Ky and Thieu. Although their ultimate objectives remained unstated, the Buddhists and their supporters looked forward to the creation of a neutralist government that would seek a political accommodation with the National Liberation Front and ask the United States to get out of South Vietnam. Their strong anti-American attitudes found expression in numerous banners calling for an end to the foreign domination of South Vietnam. Along with their American patrons, Ky and Thieu became increasingly alarmed when many ARVN soldiers stationed in the northern provinces showed their support for the democratic movement to elect a civilian government.

The military rulers of South Vietnam were determined to maintain their political authority and to sustain the war effort against the Vietcong. After obtaining American approval and support, Ky decided to suppress the Buddhists and those who had rallied around them in Danang, Hué, and Saigon. His troops moved into these Buddhist strongholds during May and June 1966, arresting several hundred monks and students. Then, as soon as order was restored, the military chiefs turned to the political arena to consolidate their power. They carefully selected a list of candidates, and in September 1966, elections were held for a constituent assembly. After deliberating for a few months, the assembly drafted a new constitution that disqualified anyone branded as a communist or neutralist sympathizer from running for president. The military junta subsequently decided that Thieu should replace Ky as the highest authority in Saigon, and in September 1967, Thieu was elected president by a small plurality of votes in a highly circumscribed contest.

The United States was by then waist deep in a bloody struggle that many had come to call "Mr. McNamara's War." After a brief visit to Saigon in November 1965, the secretary of defense made a bleak assessment of the military situation in South Vietnam. He predicted a rapid expansion of communist forces both by heavy recruitment in South Vietnam and by increased infiltration from North Vietnam. To hold the line against the contemplated enemy buildup, McNamara recommended that the United States intensify the bombing of North Vietnam and send a substantial number of additional troops to South Vietnam. He admitted that his recommendations might simply lead to a military standoff at a higher level. If President Johnson followed his advice, McNamara estimated that the American death rate in South Vietnam would reach 1,000 a month. He also calculated that the odds were even that the United States would still not achieve a victory. Yet McNamara concluded that the American force level should be brought up to 400,000 by the end of 1966 and that the deployment of 200,000 more American troops might be needed during the following year.

Acting on the advice of his influential defense secretary, Johnson carefully laid the political foundations for a sharp escalation in the American war effort. The president hoped to defuse his domestic and foreign critics by calling a temporary halt to the aerial bombardment of North

Vietnam. And during this pause, which began on Christmas Eve 1965 and lasted for thirty-seven days, Johnson launched a dramatic peace offensive. He dispatched prominent envoys to more than forty different countries to spread the word that the United States desired peace. Hoping to convince the American people that he had explored every alternative to escalation, Johnson repeatedly insisted that he was ready to enter into discussions to bring an end to the fighting. But his peace gestures were bogus. Johnson was not willing to negotiate a peace settlement that would allow the formation of a neutralist government in Saigon and the reunification of Vietnam under communist leadership. Indeed, his public relations campaign was primarily designed to provide a justification for a major American military escalation.

During the months following the well-advertised bombing pause, Operation Rolling Thunder gradually assumed massive proportions. The number of American air strikes grew from 25,000 to 108,000 a year between 1965 and 1967, while the tonnage of bombs dropped on North Vietnam increased from 63,000 to 226,000. As the list of targets expanded, the steadily intensifying air campaign against North Vietnam destroyed factories, disrupted agriculture, leveled cities, and scarred the countryside. Besides inflicting severe economic damage, the bombing raids maimed and killed many noncombatants in North Vietnam. American pilots did not direct their attacks against major population centers, but the huge payloads dropped from high altitudes by giant B-52 bombers seldom hit targets with pinpoint accuracy. And although American officials publicly maintained that civilian casualties were minimal, Secretary of Defense McNamara privately estimated that they were as high as 1,000 a month during peak bombing periods.

The widespread bombardment did not destroy the morale of the North Vietnamese people, however. They responded to the American onslaught in much the same way that the British had reacted to the Nazi air assault during World War II. Rather than disheartening the people of North Vietnam, the bombing missions seemed to stiffen their will to resist the American colossus. The North Vietnamese demonstrated remarkable determination in coping with the aerial attacks on their homeland. After evacuating many civilians from the cities, they constructed individual bomb shelters along the streets to protect those who remained to perform essential tasks. Small factories and storage facilities were dispersed across the countryside and often concealed in underground tunnels, while trenches were cut through rice paddies to safeguard peasants from shrapnel and napalm. Major roads were repaired within hours after bombs dotted them with craters, and damaged bridges were quickly replaced by bamboo pontoons and ferryboats. And while hundreds of thousands of North Vietnamese civilians and Chinese soldiers worked full time to keep key transportation routes open, truck drivers traveled at night, without headlights, to avoid detection.

Although the American bombing attacks crippled industrial production in North Vietnam, Rolling Thunder had very little impact on the ground war in South Vietnam. The communist forces needed only about fifty tons of supplies per day to sustain their military operations in South Vietnam, and the bulk of the heavy equipment that they received came from a vast stockpiling area on the Chinese side of the Tonkin border. Between 1964 and 1968, the number of guns and the amount of ammunition that China sent to North Vietnam per year increased rapidly: guns from 80,500 to 219,899, artillery pieces from 1,205 to 7,087, bullets from 25.2 million to 247.9 million, and artillery shells from 335,000 to 2 million. Some of these supplies were carried by ships from the Chinese coast to the Cambodian port of Sihanoukville and then transported overland into South Vietnam. But most of the military supplies coming from China were shipped by rail and truck into Tonkin and then stored in scattered dumps until they could be reshipped down the Ho Chi Minh Trail to their final destination in South Vietnam. Despite the intensification of the American air campaign, therefore,

North Vietnam continued to serve as a vital highway carrying ample amounts of weapons and munitions into South Vietnam.

The United States also paid a high price for the physical damage that Rolling Thunder caused in North Vietnam. In response to the American bombing campaign, the Soviet Union provided North Vietnam with antiaircraft guns, surface-to-air missiles, MIG fighters, and sophisticated radar equipment. Thus, American pilots encountered stiff resistance as they flew closer to Hanoi and Haiphong. Armed with Russian weapons, the North Vietnamese were frequently able to drive off American warplanes or even shoot them down before they reached their targets. The United States lost more than 500 aircraft between 1965 and 1966, and in these two years alone the total cost of the air war mounted to well over $1 billion. Summarizing the effectiveness of American air strikes conducted during 1966, the Central Intelligence Agency calculated that the United States spent nearly $10 on bombing missions and warplane replacements for each $1 in damage inflicted on North Vietnam.

The United States was similarly engaged in an expensive big-unit ground war in South Vietnam. After making the momentous decision to dive into full-scale warfare in July 1965, President Johnson rushed logistical experts to South Vietnam to construct facilities to handle huge numbers of American troops and enormous quantities of military equipment. Soon, supplies at the rate of 1 million tons a month were pouring into South Vietnam to provide American soldiers with a mighty arsenal of weapons and a vast array of luxuries rarely ever seen on a battlefield. The number of American combatants in South Vietnam simultaneously jumped from just under 185,000 at the end of 1965 to more than 485,000 by the end of 1967. As the American military buildup proceeded apace, General Westmoreland ordered his troops to conduct massive sweeps through the South Vietnamese countryside in an effort to entrap and eliminate main force enemy units. He sought to engage large concentrations of Vietcong and North Vietnamese soldiers in relatively unsettled areas where mobile American forces would be able to use maximum firepower while keeping civilian casualties to a minimum.

Despite their ability to move with tremendous speed, however, American troops seldom enjoyed the advantage of surprise. The mechanized American forces made a lot of noise, and they were often detected before they could pounce on their prey. Upon hearing the roar of American vehicles charging down the roads, the Vietcong and North Vietnamese soldiers could choose to flee if the odds were against them. Only 1 percent of American search-and-destroy sweeps in South Vietnam actually resulted in contact with enemy forces. Their ability to avoid combat was enhanced by information about American military plans that they received from agents who had worked their way into the highest ranks of the Saigon government and the South Vietnamese army. Aided by an impressive intelligence network, communist infantry units could choose to fight when they had superior numbers. In fact, they fired the first shot in 85 percent of all firefights with American troops in South Vietnam. But if their casualties reached unacceptable levels, they could melt away into the jungle or retreat across the border into sanctuaries in Laos and Cambodia. Thus, American soldiers, as they scoured the countryside in search of the enemy, typically experienced long periods of boredom followed by short intervals of tremendous excitement when they found themselves facing death while trying to kill their adversaries during firefights.

Although the communists could usually determine the location, timing, size, and duration of each battle that they fought against troops from the United States, General Westmoreland continued to pursue a strategy of attrition. He aimed to achieve a military victory by destroying enemy units faster than they could be replaced through either recruitment in South Vietnam or infiltration from North Vietnam. Engaged in a war without front lines,

American troops moving through the Vietnamese Countryside. AP Photo/Phuoc.

American army officers measured progress by counting cadavers rather than by taking and holding territory. Their gruesome goal was to locate and liquidate the enemy. And having no territorial objectives to attain in South Vietnam, American ground troops found themselves in a killing contest on the Asian mainland against elusive opponents who could control the rate of their losses.

American field commanders sought a favorable kill ratio by exterminating a large number of enemy soldiers without losing a correspondingly high number of their own men. With the body count serving as the primary index of success on the battelfiels of South Vietnam, American army officers were not inclined to risk heavy casualties in close combat. Thus, it became standard policy for the United States army to use foot soldiers to help find the foe and then to use an avalanche of fire in an attempt to annihilate him. As the motto "expend shells, not men" was applied with a vengeance, the number of B-52 sorties in South Vietnam leaped from 60 a month in 1966 to over 800 a month in 1967. American infantry units were seldom prodded into practicing their traditional mission of closing in on the enemy and destroying him in place. After making contact with Vietcong regulars or North Vietnamese forces, American ground troops generally fell back into a defensive perimeter to call for air strikes and artillery support. Large enemy units were therefore rarely pinned down by American infantrymen.

Given their ability to choose when and where to fight, the Vietcong and North Vietnamese maintained the initiative on the battlefield throughout most of the war. The communists employed hit-and-run tactics with the hope that American troops would dissipate their energy in endless search-and-destroy operations. While avoiding major clashes unless they had a clear numerical advantage, these agile warriors were constantly darting out of tunnels and bunkers to ambush American patrols. They not only depended on the element of surprise, they also tried to maintain close and continuous contact when attacking isolated platoons so that American officers could not call for air strikes or artillery support without endangering their own men. To compensate for their military inferiority, the communists likewise relied on an assortment of ingenious mines and booby traps that took a heavy toll on American grunts tramping through the rice paddies and along the jungle trails of South Vietnam.

As the number of casualties steadily mounted on both sides, the conflict became a protracted war of attrition. General Westmoreland clung to his assumption that American forces could sap the strength of the enemy by attacking him with a phalanx of fire. But General Giap remained confident that he could overcome American firepower with Vietnamese manpower. Although a great many of his men were killed or wounded, Giap continued to replace his losses with fresh North Vietnamese as well as Vietcong troops. American intelligence experts estimated that the infiltration of North Vietnamese soldiers into South Vietnam increased from about 35,000 during 1965 to around 90,000 during 1967, even as the bombing of the Ho Chi Minh Trail grew in intensity. Giap had the capacity to match each American troop increment in South Vietnam with one of his own because approximately 200,000 potential recruits reached draft age every year in North Vietnam. Realizing that he could draw from a vast pool of men, Giap hoped to exhaust the patience of the American people in a prolonged struggle far away from their homeland.

President Johnson offered to make a deal with North Vietnam when he began to comprehend just what the United States was up against. In a letter to Ho Chi Minh in February 1967, Johnson indicated that the United States would cease bombing North Vietnam and refrain from augmenting its troop strength in South Vietnam as soon as North Vietnam stopped sending men and materiel into South Vietnam. He concluded that such acts of restraint on each side could set the stage for serious peace discussions. In a telegram to the American embassy in Saigon, Secretary of State Rusk explained the rationale underlying the proposal. "Deprived of additional men and of urgently needed equipment from the North," he cabled, "we believe NVA/VC [North Vietnamese Army/Vietcong] forces would be significantly weakened in concrete terms and would probably suffer serious adverse effects on their morale." But Ho Chi Minh refused to take the bait. He replied to Johnson that before peace talks could begin, the United States would have to stop unconditionally its bombing raids and all other acts of war against North Vietnam. "The Vietnamese people will never submit to force," Ho declared. "They will never accept talks under the threat of bombs."

THE AMERICAN ANTIWAR MOVEMENT

With no end to the military struggle in sight, the American people found themselves paying an escalating price for the war both in terms of men and money. More than 13,000 Americans had died in Vietnam by the summer of 1967, and draft calls exceeded 30,000 each month. While deploying nearly a half-million troops in South Vietnam, the United States was spending over $2 billion a month on the conflict. Yet President Johnson insisted that the United States could afford to support a comprehensive domestic welfare program while simultaneously financing an open-ended war across the Pacific. Determined to build a Great Society at home without withdrawing from the New Frontier in Southeast Asia, Johnson decided in August 1967 that a 10 percent surtax needed to be placed on individual and corporate incomes. The American people were subsequently forced to bear the burden of higher tax levies as well as continuously rising conscription quotas and death rates.

These mushrooming costs of the Vietnamese conflict made the American people increasingly critical of the Johnson administration. Only a few had objected in March 1965, when the United States began dispatching combat troops to South Vietnam. But when the American military effort failed to yield quick results, public support for the war gradually eroded. While some militants advocated even greater effort to achieve victory, most Americans simply did not understand why their country was plunging deeper and deeper into the quagmire in Southeast Asia. Nor were many in the United States willing to trust the rosy statements emanating from the White House. As the drain of dollars and the flow of blood produced a crisis of confidence, more and more Americans came to the conclusion that the decision to intervene in Vietnam had been a mistake. As their confusion and disenchantment continued to grow, public approval of the way President Johnson was handling the war plummeted to only 28 percent by October 1967, even though television coverage of the conflict remained overwhelmingly favorable.

As the struggle in South Vietnam became an escalating military stalemate, the rippling antiwar movement in the United States swelled into a tidal wave that threatened to swamp the Johnson administration. Antiwar rallies on university campuses increased enormously in size and intensity during 1966 and 1967 as the death toll mounted in Vietnam and draft calls soared in the United States. College students expressed their opposition to the war in a variety of ways. While only a small number burned their draft cards, disrupted classrooms, blew up Reserve Officers' Training Corps [ROTC] buildings, and engaged in other acts of civil disobedience or violence, a great many participated in public demonstrations that were both peaceful and lawful. Furthermore, the vast majority of middle-class and upper-class men of draft age found a way to evade conscription. Many obtained educational deferments or occupational exemptions, while others claimed to be conscientious objectors or persuaded sympathetic doctors to declare that they were disabled. A student at the University of Wisconsin, for example, took drugs in hopes of raising his blood pressure to an abnormal level before reporting for his army physical, and when that ploy failed, he convinced an army doctor to rule that he was psychologically unfit for military service. Determined to avoid fighting in Vietnam, many joined the Reserves or National Guard, and about 40,000 draft dodgers fled to Canada. Some even preferred serving jail sentences in the United States rather than risking their lives or killing others in a war they thought lacked moral justification.

The antiwar campaign spread far beyond the academic community. It received strong backing from many prominent figures, including Dr. Benjamin Spock, Muhammad Ali, Jane Fonda, Bishop Fulton J. Sheen, Joan Baez, and Dr. Martin Luther King, Jr. At the same time, numerous metropolitan newspapers shifted their editorials on the war from support to opposition. And television news reports, even if they were uncritical of American policy, slowly eroded public support for the war by repeatedly broadcasting into living rooms throughout the United States graphic pictures of the death and destruction in Vietnam. Some older Americans joined hands with college students and marched side by side down the streets of New York, Washington, and other major cities in huge demonstrations protesting American military involvement in that country. But most Americans who opposed the war remained passive and did not participate in public demonstrations. In fact, many passive opponents were turned off by student activists who wore long hair, dressed in grubby clothes, used foul language, smashed windows, and clashed with the police. They quietly opposed the war despite their visceral antipathy toward loud protesters who seemed disrespectful, if not disloyal, as they paraded around the White House, the Pentagon, and other symbols of government authority.

Americans from different walks of life seriously debated whether or not the United States should remain involved in the Vietnam War. Many continued to accept the official State Department argument: The United States had a commitment to protect democracy in South Vietnam against a communist invasion from North Vietnam, and if South Vietnam fell to the forces of communism, China and the Soviet Union would be encouraged to sponsor aggression in other parts of the world. But as the Sino-Soviet rift widened, an increasing number of Americans began to challenge the State Department position. Critics insisted that the Vietnam

War could best be described as either a civil war or a social revolution rather than as a crucial front in a global struggle against communist aggression. They also charged that the United States was supporting a corrupt and repressive dictatorship in South Vietnam. Their accusations received strong support when Nguyen Cao Ky told American news reporters that Adolf Hitler had been his boyhood hero.

Those opposed to the war questioned both the morality and the rationality of American military action in Vietnam. Some argued from a humanitarian perspective that American bombs and shells were killing or maiming thousands of innocent civilians each month. Others argued on pragmatic grounds that the costs of the conflict far exceeded the benefits for the United States. Denying that the spread of communism in Southeast Asia would endanger the physical security of the United States, the peace advocates complained that the Vietnam War was diverting funds away from urgent domestic problems. General James M. Gavin, in his testimony before the Senate Foreign Relations Committee in February 1967, gave vent to the widespread belief that the United States had to choose between guns and butter. "I recommend," he declared, "that we bring hostilities in Vietnam to an end as quickly and reasonably as we can, that we devote those vast expenditures of our national resources to dealing with our domestic problems; that we make a massive attack on the problems of education, housing, economic opportunity, lawlessness, and environmental pollution."

As the antiwar movement gained momentum, Secretary of Defense McNamara himself started to search for a way out of the conflict that had come to bear his name. He realized that the American bombing program had failed either to break the will of the communist leaders in North Vietnam or to prevent them from increasing the infiltration of soldiers and supplies into South Vietnam. In a memorandum prepared for President Johnson in October 1966, he warned that a more intensive bombardment of North Vietnam would provoke tremendous public criticism and "involve a serious risk of drawing us into open war with China." McNamara soon began to advocate restraint in the exercise of American military power in Southeast Asia. In private meetings, he urged Johnson to limit the area of bombing in North Vietnam and to place a ceiling on the level of American troops deployed in South Vietnam. McNamara also proposed a basic shift in American military operations away from pursuing Vietcong and North Vietnamese forces and toward controlling South Vietnamese population centers.

General Westmoreland, however, was still confident that his strategy of attrition would prove successful. During a meeting at the White House in April 1967, he warned President Johnson that without a major increase in American troop strength in South Vietnam, the war might drag on for another five years or more. But the president seemed reluctant to escalate. "When we add divisions, can't the enemy add divisions," Johnson asked. "If so, where does it all end?" Westmoreland replied that during the last month, it appeared that the "crossover point" had been reached in most parts of South Vietnam. Defining the "crossover point" as the moment when enemy attritions became greater than enemy additions, he argued that in the future, U.S. forces would be destroying enemy units faster than they could be replaced. The more troops he had under his command, Westmoreland reasoned, the sooner he could win the war. Westmoreland calculated that he needed another 200,000 American soldiers in order to achieve a victory in the next two or three years.

The Joint Chiefs of Staff, besides supporting Westmoreland's request for additional troops in South Vietnam and urging a limited mobilization of the Reserves, advocated stepped-up attacks against North Vietnam. In a memorandum drafted in May 1967, the JCS recommended the interdiction of land and sea lines of communication entering and departing from the Hanoi-Haiphong area. They urged first the shouldering out of foreign ships from Haiphong by a series of air attacks around the port and then the mining of approaches to the harbor. In addition, they called for a systematic attack on the eight operational airfields in North Vietnam and an intensive bombing campaign against the roads and railroads extending down from China. But the Central Intelligence Agency responded negatively to these proposals. While acknowledging that such a program of mining and bombing would have serious economic consequences, the CIA concluded that it probably would not significantly weaken the military establishment in North Vietnam or prevent Hanoi from supporting the struggle against the Saigon government and its armed forces in South Vietnam.

President Johnson was torn by divided counsel. While Westmoreland and the Joint Chiefs of Staff advocated the application of greater American military force, McNamara warned the president that an expanded bombing campaign against North Vietnam would generate increased antiwar sentiment in the United States: "The picture of the world's greatest superpower killing or seriously injuring 1,000 non-combatants a week, while trying to pound a tiny, backward nation into submission on an issue whose merits are hotly debated, is not a pretty one." Civilians in the Department of State and in the Department of Defense also warned that a major American escalation might provoke a massive Chinese intervention. Johnson responded to the barrage of conflicting advice by taking a middle course. To increase the pressure on North Vietnam, he decided in June 1967 to authorize expanded air strikes in the Hanoi-Haiphong region. But Johnson remained reluctant to call up the Reserves, and in July 1967, he approved only a 55,000 increase in American troop strength in South Vietnam instead of the 200,000 additional men General Westmoreland had requested. Thus, Johnson proceeded with caution in hopes of achieving a victory without risking a war with China or adding fuel to the flames of the antiwar crusade in the United States.

President Johnson became increasingly concerned about his waning popularity and the lack of public support for the war. "The major threat we have," he told his advisers in September 1967, "is from the doves." Convinced that the peace activists were turning the American people against the war, Johnson ordered the Central Intelligence Agency to search for evidence indicating that antiwar protesters were controlled by communists. When the CIA found none, the Federal Bureau of Investigation (FBI) began infiltrating antiwar groups and provoking violent actions in an attempt to discredit them. Then, the president asked the so-called Wise Men, a distinguished group of former government officials and military leaders, for advice on what could be done to unite the American people behind the war. Responding on November 2, the Wise Men suggested that the United States should abandon big-unit search-and-destroy operations in order to reduce American casualties in South Vietnam and force the ARVN to assume greater responsibility for the fighting. Although he was not ready to scrap the strategy of attrition, Johnson worried that rising casualty rates would exhaust the patience of the American people. "The weakest chink in our armor is American public opinion," he told an aide. "Our people won't stand firm in the face of heavy losses, and they can bring down the government."

Hoping to shore up the home front, Johnson summoned Westmoreland to Washington in November 1967 to assure the American people that his troops were making real progress in Vietnam. Westmoreland played his role to the hilt. In a command performance before Congress, he claimed that "we have reached an important point when the end begins to come into view." Westmoreland continued to exude great optimism during his campaign to win public support for the American war effort. In a television appearance, he said that the United States might be able to start withdrawing troops from Vietnam within two years or less. Westmoreland repeatedly professed to see "light at the end of the tunnel" in an attempt to convince the American people that his forces had the Vietcong and North Vietnamese on the run. "I hope they try something," he told an American journalist, "because we are looking for a fight." It would not be long before Westmoreland got his wish.

THE TET OFFENSIVE

During the summer of 1967, the communist leaders in Hanoi decided to abandon their protracted war strategy and make an all-out effort to win a quick victory. General Giap promptly began developing plans for a massive offensive scheduled to take place in the winter of 1968 after the rainy season ended. He aimed to precipitate a general uprising by launching a general offensive throughout South Vietnam. During Phase I, North Vietnamese soldiers would conduct aggressive operations near the borders of Laos and Cambodia in an attempt to draw American troops away from the centers of population in South Vietnam. During Phase II, after the United States had rushed forces to the mountainous regions on the periphery, the Vietcong would begin coordinated attacks on the major cities and towns sprinkled along the seacoast. Giap hoped that the South Vietnamese government and army would collapse during the urban assaults and that the South Vietnamese people would rise up and support the Vietcong insurgents.

The first phase of the offensive worked to perfection. In the autumn of 1967, Giap ordered North Vietnamese army units to go into action in remote areas along the western frontier of South Vietnam. His troops mounted a series of attacks, though they sustained heavy losses in order to accomplish their objective. While these bloody battles were raging, American intelligence reports indicated that about 40,000 North Vietnamese soldiers were converging on a small U.S. marine base located on the Khe Sanh plateau in the far northwest corner of South Vietnam. Westmoreland immediately sent reinforcements into the region, and he soon had half of his combat troops stationed in the northern sector of South Vietnam. Westmoreland looked forward to a decisive engagement. Delighted by the prospect of using American firepower on a large concentration of enemy soldiers, he eagerly drafted plans to deluge the North Vietnamese forces in a spectacular bombing cascade appropriately code-named Operation Niagara.

During the first month of 1968, Americans became fixated on Khe Sanh. The North Vietnamese attacked one of the hills serving as an outpost for the American marines on January 21, and then they began a continuous shelling of the base at Khe Sanh. As the North Vietnamese assailants crept closer and closer in approaching trenches and tunnels to the beleaguered marines, Westmoreland assumed that Giap was maneuvering to grab as much territory as possible prior to the opening of peace negotiations, just as he had done when fighting the French a decade and a half earlier. The American press noted that the similarities between Khe Sanh and Dien Bien Phu were striking in terms of both physical terrain and enemy tactics. As public interest in the battle flared, officials in Washington feared that the United States might suffer a humiliating defeat. President Johnson became so preoccupied with the battle that he had a detailed photomural of the Khe Sanh plateau mounted on the walls of the Situation Room in the basement of the White House. Demanding that the Joint Chiefs of Staff assure him that Khe Sanh would not fall, Johnson barked that he did not want "any damned Dien Bien Phu."

Confident that he possessed ample firepower to hold the line at Khe Sanh, Westmoreland hoped that Giap would go all out in an attempt to take the marine base. American forces stood poised to strike a dramatic blow that would cripple the North Vietnamese army. But Giap never had any intention of asking his troops to capture the encircled base. He simply wanted to direct American resources away from the population centers in the lowlands of South Vietnam. So while American eyes were riveted on Khe Sanh, Vietcong units moved into position around the principal cities and towns in preparation for the second phase of the offensive. And they succeeded in taking the Americans and their South Vietnamese allies by complete surprise. In fact, when the Vietcong attack on the urban areas commenced, Westmoreland thought it was a trick to distract him from the battle at Khe Sanh. He had fallen for Giap's ruse. Noting that the siege of Khe Sanh was only a feint, a military textbook used at West Point after the war ended taught cadets that the American failure to anticipate the urban attacks was an "intelligence failure ranking with Pearl Harbor."

The general offensive erupted on the eve of the Tet holidays in 1968, just as the Vietnamese people were preparing to celebrate the beginning of the lunar new year. Shortly after midnight on January 30, Vietcong assailants stormed the American embassy in Saigon, and during the next few days, their comrades surged into more than 100 different cities and towns scattered across South Vietnam. The carefully coordinated series of attacks exploded throughout the country like a string of firecrackers announcing the arrival of the Year of the Monkey. The Vietcong expected that the townspeople would hail them as liberators and that the South Vietnamese army units patrolling the cities would flee rather than fight. But the ARVN defenders did not run. Nor did the urban dwellers take to the streets to support the Vietcong. Contrary to the high hopes of the insurgents, the general offensive failed to precipitate a general uprising.

The Tet offensive, rather than resulting in a communist victory, turned into a military disaster for the Vietcong and the North Vietnamese. Although caught by surprise, ARVN units succeeded in holding their positions in a sequence of intense firefights while American troops were airlifted into critical areas to help them reestablish control of the besieged cities and towns. The Vietcong attacks were quickly repulsed in every major South Vietnamese city except Hué, where savage fighting continued for nearly three weeks. During the bloody battles of Tet, the Vietcong and North Vietnamese may have lost as many as 40,000 men—compared with only 1,100 American and 2,300 ARVN soldiers killed in action. The Tet campaigns left the Vietcong in a permanently weakened condition. Their regular units were so thinned that they would never regain their full strength, and their political cadres were so exposed that they could never completely rebuild their underground network. Consequently, after Tet, North Vietnamese troops assumed a much greater role in the fighting in South Vietnam.

Yet while the Tet offensive was a serious military setback for the Vietcong and North Vietnamese, it was at the same time a great psychological and political defeat for the United States. Both the suddenness and the magnitude of the attacks on supposedly secure urban areas stunned the American people. Having been led to believe by recent statements from General Westmoreland that the enemy was on the run, they were shocked by vivid television accounts of the assault on the American embassy in Saigon and the bloody street fighting in Hué. People in every part of the United States wanted to know how a foe who was on the ropes could have carried out attacks against so many cities and towns in South Vietnam. "What the hell is going on?" CBS newscaster Walter Cronkite asked in disbelief. "I thought we were winning the war!" Tet shattered official assurances that the United States was making steady progress in Vietnam, and it convinced more and more Americans that their country was bogged down in an endless stalemate. As the credibility gap widened, the American people became even more disenchanted with the military struggle in Vietnam. Tet also marked an important psychological turning point for U.S. soldiers. When American combat troops began pouring into South Vietnam in 1965, they were filled with optimism about their ability to achieve a quick and decisive victory. But after the vigorous ememy offensive in 1968, American grunts became increasingly pessimistic about their ability to prevent South Vietnam from eventually falling into communist hands.

Major battles of the Tet offensive in January 1968.

In the aftermath of the Tet offensive, however, General Westmoreland decided to ask for a significant expansion in the size of his ground forces. He wanted to take advantage of the enemy losses and seize the initiative in an effort to achieve a military victory. Concerned about their global military responsibilities, the Joint Chiefs of Staff hoped to grasp the opportunity to induce President Johnson to call up the Reserves. General Wheeler, the chairman of the JCS, flew to

Saigon in late February 1968 to confer with Westmoreland. The two generals agreed to recommend that an additional 206,000 American combat troops be deployed in Vietnam. When Wheeler formally presented Westmoreland's request for a large number of reinforcements on February 27, he described the Tet offensive as a "very near thing." Wheeler and the Joint Chiefs not only wanted to strengthen the American military position in Vietnam, they also hoped to rebuild their strategic reserve to enable the United States to meet any contingencies that might arise elsewhere in the world.

Many civilian leaders, however, were worried about the economic position of the United States in the liberal capitalist world system. Wall Street spokesmen complained that the huge military expenditures in Vietnam were creating an inflationary spiral that was not only decreasing the purchasing power of the dollar in the United States but also making American goods less competitive in foreign markets. Believing that prosperity at home depended on the sale of surplus products abroad, many members of the American business community had backed the decision to send combat troops to Vietnam. But it became clear by the early months of 1968 that the mounting costs of the conflict were sowing the seeds for a balance of payment problem that would plague the United States. As their anxiety about the impending foreign trade deficit grew, business leaders increasingly feared that the military campaign to prevent the spread of communism in Southeast Asia threatened to undermine the successful functioning of capitalism in the United States. Consequently, more and more top corporate managers and their associates in government concluded that it was time to start withdrawing American troops from Vietnam.

President Johnson promptly turned the problem over to Clark Clifford, who had just replaced Robert McNamara as secretary of defense. Doubtful that Westmoreland could win the war even if his troop requests were met, Clifford and his civilian aides in the Pentagon believed that the South Vietnamese would have to assume a greater responsibility for their own fate. They thought that the United States should not only help the South Vietnamese army become an effective fighting force but also pressure the Saigon government to make essential political reforms. Concluding that Westmoreland must not receive more than a token increase in troops, Clifford wrote Johnson on March 4, 1968, that the United States should dispatch only 22,000 additional soldiers to South Vietnam. His recommendation was accepted without serious debate. The president and his top civilian advisers agreed that American military forces in South Vietnam should not be significantly enlarged and that the ARVN would have to shoulder a greater burden of the fighting in the future. Encouraged by the performance of the ARVN during the Tet attacks, Johnson decided to inform Thieu and Ky that the United States would send only limited troop reinforcements to South Vietnam.

Even before Johnson announced his decision against a major troop increase, however, he was besieged by mounting evidence that the American people had grown tired of the war. Opinion polls taken in the wake of the Tet offensive indicated that an overwhelming majority of Americans believed that their country was hopelessly mired in an increasingly costly military stalemate. As war-weariness engulfed the United States, Senator Eugene McCarthy embarked on a campaign for president, and on March 12, the outspoken peace candidate from Minnesota made a surprisingly strong showing in the Democratic primary in New Hampshire. Johnson was even more concerned when Senator Robert Kennedy of New York announced on March 16 that he would seek the Democratic nomination and run for president on an antiwar platform. Then, the Wise Men delivered the final blow. After a series of private briefings on March 26, this elite group of foreign policy advisors told Johnson that time had run out for the American war effort in Vietnam. Former Secretary of State Dean Acheson summarized the majority view when he said that "we can no longer do the job we set out to do in the time we have left and we must begin to take steps to disengage."

President Johnson kept silent until the evening of March 31 when he made a dramatic television address to the American people. Johnson announced that henceforth the bombardment of North Vietnam would be limited to the enemy staging area just above the demilitarized zone. Noting that the United States had recently sent approximately 11,000 combat troops to help counter the Tet offensive, Johnson explained that he would dispatch only about 13,500 additional soldiers to South Vietnam. He emphasized that the United States was ready to send representatives to any place at any time to discuss peace. In a strong appeal for national unity, Johnson said that he had decided not to devote any of his time to partisan causes. "Accordingly," he declared, "I shall not seek, and I will not accept, the nomination of my party for another term as your president."

Despite his conciliatory language, Johnson was not about to abandon his effort to assure the survival of an independent, noncommunist South Vietnam. Johnson believed that the prospects for a satisfactory peace settlement remained bleak, but he hoped that the partial bombing halt would convince domestic critics that he was doing everything possible to bring about negotiations. "It is hoped," General Wheeler cabled American military commanders in the Pacific, "that this unilateral initiative to seek peace will reverse the growing dissent and opposition within our society to the war." In a message to American ambassadors in Southeast Asia, the State Department noted that the peace gesture would cost the United States nothing since weather conditions over the northern portion of North Vietnam would continue to be unsuitable for air operations for at least the next four weeks. The State Department further explained that Hanoi would be "most likely to denounce the project and thus free our hand after a short period."

President Johnson was therefore caught by surprise when the North Vietnamese responded positively to his plea for peace. They hoped to put an end to the American bombing, to encourage further antiwar sentiment in the United States, and to promote discord between Washington and Saigon. Although he had no choice but to accept their proposal for direct negotiations, Johnson still hoped to blame Hanoi if the peace discussions proved fruitless. Secretary of State Rusk reasoned that if the North Vietnamese refused to make concessions, they would have to take "responsibility for breaking off the talks." But when formal negotiations opened in Paris in May 1968, neither side showed any willingness to compromise on fundamental issues. The American delegation said that the United States would call a complete halt to the bombing of North Vietnam if Hanoi would take reciprocal steps of deescalation in South Vietnam. But the representatives from Hanoi insisted on the unconditional cessation of American bombing raids and all other acts of war against North Vietnam. With each side repeating past arguments, the dialogue quickly reached an impasse.

While maintaining a firm stand in Paris, the Johnson administration began the process that came to be called Vietnamization. General Creighton Abrams was sent to Saigon in July 1968 to replace General Westmoreland, who had been recalled to Washington to serve as the army chief of staff. Upon assuming command of the MACV, General Abrams began scaling down American military operations and preparing the South Vietnamese army to take primary responsibility for the ground war. The United States provided ARVN units with modern weapons and urged the Saigon government to make political reforms to win popular support. At the same time, Abrams shifted military tactics in the direction of small-unit patrols in an attempt to keep pressure on the enemy while avoiding the heavy casualties that often resulted from big-unit search-and-destroy sweeps. Abrams also committed a major share of his military resources to an accelerated pacification campaign to extend American and ARVN control over a greater portion of the South Vietnamese countryside.

Neither the government nor the army of South Vietnam, however, appeared ready to live up to American expectations. Although its force level was rapidly expanded from 685,000 to 850,000 men, the ARVN continued to suffer from incompetent leadership and low morale. Desertions from the South Vietnamese army reached an all-time high after the bitter fighting during the Tet offensive. The performance of the Thieu regime was equally disappointing. In response to American pressure, Thieu launched an anticorruption campaign and promised to give civilians a larger voice in his government. But Thieu did little to promote land reform in the countryside or to improve living conditions for the throngs of refugees who had flocked into the cities. Nor did he try to satisfy the widespread desire for peace in South Vietnam. As the fighting continued and draft calls rose, the Buddhist militants openly demanded the formation of a peace cabinet in Saigon and urged ARVN soldiers to lay down their arms. Thus, it became apparent that Thieu could not create unity within South Vietnam by promising cosmetic changes.

While causing deep political divisions in South Vietnam, the war also produced growing discord among Americans as they prepared to elect a new president. The Democratic convention was held in August 1968 amid great turbulence in Chicago. While antiwar protesters clashed with local policemen and national guardsmen on the streets outside the convention hall, the delegates nominated Vice President Hubert H. Humphrey as their candidate to succeed Johnson in the White House. Humphrey wanted to run on a compromise platform that would satisfy Johnson loyalists yet appeal to those who had supported Robert Kennedy before his assassination two months earlier. But Humphrey capitulated when Johnson insisted on a Vietnam plank that endorsed his policies. As Richard M. Nixon launched a vigorous campaign after accepting the Republican nomination, some Democratic Party leaders urged Johnson to make a dramatic peace move to assist Humphrey at the polls. Johnson finally complied. On October 31, he announced a complete halt to the bombing of North Vietnam. But Nixon won the election five days later by a very close margin, and now, he would have the chance to make good on his campaign pledge to "end the war and win the peace."

DOCUMENT 6-1
Memorandum on Combat Troops in South Vietnam, July 1, 1965

Under Secretary of State George W. Ball argued against a major increase in the number of American combat troops in South Vietnam in a memorandum for President Johnson on July 1, 1965.

A Compromise Solution in South Vietnam

1. *A Losing War:* The South Vietnamese are losing the war to the Viet Cong. No one can assure you that we can beat the Viet Cong or even force them to the conference table on our terms, no matter how many hundred thousand *white, foreign* (U.S.) troops we deploy.

No one has ever demonstrated that a white ground force of whatever size can win a guerrilla war—which is at the same time a civil war between Asians—in jungle terrain in the midst of a population that refuses cooperation to the white forces (and the South Vietnamese) and thus provides a great intelligence advantage to the other side. Three recent incidents vividly illustrate this point: (a) the sneak attack on the Da Nang Air Base which involved penetration of a defensive

DOCUMENT 6-1 Continued

parameter guarded by 9,000 Marines. This raid was possible only because of the cooperation of the local inhabitants; (b) the B-52 raid that failed to hit the Viet Cong who had obviously been tipped off; (c) the search and destroy mission of the 173rd Air Borne Brigade which spent three days looking for Viet Cong, suffered 23 casualties, and never made contact with the enemy who had obviously gotten advance word of their assignment.

2. ***The Question to Decide:*** Should we limit our liabilities in South Vietnam and try to find a way out with minimal long-term costs?

The alternative—no matter what we may wish it to be—is almost certainly a protracted war involving an open-ended commitment of U.S. forces, mounting U.S. casualties, no assurance of a satisfactory solution, and a serious danger of escalation at the end of the road.

3. ***Need for a Decision Now:*** So long as our forces are restricted to advising and assisting the South Vietnamese, the struggle will remain a civil war between Asian peoples. Once we deploy substantial numbers of troops in combat it will become a war between the U.S. and a large part of the population of South Vietnam, organized and directed from North Vietnam and backed by the resources of both Moscow and Peiping.

The decision you face now, therefore, is crucial. Once large numbers of U.S. troops are committed to direct combat, they will begin to take heavy casualties in a war they are ill-equipped to fight in a non-cooperative if not downright hostile countryside.

Once we suffer large casualties, we will have started a well-nigh irreversible process. Our involvement will be so great that we cannot—without national humiliation—stop short of achieving our complete objectives. Of the two possibilities I think humiliation would be more likely than the achievement of our objectives—even after we have paid terrible costs.

4. ***Compromise Solution:*** Should we commit U.S. manpower and prestige to a terrain so unfavorable as to give a very large advantage to the enemy—or should we seek a compromise settlement which achieves less than our stated objectives and thus cut our losses while we still have freedom of maneuver to do so.

5. ***Costs of a Compromise Solution:*** The answer involves a judgment as to the costs to the U.S. of such a compromise settlement in terms of our relations with the countries in the area of South Vietnam, the credibility of our commitments, and our prestige around the world. In my judgment, if we act before we commit substantial U.S. troops to combat in South Vietnam we can, by accepting some short-term costs, avoid what may well be a long-term catastrophe. I believe we tend to grossly exaggerate the costs involved in a compromise settlement. . . .

Source: *The Pentagon Papers: Senator Gravel Edition* (Boston: Beacon Press, 1971), vol. IV, 615–619.

DOCUMENT 6-2

Notes for a Memorandum on Increasing American Troops in Vietnam, July 20, 1965

In Notes for a Memorandum to President Lyndon Johnson prepared on July 20, 1965, Secretary of Defense Robert McNamara recommended a major increase in the deployment of American combat troops in Vietnam.

Recommendations of additional deployments to VN [Vietnam]

1. Our object in VN is to create conditions for a favorable outcome by demonstrating to the

(*continued*)

DOCUMENT 6-2 Continued

VC/DRV that the odds are against their winning. We want to create these conditions, if possible, without causing the war to expand into one with China or the Soviet Union and in a way which preserves support of the American people and, hopefully, of our allies and friends.

2. In my view a "favorable outcome" has nine fundamental elements:

   a. VC stop attacks and drastically reduce incidents of terror and sabotage.

   b. DRV reduces infiltration to a trickle, with some reasonably reliable method of our obtaining confirmation of this fact.

   c. US/GVN [United States/Government of Vietnam] stop bombing of NVN [North Vietnam].

   d. GVN stays independent (hopefully pro-US, but possibly genuinely neutral).

   e. GVN exercises governmental functions over substantially all of SVN [South Vietnam].

   f. Communists remain quiescent in Laos and Cambodia.

   g. DRV withdraws PANV [Peoples'Army of North Vietnam] forces and other NVNese infiltrators (not regroupees) from SVN.

   h. VC/NLF transform from a military to a purely political organization.

   i. US combat forces (not advisers or AID) withdraw. . . .

3. Estimate: The situation in SVN is worse than a year ago (when it was worse than a year before that). After a few months of stalemate, the tempo of the war has quickened. . . . The central highlands could well be lost to the NLF during this monsoon season. Since June 1, the GVN has been forced to abandon six district capitals; only one has been retaken. US combat troop deployments and US/VNAF [United States/Vietnamese Air Force] strikes against the North have put to rest most SVNese fears that the US will forsake them, and US/VNAF air strikes in-country have probably shaken VC morale somewhat. Yet the government is able to provide security to fewer and fewer people in less and less territory as terrorism increases.

   . . .The odds are less than even that the Ky government will last out the year. Ky is "executive agent" for a directorate of generals.

   . . .The Govt-to-VC ratio overall is now only a little better than 3-to-1, and in combat battalions little better than 1.5-to-1.

   Nor have our air attacks in NVN produced tangible evidence of willingness on the part of Hanoi to come to the conference table in a reasonable mood. The DRV/VC seem to believe that SVN is on the run and near collapse; they show no signs of settling for less than complete takeover.

4. Options open to us:

   a. Cut our losses and withdraw under the best conditions that can be arranged—almost certainly conditions humiliating the US and very damaging to our future effectiveness on the world scene.

   b. Continue at about the present level, with the US forces limited to say, 75,000, holding on and playing for the breaks—a course of action which, because our position would grow weaker, almost certainly would confront us later with a choice between withdrawal and an emergency expansion of forces, perhaps too late to do any good.

   c. Expand promptly and substantially the US military pressure against the VC in the South and maintain the pressure against the NVNese in the North while launching a vigorous effort on the political side to lay the groundwork for a favorable outcome by clarifying our objectives and establishing channels of communication. (Amb. Lodge states "any further initiative by us now—before we are strong—would simply harden the Communist resolve not to stop fighting." Ambs. Taylor and Johnson would maintain discrete contacts with the Soviets, but otherwise agree with Amb. Lodge.) This alternative would stave off defeat in the short run and offer a good

DOCUMENT 6-2 Continued

chance of producing a favorable settlement in the longer run; at the same time, it would imply a commitment to see a fighting war clear through at considerable cost in casualties and materiel and would make any later decision to withdraw even more difficult and even more costly than would be the case today.

My recommendations in par. 5 below are based on the choice of the third alternative as a course of action involving the best odds of the best outcome with the most acceptable cost to the US.

5. There are now 15 US (and 1 Australian) combat battalions in VN; they together with other combat and non-combat personnel, bring the total US personnel in VN to approx. 15,000.

   a. Increase by October to 34 maneuver battalions; plus other reinforcements, up to approx. 175,000. . . . It should be understood that the deployment of more men (perhaps 100,000) may be necessary in early 1966, and that the deployment of additional forces therefore is possible but will depend on developments. (Ask congress to authorize call up of 235,000 men in Reserves and National Guard; increase regular forces by 375,000 men. By mid-66 US would have 600,000 additional men as protection against contingencies.)

((VNese have asked for forces: for 53 bns.))

. . .The DRV, on the other hand, may well send up to several divisions of regular forces in SVN to assist the VC if they see the tide turning and victory, once so near, being snatched away. This possible DRV action is the most ominous one, since it would lead to increased pressures on us to "counter-invade" NVN and to extend air strikes to population targets in the North; acceding to these pressures would bring the Sovs and Chinese in.

. . .The success of the program from the military point of view turns on whether the VNese hold their own in terms of numbers and fighting spirit, and on whether the US forces can be effective in a quick-reaction reverse role, a role in which they are only now being tested. The number of US troops is too small to make a significant difference in the traditional 10-to-1 government-guerrilla formula, but it is not too small to make a significant difference in the kind of war which seems to be evolving in Vietnam—a "Third Stage" or conventional war in which it is easier to identify, locate and attack the enemy.

. . .The SVNese under one government or another will probably see the thing through (Amb. Lodge points out that we may face a neutralist government at some time in the future and that in those circumstances the US should be prepared to carry on alone) and the US public will support the course of action because it is a sensible and courageous military-political program designed and likely to bring about a success in Vietnam.

It should be recognized, however, that success against the larger, more conventional, VC/PAVN forces could merely drive the VC back into the trees and back to their 1960–64 pattern—a pattern against which US troops and aircraft would be of limited value but with which the GVN, with our help, could cope. The question here would be whether the VC could maintain morale after such a setback, and whether the SVNese would have the will to hang on through another cycle. It should be recognized also that even in "success" it is not obvious how we will be able to disengage our forces from Vietnam. It is unlikely that a formal agreement good enough for the purpose could possibly be negotiated—because the arrangement can reflect little more than the power situation. A fairly large number if US (or perhaps international) forces may be required to stay in Vietnam

The overall evaluation is that the course of action recommended within this memo . . . stands a good chance of achieving an acceptable outcome within a reasonable time in Vietnam.

Source: *The Pentagon Papers: Senator Gravel Edition* (Boston: Beacon Press, 1971), vol. IV, 619–622.

DOCUMENT 6-3

Notes from Lyndon Johnson's Meeting with Advisory Group, March 26, 1968

President Lyndon Johnson met with a group of so-called Wise Men to discuss American involvement in Vietnam. The group included several distinguished civilian and military leaders, including McGeorge Bundy (former National Security Adviser), George Ball (former Under Secretary of State), Arthur Dean (former American diplomat), Cyrus Vance (former Deputy Secretary of Defense), Douglas Dillon (former Secretary of the Treasury), General Omar Bradley (former Chairman of the Joint Chiefs of Staff), General Maxwell Taylor(former American Ambassador to South Vietnam), Robert Murphy (former American diplomat), Henry Cabot Lodge, Jr. (former American Ambassador to South Vietnam), Abe Fortas (close adviser to President Johnson), and Dean Acheson (former Secretary of State).

Summary of Notes

McGEORGE BUNDY: There is a very significant shift in our position. When we last met we saw reasons for hope.

We hoped then there would be slow but steady progress. Last night and today the picture is not so hopeful particularly in the countryside.

Dean Acheson summed up the majority feeling when he said that we can no longer do the job we set out to do in the time we have left and we must begin to take steps to disengage.

That view was shared by:

George Ball

Arthur Dean

Cy Vance

Douglas Dillon

and myself (McGeorge Bundy)

We do think we should do everything possible to strengthen in a real and visible way the performance of the Government of South Vietnam.

There were three of us who took a different position:

General Bradley

General Taylor

Bob Murphy

They all feel that we should not act to weaken our position and we should do what our military commanders suggest.

General Ridgway has a special point of view. He wanted to so strengthen the Army of South Vietnam that we could complete the job in two years.

On negotiations, Ball, Goldberg and Vance strongly urged a cessation of the bombing now. Others wanted a halt at some point but not now while the situation is still unresolved in the I Corps areas [northern region of South Vietnam].

On troop reinforcements the dominant sentiment was that the burden of proof rests with those who are urging the increase. Most of us think there should [not] be a substantial escalation. We all felt there should not be an extension of the conflict. This would be against our national interest.

The use of atomic weapons is unthinkable.

Summary

RIDGWAY: I agree with the summary as presented by McGeorge Bundy.

[ARTHUR] DEAN: I agree. All of us got the impression that there is no military conclusion in sight. We felt time is running out.

DEAN ACHESON: Agree with Bundy's presentation. Neither the effort of the Government of Vietnam or the effort of the U.S. government can succeed in the time we have left. Time is limited by reactions in this country. We cannot build an independent South Vietnam; therefore, we should do something by no later than late summer to establish something different.

HENRY CABOT LODGE: We should shift from a search-and-destroy strategy to a strategy of using our military power as a shield to permit the South Vietnamese society to develop

DOCUMENT 6-3 Continued

as well as North Vietnamese society has been able to do. We need to organize South Vietnam on a block-by-block, precinct-by-precinct basis.

DOUGLAS DILLON: We should change the emphasis. I agree with Acheson. The briefing last night led me to conclude we cannot achieve a military victory. I would agree with Lodge that we should cease search-and-destroy tactics and head toward an eventual disengagement. I would send only the troops necessary to support those there now.

GEORGE BALL: I share Acheson's view. I have felt that way since 1961—that our objectives are not attainable. In the U.S. there is a sharp division of opinion. In the world, we look very badly because of the bombing. That is the central defect in our position. The disadvantages of the bombing outweigh the advantages. We need to stop the bombing in the next six weeks to test the will of the North Vietnamese. As long as we continue to bomb, we alienate ourselves from the civilized world. I would have the Pope or U Thant [Secretary-General of the United Nations] suggest the bombing halt. It cannot come from the President. A bombing halt would quiet the situation here at home.

CY VANCE: McGeorge Bundy stated my views. I agree with George Ball. Unless we do something quick, the mood in this country may lead us to withdrawal. On troops, we should send no more than 13,000 support troops....

GENERAL TAYLOR: I am dismayed. The picture I get is a very different one from that you have. Let's not concede the home front; let's do something about it.

[ABE] FORTAS: The U.S. has never had in mind winning a military victory out there; we always have wanted to reach an agreement or settle for the status quo between North Vietnam and South Vietnam. I agree with General Taylor....This is not the time for an overture on our part. I do not think a cessation of the bombing would do any good at this time. I do not believe in drama for the sake of drama.

ACHESON: The issue is not that stated by Fortas. The issue is can we do what we are trying to do in Vietnam. I do not think we can. The issue is can we by military means keep the North Vietnamese off the South Vietnamese. I do not think we can. They can slip around and end-run them and crack them up.

Source: *Meeting with Special Advisory Group,* March 26, 1968, Lyndon B. Johnson Library.

Chronological List of Main Events

March 1965   The dispatch of American marines to Danang

May 1965   The beginning of a successful Vietcong offensive

July 1965   The decision to Americanize the Vietnam War

September 1967 The election of Nguyen Van Thieu as President of South Vietnam

November 1967   The optimistic war report by General William C. Westmoreland

January 1968   The beginning of the Tet offensive

March 1968   The announcement that President Johnson would not seek reelection

July 1968   The change in American military leadership in Saigon

November 1968   The election of Richard M. Nixon as president after his campaign promise to end war the war and win the peace

Study Questions

1. What was the strategy of attrition?
2. What advice did the Wise Men give to President Johnson?
3. What were the military and political consequences of the Tet offensive?
4. Would China have dispatched combat troops to fight American forces if the United States had invaded North Vietnam?

7

Withdrawal Without Victory

The bastards have never been bombed like they're going to be bombed this time.

PRESIDENT RICHARD M. NIXON, 1972

THE MADMAN THEORY

When he took the oath of office in January 1969, President Richard M. Nixon was determined to extricate the United States from the military stalemate in Indochina before the rapidly growing antiwar movement wrecked his administration. Nearly 300 American soldiers were dying each week in Vietnam, and the desire for peace was pervasive in the United States. But Nixon was not about to abandon the long-standing American policy of integrating Southeast Asia into the liberal capitalist world system. Convinced that he could not win the war in Vietnam without risking a military clash with China or the Soviet Union, Nixon decided to seek a diplomatic solution that would end the protracted conflict without undermining the prestige and credibility of the United States. Thus, he aimed to negotiate a peace settlement that would enable South Vietnam to survive as an independent, noncommunist nation. By engineering an American disengagement from the bloody struggle in Vietnam while avoiding even the slightest appearance of defeat for the United States, Nixon hoped to go down in history as a great American president who had succeeded in achieving "peace with honor."

Nixon realized that huge military expenditures were eroding the commercial supremacy of the United States in the global marketplace. After the Cuban missile crisis in 1962, the Soviet Union had embarked on a massive rearmament program, and by 1969, it had achieved nuclear parity with the United States. Congressional appropriations in Washington to support both the arms race with the Russians and the war in Vietnam were generating an inflationary spiral and making American goods more expensive at home and abroad. Determined to keep the United States competitive in the international trading network, Nixon decided not only to disengage from Vietnam but also to establish a peaceful world order based on harmonious relations with the Soviet Union and China. The three great powers were all ready for détente—a new era of mutual cooperation and accommodation. Burdened by the enormous cost of the Cold War, the Russians wanted a nuclear disarmament agreement with the United States. The Chinese wanted to end the breach with Washington that had existed since the Korean War because they had come to regard the Soviet Union rather than the United States as the major threat to their security. And in return

145

for American friendship, Nixon hoped that Moscow and Beijing would be willing to exert pressure on the North Vietnamese to negotiate a peace settlement that would allow South Vietnam to remain free from communist domination.

Even before he assumed the reins of power in Washington, Nixon had devised a plan to end the Vietnam War during his first year in the White House. Nixon figured that he could scare the North Vietnamese into accepting American peace terms by employing a tactic that President Eisenhower had used to bring the Korean War to a satisfactory conclusion. When Nixon was serving as vice president under Eisenhower in 1953, the Chinese and North Koreans were stalling at the conference table while fighting to improve their position on the battlefield. But negotiations moved swiftly toward an armistice after Stalin died and Eisenhower hinted that the United States might use atomic weapons if the communists continued to drag their feet. It was a lesson that Nixon would never forget. With peace discussions now languishing in Paris, he intended to emulate his former boss. Nixon reasoned that he could intimidate the communist leaders in Hanoi by implying that the United States might bomb North Vietnam into the Stone Age.

Nixon intended to portray himself as a rabid anticommunist who might lose all sense of proportion and order the annihilation of North Vietnam. By appearing irrational and unpredictable, Nixon thought that he could frighten Ho Chi Minh into accepting a political settlement that would leave Nguyen Van Thieu firmly in control of South Vietnam. "I call it the Madman Theory," he confidently told one of his aides. "I want the North Vietnamese to believe I've reached the point where I might do *anything* to stop the war. We'll just slip the word to them that 'for God's sake, you know Nixon is obsessed about Communism. We can't restrain him when he's angry—and he has his hand on the nuclear button'—and Ho Chi Minh himself will be in Paris in two days begging for peace." Nixon decided to test his reputation as an anticommunist fanatic shortly after he became president.

Using a French intermediary, Nixon proposed the mutual withdrawal of North Vietnamese and American troops from South Vietnam as a first step toward an enduring peace. To supplement his overture to Hanoi, Nixon made a parallel approach to Moscow. He hoped to persuade Soviet leaders to put pressure on Ho Chi Minh to come to terms with the United States. In exchange for Russian diplomatic support, Nixon was prepared to offer the Soviet Union such commodities as wheat and modern technology and an agreement to limit strategic armaments. Nixon called on National Security Adviser Henry A. Kissinger to put his concept of "linkage" into practice. In March 1969, Kissinger sent Cyrus Vance to Moscow to open preliminary discussions on the control of nuclear weapons. He instructed Vance, a member of the American negotiating team in Paris, to tell the Russians that their cooperation in Vietnam would facilitate an arms deal with the United States. Complementing Vance's positive message with a negative one of his own, Kissinger personally warned the Soviet ambassador in Washington that the United States would intensify the war unless a peace settlement could be reached in the near future.

To convince both Hanoi and Moscow that the United States meant business, President Nixon ordered massive air strikes against North Vietnamese bases inside Cambodia. General Wheeler and General Abrams had been urging the bombardment of the North Vietnamese sanctuaries in Cambodia to make it harder for General Giap to direct attacks against South Vietnam. But Nixon was primarily interested in implementing his Madman Theory. On March 16, the president told his top foreign policy aides that the only way to get the communists to negotiate was to do something on the military front that they would understand. The Cambodian bombing began a day later. During the next fourteen months, American B-52s would make 3,630 raids, dropping more than 100,000 tons of bombs on Cambodia. Complying with White House demands that the bombing remain secret, the air force devised a deceptive reporting system to make it appear that the giant B-52s were dropping their payloads in South Vietnam. Nixon wanted to conceal the Cambodian bombing from the American people because he feared a national uproar if they knew that he was widening the war.

While secretly bombing Cambodia to get Hanoi to comply with his desire for a cease-fire, President Nixon decided to advertise his efforts to achieve an "honorable" settlement in Vietnam. Nixon hoped to counter the spread of antiwar sentiment in the United States by going public with the proposal that he had made in private to the North Vietnamese. During a nationally televised address delivered on May 14, the president issued a call for "the withdrawal of all non-South Vietnamese forces from South Vietnam." Nixon assumed that the Vietcong, after having suffered such terrible losses during the Tet offensive, would never again be able to stand alone against the armed forces of the Saigon government. He therefore concluded that if the North Vietnamese troops discontinued their operations below the seventeenth parallel, the Thieu regime would be able to regain control of the South Vietnamese countryside.

The communist leaders in Hanoi, however, were not about to recognize the demilitarized zone as a permanent boundary separating the northern and southern halves of Vietnam. Acting on instructions from home, the North Vietnamese delegates at the Paris discussions publicly denounced the American proposal as a "farce." And they continued to insist on the unconditional withdrawal of all U.S. forces from South Vietnam and the establishment of a new coalition government in Saigon. While maintaining a rigid negotiating posture in Paris, the North Vietnamese reverted to a protracted war strategy so that they could rebuild their military strength to the level reached prior to the Tet attacks. The North Vietnamese believed that time was on their side. Adopting a familiar ploy, they continued fighting in South Vietnam and talking in Paris in an effort to exhaust the patience of the American people.

Hoping to outmaneuver the North Vietnamese, President Nixon tried to convince domestic opponents of the war that he was winding down American military operations in Southeast Asia.

President Nixon meeting with Nguyen Van Thieu at Midway Island on June 8, 1969. From National Archives (Nixon Collection).

Nixon met with Thieu on Midway Island in early June 1969 and announced that he would immediately repatriate 25,000 American troops from South Vietnam. A month later, during a talk with journalists in Guam, he proclaimed a principle widely publicized as the Nixon Doctrine. The president told the reporters that in the past, the United States had committed men as well as money to protect Asian countries against the threat of communism. Although the United States would continue to provide Asian nations with economic and military assistance, he explained, henceforth they would have to rely on their own troops. Thus, Nixon hoped to shore up the home front by ordering a token disengagement of American forces from South Vietnam and by promising to shift the burden of ground combat throughout the Far East to Asian soldiers.

While indicating to the American people that he would pursue a policy of deescalation, however, Nixon was threatening the North Vietnamese with total devastation. First, to strengthen his hand, he ordered the chief of naval operations to prepare a top secret study for a massive bombing campaign against North Vietnam. Then, through a French intermediary on July 15, Nixon delivered an ultimatum to Ho Chi Minh. The president warned that unless some progress toward a peace settlement was made by November 1, he would resort to "measures of great consequence and force." But the North Vietnamese leader refused to be intimidated. In a personal letter to Nixon on August 25, Ho again demanded the withdrawal of all American troops from South Vietnam and the dissolution of the Thieu government in Saigon. He insisted that there could be no peace until the United States ended its "war of aggression" and allowed the Vietnamese people the right to resolve their own political differences "without foreign influence." Although Ho died on September 3 at the age of seventy-nine, his comrades in Hanoi pledged to carry on their struggle for national reunification.

President Nixon was infuriated when the "cold rebuff," as he termed it, arrived from Hanoi. Acting under White House orders, Kissinger promptly assembled a special work group to consider the bombing plan that had been developed by the chief of naval operations. "I refuse to believe that a little fourth-rate power like North Vietnam does not have a breaking point," Kissinger declared at the opening meeting. "It shall be the assignment of this group to examine the option of a savage, decisive blow against North Vietnam." But the study group quickly concluded that the plan to bomb North Vietnam would lead to heavy civilian casualties without seriously diminishing Hanoi's capacity to continue the war in South Vietnam. A savage blow, in other words, would not be decisive. Worse yet, Secretary of Defense Melvin R. Laird warned that the proposed air strikes would provoke strong antiwar protests in the United States. Nixon consequently decided, at least for the moment, to shelve the plan for the massive bombardment of North Vietnam.

THE VIETNAMIZATION POLICY

Having failed to frighten Hanoi into complying with his wishes, Nixon fell back on the Vietnamization policy that he had inherited from Johnson. Like his predecessor in the White House, Nixon believed that the army fighting for the Saigon government should assume primary responsibility for the conduct of ground operations in South Vietnam. But he realized that in the immediate future, the ARVN would not be able to stand up against both the Vietcong and North Vietnamese forces without American combat support. Therefore, despite his desire to stifle the antiwar movement in the United States, Nixon refused to authorize a rapid withdrawal of American troops from South Vietnam. Instead, he decided that the American disengagement should proceed very gradually, while the ARVN steadily gained strength. If the United States continued to provide the Thieu regime with economic and military assistance, Nixon concluded, American infantry units eventually might not be needed to prevent a communist takeover in Saigon.

Such reasoning prompted the United States to make a concerted effort to alter the balance of forces in South Vietnam before too many American troops were brought home. While the Saigon government increased its force level to over 1 million men, the United States furnished the ARVN with a vast array of modern weapons. The South Vietnamese received automatic rifles, machine guns, grenade launchers, heavy mortars, armored vehicles, jets, gunboats, and helicopters. The United States also expanded the campaign to pacify the South Vietnamese countryside. Americans repaired bridges and roads, established schools and hospitals, and provided other basic services in an attempt to help Thieu win popular support. At the same time, CIA operatives trained South Vietnamese agents to mix with the peasant population to gather information on Vietcong organizers. As a result of this so-called Phoenix Program, at least 20,000 enemy suspects—innocent civilians along with Vietcong cadres—were arrested and slain.

While endeavoring to cripple the enemy in Vietnam, President Nixon also sought to quiet his critics at home. Hence, he announced in September 1969 that 35,000 more American troops would be pulled out of Vietnam by the end of the year. Hoping to quell antiwar protests by students returning to college, Nixon simultaneously noted that he had ordered a reduction in draft calls. But the president could not stop antiwar sentiment from spreading among vocal elements in American society. Press commentators, religious leaders, corporate executives, and other prominent figures increasingly spoke out against the war. On October 15, young liberals staged a peaceful "moratorium" to express their opposition to the war. Huge crowds of somber middle-class citizens assembled in cities across the country to listen to antiwar speakers. In Washington, thousands of protesters marched by candlelight in a solemn procession from Arlington Cemetery to Capitol Hill. Nixon was alarmed. He immediately ordered his staff to draft a speech that would isolate his domestic opponents before they could stage another moratorium a month later.

In a nationally televised address on November 3, Nixon tried to rally the American people behind his long-range Vietnamization program. The president spelled out his plan for the gradual withdrawal of American troops from Vietnam as ARVN units steadily gained strength. Realizing that most of his listeners wanted the United States to disengage from the fields of fire in Vietnam without losing the war, Nixon offered them a policy that promised to reduce American casualties yet avoid a defeat for the United States. But he warned that the enemy would be less likely to negotiate if Americans became more divided at home. Thus, Nixon appealed to the "great silent majority" in the United States to support his efforts to end the war and win the peace. "Let us be united for peace," he declared. "Let us also be united against defeat. Because let us understand: North Vietnam cannot defeat or humiliate the United States. Only Americans can do that." His plea for national unity initially paid handsome dividends. Although the second moratorium on November 15 was even bigger than the one held a month earlier, opinion polls showed that most Americans approved of the way the president was handling the war. "We've got those liberal bastards on the run," Nixon boasted, "and we're going to keep them on the run."

After gaining public backing for his Vietnamization policy, Nixon pushed ahead with a phased American disengagement from the war. The number of U.S. servicemen stationed in Vietnam declined steadily during his first term in the White House. From a peak of 543,300, reached shortly after his inauguration in January 1969, the American force level in Vietnam fell to 475,200 by the end of the year. The pullout proceeded by fits and starts in response to public pressure in the United States. Thus, American troop strength decreased from 334,000 in December 1970 to 156,800 in December 1971, and by the end of 1972, only 24,000 American soldiers remained in Vietnam. The number of casualties suffered by the United States also declined in a dramatic fashion. While 222,351 Americans were killed or wounded in Vietnam during the years of escalation under Johnson between 1964 and 1968, the U.S. casualty count dropped to 122,709 during the period of deescalation under Nixon between 1969 and 1972.

With the American involvement in the war slowly winding down, however, the United States Army confronted a crisis of discipline in Vietnam. The gradual withdrawal of American troops led those who were still fighting in Vietnam to conclude that the United States would never achieve a victory. Military morale drastically deteriorated as more and more American grunts decided that they did not want to die for what they regarded as a lost cause. While many American soldiers went on "search-and-evade" (as opposed to "search-and-destroy") missions, others deserted or went on strike to avoid combat. Some American officers who persisted in giving orders to fight were killed or injured by fragmentation grenades that their own men had lobbed into their bunks. The Defense Department has admitted that as many as 788 such "fraggings" occurred in Vietnam during the period from 1969 to 1972. At the same time, racial tension between white and black soldiers in the U.S. Army increased sharply, and the number of American troops using hard drugs became so great that several hundred thousand soldiers became addicted while serving in Vietnam. "What the hell is going on?" asked General Abrams. "Officers are afraid to lead their men into battle, and the men won't follow."

The crisis of discipline in Vietnam was compounded by the rampant growth of careerism in the U.S. Army. By the time Nixon entered the White House, many American army officers had become more interested in personal advancement than in military accomplishment. Upwardly mobile officers competed for command assignments in Vietnam to get promotions without risking their lives in combat. The statistics speak for themselves. The ratio of medals distributed to army officers serving in Vietnam was higher than ever before, but the ratio of officer deaths was lower than in any other American war. As a result of its careerist orientation, the U.S. officer corps was plagued by incompetence. The army usually rotated senior officers out of Vietnam after only a six-month tour of duty to provide their replacements with an opportunity to get their tickets punched and move up the ranks in the military bureaucracy. Since army officers were transferred before they could learn their jobs, they frequently made mistakes that endangered the men under their command. And the poor performance of the officer corps contributed to the general demoralization of the American military establishment in Vietnam.

Even as the process of disengagement and demoralization undermined American military strength, however, conditions in Cambodia provided an opening for the United States to weaken the enemy before the South Vietnamese army assumed greater responsibility for the fighting. Cambodian Prime Minister Lon Nol had become disenchanted with the neutralist policy pursued by the Phnom Penh government, and in March 1970, in anticipation of obtaining military aid from the United States, he led a coup against Prince Norodom Sihanouk. After seizing power, Lon Nol immediately insisted on the withdrawal of North Vietnamese troops from Cambodia. The North Vietnamese responded by increasing their support for the Khmer Rouge guerrillas, and before long, the communist forces were pushing deep into the interior of Cambodia. On April 14, with the communists closing in around Phnom Penh, Lon Nol asked the United States for military help. President Nixon jumped at the chance to buy time for his Vietnamization program, and on April 30, he appeared on television to announce an incursion into Cambodia. While Nixon was speaking, 20,000 American and ARVN troops began attacking North Vietnamese base areas and logistical networks in Cambodia.

This combined U.S. and South Vietnamese military operation produced mixed results. During their two-month stay in Cambodia, American and ARVN soldiers captured large stores of rice, weapons, and ammunition abandoned by North Vietnamese troops who temporarily fled from their sanctuaries near the border of South Vietnam. But the Nixon administration paid a heavy political price for these minor military gains. Colleges all across the United States erupted in protest when it became clear that Nixon was actually widening the war in Indochina. Then, on May 4, at Kent State University, four student demonstrators were shot to death by overzealous members of the Ohio National Guard. Coming like thunderbolts on a spring day, the Kent State killings sent shock waves throughout the American academic community. Students and professors at hundreds of colleges went on strike, and many campuses were officially closed to avert further violence. And when more than 100,000 antiwar protestors marched on Washington and encircled the White House, a siege mentality began to pervade the Nixon administration.

The Cambodian adventure also aroused the wrath of political leaders on Capitol Hill. Senators John Cooper of Kentucky and Frank Church of Idaho sponsored an amendment that would cut off all funds for American military operations in Cambodia. Advocating even greater restrictions on executive authority, Senators George McGovern of South Dakota and Mark Hatfield of Oregon sponsored an amendment that would require the president to withdraw all American forces from Vietnam. Neither amendment could secure enough support to be translated into legislation that would immediately limit the power of the president to wage war. But in a symbolic act of defiance, the Senate voted overwhelmingly in June 1970 to terminate the Gulf of Tonkin Resolution. The House, moreover, soon joined with the Senate in reducing appropriations for the defense budget and in lowering quotas for the Selective Service. And in December 1970, while permitting the president to continue the air campaign in Cambodia, Congress prohibited the use of funds to support the deployment of any American combat forces or military advisers in ground operations outside South Vietnam.

The conflict in Indochina, however, continued to spread despite the rapid expansion of antiwar sentiment in the United States. After Lon Nol closed the Cambodian port of Sihanoukville to Chinese and Russian ships carrying weapons for North Vietnamese and Vietcong soldiers, the land route winding down the Laotian panhandle became the only remaining way to supply communist troops fighting in South Vietnam. The North Vietnamese reacted quickly by reinforcing their base camps in Laos and renovating the Ho Chi Minh Trail. In response, President Nixon immediately ordered the heavy bombardment of North Vietnamese staging areas and supply lines in Laos. He also authorized American air strikes against targets in the Hanoi-Haiphong area and other parts of North Vietnam. Finally, after considerable deliberation, Nixon decided in February 1971 to sponsor an invasion of Laos. The military campaign in Laos, like the earlier one in Cambodia, was designed to buy time for Vietnamization by disrupting enemy logistical facilities. But the congressional prohibition against the deployment of American infantry units or military advisers outside South Vietnam meant that the ground operations in Laos would have to be conducted solely by ARVN soldiers.

Launched amid great optimism on February 8, the Laotian invasion quickly turned into a complete disaster. The original plan called for the South Vietnamese forces to remain in Laos until May, when the onset of heavy rains would make further military operations impractical. But after his troops encountered fierce resistance from North Vietnamese army units, President Thieu abruptly decided on March 9 to pull out of Laos. The South Vietnamese took a terrible beating during their hasty twelve-day retreat. Despite extensive American air support, the expeditionary forces of the Saigon government suffered a casualty rate approaching 50 percent before they could complete their disorganized withdrawal. Television viewers in the United States were disturbed by pictures of ARVN soldiers clinging desperately to the skids of American helicopters departing from Laos. And many American observers worried that the Thieu regime might not be able to carry out the Vietnamization program once the last contingent of U.S. combat troops returned home.

The poor ARVN performance in Laos during the winter of 1971 raised a fundamental question: Why did the Vietcong and North Vietnamese fight so much better than the South Vietnamese?

The answer lay partially in the fact that ARVN lacked honest and effective leadership. Like Diem before him, Thieu promoted officers from privileged urban backgrounds to the top positions in the South Vietnamese army as a reward for their personal loyalty rather than for their military competence. But the weakest links in the military chain girdling Saigon were the peasant soldiers who saw no reason to risk their lives to protect the social and political system that paid them to fight. "These people don't need advisers; or if they do, then we have already failed," a senior American military adviser explained. "Charlie doesn't need advisers when he conducts a sapper attack. He doesn't need Tac air or gunships or artillery. He's hungry and he's got a cause and he's motivated. Therein lies the difference. On our side, nobody is hungry and few are motivated."

Painfully aware of this contrast, the Nixon administration was further distraught by a series of events that came fast on the heels of the Laotian fiasco. After a highly publicized trial ending on March 29, a military court found Lieutenant William Calley guilty of the premeditated murder of at least twenty-two South Vietnamese civilians in the village of My Lai. The Vietnam Veterans Against the War movement wanted to make the American people realize that the massacre at My Lai was not a unique incident. After arriving in Washington on April 20, several hundred Vietnam veterans testified to their own war crimes and threw their medals down on the steps of the Capitol. The American public then learned that Washington officials had repeatedly issued misleading statements about the Vietnam War when on June 13 the *New York Times* began publishing secret Defense Department documents that had been stolen by Daniel Ellsberg when he worked at the Pentagon. President Nixon secured an injunction to prevent the publication of these so-called *Pentagon Papers*, which revealed many embarrassing things, such as the American involvement in the coup that toppled Diem. But the Supreme Court overturned the order. Hoping to prevent future disclosures, Nixon approved the creation of a clandestine group of "plumbers" to plug leaks within the government.

Nixon could not, however, stop the continuous barrage of shocking stories about American conduct in Vietnam from generating even greater war-weariness in the United States. Public opinion polls taken in the summer of 1971 indicated that disillusionment with the war had reached an all-time high among the American people. While over 70 percent thought that the United States had made a mistake by sending armed forces to Vietnam, nearly 60 percent regarded American military operations in Indochina as immoral. A mere 31 percent of the American population expressed approval for the way that Nixon was handling the war. Disenchantment with the prolonged military ordeal had become so widespread that a substantial majority of those surveyed said they favored the removal of all American troops from Southeast Asia by the end of 1971—even if the result would be a communist takeover in South Vietnam.

THE PARIS PEACE TREATY

Faced with such overwhelming domestic opposition to the war, President Nixon sent Henry Kissinger to Paris to try to break the deadlock in peace negotiations. During secret meetings beginning in May 1971, Kissinger presented a plan calling for the withdrawal of all U.S. troops from South Vietnam in exchange for the release of American prisoners of war (POWs). But Le Duc Tho, the chief delegate from Hanoi, responded that North Vietnam would not agree to an armistice until the Thieu regime was replaced by a coalition government that included representatives of the Provisional Revolutionary Government (PRG), the political arm of the Vietcong. When the United States refused to abandon Thieu, the PRG issued a public statement explaining that the disagreement over the eventual status of the Saigon government remained the major obstacle to a peace settlement: "The U.S. Government must really respect the South Viet Nam people's right to self-determinism, put an end to its interference in the internal affairs of South Viet Nam, cease backing the bellicose group headed by Nguyen Van Thieu at present in office in Saigon, and stop all maneuvers, including tricks on elections, aimed at maintaining the puppet Nguyen Van Thieu."

While the peace talks in Paris stagnated, Nixon and Kissinger decided to try their hands at great power diplomacy. They hoped to get China and the Soviet Union to persuade Hanoi to accept a compromise settlement with the United States. In July 1971, Kissinger made a secret trip to Beijing, where he raised the Vietnam issue. But Chinese policymakers ignored his request that they exert pressure on the North Vietnamese to soften their negotiating position in Paris. Nevertheless, during a later visit to Beijing, Kissinger succeeded in scheduling a summit meeting between Nixon and Mao Zedong to be held in China early in the following year. The North Vietnamese were dismayed. Prime Minister Pham Van Dong hurried to Beijing in November 1971 to ask Mao to cancel his forthcoming meeting with Nixon. But Mao flatly refused. When the North Vietnamese learned that Kissinger was also arranging a summit meeting between Nixon and Soviet leader Leonid I. Brezhnev, they became increasingly worried about the possible consequences of a rapprochement among the superpowers. Perhaps the Chinese and Russians would reduce their shipments of weapons to North Vietnam if the war did not end soon. Thus, a major offensive might offer Hanoi a last chance to obtain a peace settlement that would result in the reunification of Vietnam under communist rule.

Still buttressed by a continuing flow of arms from China and the Soviet Union, the North Vietnamese decided to abandon their protracted war strategy and to deliver a decisive blow against the South Vietnamese army. General Giap immediately drew up plans for a military offensive to be launched in the spring of 1972 in an effort to topple the Thieu regime and to force the United States to leave South Vietnam. While Soviet ships carried hundreds of battle tanks and other heavy equipment into Haiphong harbor, Giap recruited tens of thousands of fresh troops. The balance of forces shifted rapidly in favor of the North Vietnamese as American combat units continued to withdraw from South Vietnam. Aware of the strong antiwar feelings in the United States, the communist leaders in Hanoi assumed that Nixon would not risk creating an uproar at home by sending American reinforcements to South Vietnam in an endeavor to save the Saigon government.

General Giap struck with 200,000 soldiers during the final days of March 1972 as the 6,000 American combat troops who still remained in South Vietnam were observing the start of the Easter weekend. Although the Central Intelligence Agency had gathered information about the North Vietnamese military buildup, the American and ARVN field commanders were stunned by both the magnitude and the method of the communist offensive. They expected that the North Vietnamese would employ traditional guerrilla tactics, but Giap launched a conventional, three-pronged attack against ARVN units in an attempt to prove that the Vietnamization policy was a failure: The first group of North Vietnamese soldiers raced across the seventeenth parallel and penetrated deep into the northern provinces of South Vietnam; the second group swept through the Central Highlands; and the third group rushed into the area above Saigon. Despite suffering heavy losses, the North Vietnamese attackers steamrolled over the ARVN defenders. Nixon was distressed. "The real problem," he noted in his diary, "is that the enemy is willing to sacrifice in order to win, while the South Vietnamese simply aren't willing to pay that much of a price in order to avoid losing."

President Nixon responded quickly and vigorously to the Easter offensive. On April 6, he ordered the resumption of full-scale bombing attacks against North Vietnam. The American air campaign, code-named Operation Linebacker, was designed to prevent Giap from resupplying his advancing forces in South Vietnam. During the intensive raids, B-52s dropped new "smart" bombs, guided by small computers receiving signals from laser beams, on fuel depots and ammunition dumps in North Vietnam. Nixon wanted to punish the North Vietnamese. "The bastards," he bellowed, "have never been bombed like they're going to be bombed this time." On May 8, the president announced that he had ordered the mining of Haiphong and the imposition of a naval blockade against North Vietnam. Nixon also declared that American planes would continue plastering targets above the seventeenth parallel. During the next month, B-52s dropped more than 100,000 tons of bombs on North Vietnam in an effort to blunt the communist offensive.

Besides conducting strategic bombing missions against North Vietnamese base areas and supply lines, American planes provided tactical air support for the beleaguered ARVN forces in South Vietnam. The United States used massive aerial assaults and heavy naval gunfire to hammer the aggressive armored units charging down from North Vietnam. American tactical air strikes alone were responsible for approximately half of the tank losses and personnel casualties suffered by the enemy. As in previous engagements, the combat effectiveness of the ARVN was mixed, with some units fighting much better than others. The struggling South Vietnamese defenders finally managed to hold the line against the ferocious North Vietnamese attackers, but only after receiving crucial aid from American air crews along with strong encouragement from American ground advisers. Since American air power ultimately saved the day for the Thieu regime by enabling the ARVN to cope with the communist onslaught, the bloody fighting during the spring and summer of 1972 did not constitute a real test of the Vietnamization policy.

Nor did American military actions during the Easter offensive derail the movement toward détente. China and the Soviet Union merely issued pro forma criticisms of the American bombardment of North Vietnam. And during a secret meeting in Moscow on April 20, Kissinger insisted that Brezhnev put pressure on North Vietnam to make peace with the United States. Brezhnev refused to ask Hanoi to stop its offensive, but he did send an envoy to urge the North Vietnamese to come to terms with Washington. The Soviets received their reward during the summit meeting in Moscow a month later, when Nixon and Brezhnev signed a trade agreement and a strategic arms limitation treaty. Hoping to normalize their relations with Washington, Chinese leaders also began quietly pressing Hanoi to negotiate a peace settlement that would be acceptable to the United States. Policymakers in Beijing were becoming increasingly concerned about prospects for the postwar domination of Indochina by the smaller Vietnamese dragon in alliance with the powerful Russian bear, which had been supplying Hanoi with tanks, surface-to-air missiles, and MIG fighters. Viewing the United States as a counterweight against the Soviet Union, the Chinese wanted to see a quick conclusion to the Vietnam War in order to preserve American military strength.

Neither side emerged from the Easter offensive stronger than before. Still hoping to obtain a negotiated settlement favorable to the United States, President Nixon was relieved when the American people remained relatively passive as he renewed the bombardment of North Vietnam. And he continued to withdraw American ground forces from South Vietnam in order to minimize public criticism of his administration in the United States. But while the last contingent of actual American combat troops was returning home in August 1972, the United States was making a strenuous effort to strengthen the South Vietnamese army. Nixon eagerly authorized Operation Enhance to provide Thieu with large numbers of aircraft and other military equipment to replace what his forces had lost during the recent fighting. As the United States continued shipping supplies to South Vietnam, the North Vietnamese realized that their energetic offensive had merely escalated the military stalemate to a higher level of violence.

After their campaign to crush the South Vietnamese army had failed, the communist leaders in Hanoi decided in the autumn of 1972 to make a major concession in an attempt to break the diplomatic deadlock with the United States. The North Vietnamese dropped their persistent demand that Thieu be removed from his position of authority in Saigon before the fighting could stop. During a secret meeting in Paris on October 8, Le Duc Tho handed Kissinger a new peace proposal calling for an immediate cease-fire and the opening of negotiations for a future political settlement. There would be an exchange of all war prisoners and a total withdrawal of American and other foreign troops from South Vietnam. The United States would be allowed to provide the ARVN with replacements for weapons and supplies worn out or damaged after the cease-fire. Following the truce, the Thieu regime, the Provisional Revolutionary Government, and neutral elements in South Vietnam would establish a Council of National Reconciliation and Concord, and this tripartite body would arrange for "genuinely free and democratic general elections" to be held under international supervision. The United States would contribute to the postwar economic reconstruction of North Vietnam, and finally, both halves of Vietnam would be reunited "step by step through peaceful means."

The U.S. government was elated with the North Vietnamese proposal. Kissinger promptly put forth a schedule for implementing the accord, and on October 20, Nixon sent Prime Minister Pham Van Dong a personal message confirming that the text of the agreement could be considered essentially complete. Nixon also pledged that on October 31, the United States would formally sign the peace treaty. While still working in Paris on the wording of the pact, Kissinger advised Thieu in repeated cables that his troops should seize as much territory as possible, especially in the densely populated areas around Saigon, in advance of the truce. Nixon simultaneously issued orders for the quick delivery to South Vietnam of new aircraft, tanks, armored personnel carriers, trucks, and heavy artillery pieces. During the six-week program, named Operation Enhance Plus, the United States airlifted to South Vietnam more than $1 billion worth of military equipment. The massive American operation also provided Thieu with the fourth-largest air force in the world. In fact, the South Vietnamese received more planes than they could maintain or fly because of a lack of skilled mechanics and trained pilots.

As American weapons began pouring into South Vietnam, Kissinger hurried to Saigon to obtain approval for the peace plan. But Thieu was in no mood for compromise. After meeting with Kissinger on October 19, the South Vietnamese president raised two basic objections to the proposed agreement. First, Thieu said that he would not accept a cease-fire that did not require the withdrawal of North Vietnamese troops from South Vietnam. And second, Thieu indicated that he would not tolerate the implication that Vietnam was one country. He insisted that North Vietnam must recognize the independence and sovereignty of South Vietnam and acknowledge the demilitarized zone as a permanent international boundary. Kissinger was upset. And on October 22, he handed Thieu a letter written by Nixon. "Were you to find the agreement to be unacceptable at this point and the other side were to reveal the extraordinary lengths to which it has gone in meeting demands put upon them," Nixon warned, "it is my judgment that your decision would have the most serious effects upon my ability to continue to provide support for you and for the government of South Vietnam."

When Thieu remained adamant, however, President Nixon reneged on his commitment to carry out the peace plan according to the agreed schedule. Nixon wanted to avoid a public confrontation with the South Vietnamese government during the last weeks of his 1972 campaign for reelection. He therefore decided to stall for time. In a message to Hanoi on October 23, Nixon maintained that unexpected difficulties encountered in Saigon made further peace talks necessary. The North Vietnamese responded to the American maneuver on October 26 with a radio broadcast that reviewed the history of the negotiations and outlined the text of the agreement. "The Nixon administration" the Hanoi announcement concluded, "must bear before the people of the United States and the world responsibility for delaying the signing of the agreement, and thus prolonging the war in Vietnam." Kissinger immediately held a press conference at the White House in an attempt to defuse the situation. Claiming that the remaining issues could easily be settled during one more meeting with the North Vietnamese, he dramatically declared that "peace is at hand."

Nixon hoped to bring Thieu aboard before proceeding with peace negotiations. On November 14, just a week after winning a landslide victory over George McGovern in the presidential election, Nixon sent Thieu a personal letter that addressed his anxiety about the status of the North Vietnamese troops deployed in South Vietnam. Nixon said that he intended to deal with this problem in the draft agreement by proposing a clause that would provide for the withdrawal of North Vietnamese and American forces from South Vietnam on a one-for-one basis. "But far more important than what we say in the agreement on this issue is what we do in the event the enemy renews its aggression," he asserted. "You have my absolute assurance that if Hanoi fails to abide by the terms of this agreement it is my intention to take swift and severe retaliatory action." Insisting that the existing agreement was essentially sound, Nixon concluded it was imperative that the Saigon government "does not emerge as the obstacle to a peace which the American people now universally desires." But Thieu was unmoved. And on November 18, the South Vietnamese presented the United States with a list of sixty-nine amendments to the draft treaty.

When secret peace talks resumed in Paris on November 20, Kissinger demanded several substantive changes in the draft agreement, including a new clause that would make it illegal for the North Vietnamese to maintain a military presence below the seventeenth parallel. But Le Duc Tho countered by citing the Geneva Accords, which held that the demilitarized zone "should not in any way be interpreted as constituting a political or territorial boundary." And since the Saigon government had been arresting communist suspects and classifying them as common criminals, the North Vietnamese delegation proposed that civilian detainees in South Vietnam be made part of an overall prisoner exchange. The two sides were unable to resolve their differences, and when Le Duc Tho suspended the discussions on December 13, Kissinger left Paris empty-handed. During a press conference in Washington three days later, he blamed North Vietnam for the diplomatic impasse and announced that the United States "will not make a peace which is a disguised form of victory for the other side."

President Nixon had already decided to authorize a massive dose of bombing designed to inflict maximum damage on North Vietnam. The air force called the operation, carried out during the Christmas holidays of 1972, Linebacker II. During the twelve-day blitz between December 18 and 30, American planes flew over 1,700 sorties and dropped over 36,000 tons of bombs on Hanoi and Haiphong. "I don't want any more of this crap about the fact that we couldn't hit this target or that one," Nixon lectured the chairman of the Joint Chiefs of Staff. "This is your chance to use military power effectively to win this war, and if you don't, I'll consider you responsible." B-52 crews received new orders to press ahead toward their targets even if they met stiff enemy resistance. As a result, entire neighborhoods were obliterated, and as many as 1,600 civilians were killed. But the United States paid a high price for the pain inflicted on the two cities. Using Russian surface-to-air missiles, the North Vietnamese shot down fifteen B-52s and eleven other American planes. They also killed or captured nearly 100 American airmen, and the additional prisoners of war strengthened their bargaining position.

The Christmas bombing brought a torrent of denunciation that isolated the United States and weakened the Nixon administration. Bitter criticism rained down on the United States not only from Russia and China but also from England, France, and other traditional allies. While the prime minister of Sweden compared the air raids on North Vietnam with the atrocities committed by the Nazis, a German newspaper called the American action "a crime against humanity." Outrage in the United States was equally intense. Appalled by the bombing, columnists for the

New York Times charged that Nixon was acting like a "maddened tyrant" and that he was waging "war by tantrum." Members of Congress threatened to cut off funds for the war when they returned to Washington after the Christmas recess. Realizing that time was running out, Nixon indicated that he would stop the bombing if the North Vietnamese agreed to resume peace talks. He managed to avoid stern congressional action when Hanoi consented.

Nixon was determined to get out of the war during the first month of 1973. In a letter to Thieu on January 5, Nixon explained that the United States intended to conclude a settlement even if the North Vietnamese refused to remove their troops from South Vietnam. "The gravest consequences would then ensue," he warned, "if your government chose to reject the agreement and split off from the United States." Nixon then repeated his secret pledge to retaliate with full force should the North Vietnamese violate the settlement. Kissinger and Le Duc Tho began their final round of negotiations in Paris on January 8, and after six days, they were able to resolve their differences. In another letter to Thieu on January 16, Nixon warned that the United States would terminate economic and military assistance to South Vietnam in the event that the Saigon government refused to sign the peace treaty. But Thieu continued to balk until Nixon issued a blunt ultimatum. Only when Nixon threatened to have Kissinger initial the agreement without the concurrence of South Vietnam did Thieu at last capitulate.

The peace treaty, formally signed in Paris on January 27, did not fundamentally differ from the agreement that had been made two months before the brutal Christmas bombing. While obtaining a few cosmetic changes to help Thieu save face, the United States accepted the North Vietnamese description of the demilitarized zone as neither a political nor a territorial boundary. On the positive side, the Paris treaty extricated the United States from the quagmire in Vietnam and secured the return of American prisoners of war, including such prominent individuals as John McCain and Pete Peterson, who would become the first U.S. ambassador sent to Hanoi. But North Vietnamese troops remained in South Vietnam, and the fighting continued despite the truce. Above all, the treaty was flawed at the core because it did not resolve the basic political issue that had led to all the killing: Who would rule South Vietnam? Nevertheless, the Nobel Peace Prize was offered to the two diplomats who had labored in Paris to settle the conflict. Always eager to bask in the limelight, Henry Kissinger gladly accepted the award. But Le Duc Tho declined the prize. "Peace," he candidly declared, "has not yet been established in South Vietnam."

THE FALL OF SAIGON

As Le Duc Tho suggested, the Paris treaty of January 1973 had merely established a new framework for the continuation of fighting in South Vietnam without direct American participation. Just before the cease-fire went into effect, communist troops seized hundreds of hamlets that they had never controlled. They hoped that their political agents would be able to win popular support in the areas acquired during their eleventh-hour flag-raising campaign. But after the truce, the South Vietnamese army continued fighting to recapture the contested villages. These battles following the cease-fire marked the beginning of a new ARVN offensive to win control of South Vietnam. According to official statistics, more than 6,600 ARVN soldiers were killed during the first three months of the truce. And the political provisions of the peace agreement carried no greater weight than the military clauses. While the Thieu regime demanded the withdrawal of all North Vietnamese forces operating below the demilitarized zone, the Provisional Revolutionary Government insisted on the restoration of full democratic freedoms in South Vietnam. Thus, a Council of National Reconciliation and Concord was not established, and general elections to decide the future of South Vietnam were never held.

Though hoping that the Provisional Revolutionary Government and the Saigon government would settle their differences through peaceful discussions, Nixon and Kissinger were determined to provide Thieu with enough military muscle to fend off any attack from North Vietnam. Therefore, the United States did not remove its powerful fleet from the Gulf of Tonkin and the South China Sea or its awesome B-52 squadrons that were stationed in Guam and Thailand. Nor did the United States dismantle its huge military bases and storage facilities in South Vietnam. American military installations and equipment were simply turned over to the ARVN before the cease-fire took effect. At the same time, several thousand men were hastily discharged from the U.S. military service and reemployed by the Saigon government. A small American military assistance group, in other words, continued to operate in South Vietnam as a "civilian" team of advisers and technicians.

While preparing to employ the club of military retaliation, however, Nixon and Kissinger simultaneously held out the carrot of economic reconstruction to restrain the North Vietnamese. The United States had promised in Paris to help heal the wounds of war throughout Indochina, and on the February 1, 1973, Nixon wrote Pham Van Dong that the American contribution to the postwar rehabilitation of North Vietnam would fall in the range of $3.25 billion over a five-year period. Details of the financial aid program were to be worked out by a Joint Economic Commission composed of an equal number of members from the United States and North Vietnam. And although Nixon pledged that the financial assistance would be provided without any political conditions, he planned on making the American aid contingent on North Vietnamese compliance with the peace agreement. Nixon hoped that he could induce the North Vietnamese to leave their neighbors alone by slowly doling out the dollars for postwar reconstruction. But on February 7, the North Vietnamese announced that they would continue to support the Khmer Rouge struggle to turn Cambodia into a communist country.

The United States responded without delay. To buttress the Lon Nol regime in Phnom Penh, Nixon issued orders on February 9 for the resumption of American bombing in Cambodia. Waves of B-52s attacked Khmer Rouge units and North Vietnamese camps in Cambodia with far greater intensity than ever before. During the next six months, the United States dropped more than 250,000 tons of bombs on Cambodia—more than fell on Japan during all of World War II. Many of the American bombs were dropped on densely populated areas west of the Mekong River in an attempt to hit communist troops that were sweeping out from their bases in the sparsely populated mountainous region along the border of South Vietnam. As the American bombing spread across the Cambodian heartland, millions of peasants fled from their villages to seek protection in Phnom Penh. The population of the capital city swelled from around one-half million to about 3 million, while rice production declined drastically in the countryside. As a result of increasing food shortages, the Cambodian refugees suffered from hunger and malnutrition.

In the meantime, the tenuous relationship between the United States and North Vietnam began to fray. President Nixon told news reporters in the middle of March 1973 that the United States had expressed concern to Hanoi about the movement of North Vietnamese military equipment into South Vietnam. On April 3, almost immediately after the last American prisoners of war had been released in Hanoi, Nixon warned that continued North Vietnamese violations of the peace agreement "would call for appropriately vigorous reactions." The United States reinstituted reconnaissance flights over North Vietnam two weeks later. Complaining that the North Vietnamese had not withdrawn their troops from Cambodia, the United States recalled the naval task force that had been clearing mines in North Vietnamese waters and abruptly broke off the Joint Economic Commission talks concerning postwar reconstruction aid for North Vietnam. In response to these moves, authorities in Hanoi began to withhold information about American servicemen listed as missing in action (MIA).

Although Kissinger urged Nixon to resume the bombardment of North Vietnam, the imperial powers of the president had already begun to unravel. The process was accelerated by an assortment of illegal jobs that the White House plumbers had sought to do for the president. Besides breaking into the office of a psychiatrist to obtain records that might discredit Daniel Ellsberg, the plumbers attempted in June 1972 to wiretap the Democratic Party National Headquarters at the Watergate office complex in Washington, D.C. Nixon tried to cover up their effort to help assure his reelection, but in April 1973, one of his key aides resigned amid charges that the president was guilty of obstructing justice. As evidence of White House involvement in the Watergate affair mounted, Nixon found himself fighting for his political life. The president realized that he was in no position to order the renewed bombing of North Vietnam against the wishes of the American people and their representatives in Congress. Despite the militant advice coming from Kissinger, therefore, Nixon permanently shelved all plans for a new series of air strikes against North Vietnam.

During the summer and fall of 1973, as the Watergate scandal eroded the political clout of the president, Congress became bold enough to reassert its legal authority in the field of foreign affairs. Many legislators no longer felt compelled to appropriate money to support military operations in Southeast Asia since American troops had been withdrawn from Vietnam. Antibombing resolutions began to move through the House and Senate, and on June 29, Congress voted to cut off funds for any American military activity in or over Indochina after August 15. Hoping to check the unwarranted extension of executive power, more and more lawmakers drew inspiration from the constitutional principle that prohibits the president from waging war in the absence of a congressional declaration of war. Their desire to reestablish a balance between the executive and legislative branches of government manifested itself on November 7, when Congress passed the War Powers Act over a presidential veto. The measure required the president to inform Congress within forty-eight hours about the deployment of American military forces abroad, and it obligated him to withdraw those forces within sixty days unless Congress approved the undertaking. Combined with the vote terminating funds for military operations in Indochina, the passage of the War Powers Act signaled the end of direct American involvement in the Vietnam conflict.

South Vietnam soon plunged into the throes of an economic crisis. Poor rice harvests throughout Asia together with the Arab oil embargo imposed in late 1973 forced the South Vietnamese to pay sharply increased prices for their food and fuel. And as American military aid declined from $2.3 billion in 1973 to about $1 billion in 1974, ARVN soldiers suffered from a severe drop in their purchasing power. The U.S. troop withdrawal also contributed to the economic woes of South Vietnam. When American military bases closed, about 300,000 South Vietnamese civilians lost their jobs. American servicemen were no longer spending large sums in South Vietnam on goods and services, whether legal or illegal. Living costs in South Vietnam nearly doubled between January 1973 and July 1974, while the jobless rate climbed to almost 20 percent of the urban population. As the dual scourges of unemployment and inflation plagued South Vietnam, growing numbers of beggars and prostitutes roved the streets of Saigon and other major cities in a desperate effort to survive.

Military morale in South Vietnam plummeted to an all-time low. While the children of the elite purchased exemptions from military service, the sons of the poor were drafted into the army in droves. Graft and corruption pervaded the entire South Vietnamese military establishment. ARVN soldiers frequently stole from civilians because they could not provide for their families on their regular income, while South Vietnamese pilots sometimes demanded bribes to fly missions in support of ground troops. Rather than reporting the death or desertion of thousands of their men, ARVN commanders kept their names on the payroll and pocketed their wages. Discipline deteriorated even further as the death toll of the South Vietnamese army rose from around 25,000 in 1973 to nearly 31,000 in 1974. During the latter year, when more than 200,000 soldiers and militiamen deserted, the armed strength of South Vietnam declined by about one-fifth. People in every part of the country sensed that the end was near for the military forces of the Saigon government.

The curtailment of American military assistance heightened the level of anxiety in South Vietnam. Concerned about rising inflation in the United States, congressional leaders began looking for ways to reduce federal expenditures. Few reacted sympathetically, therefore, when Kissinger proposed in the spring of 1974 that the United States provide $1.45 billion to support the South Vietnamese army during the next fiscal year. Critics warned that much of the money would end up in the pockets of corrupt officers and bureaucrats. Viewing the appropriation of vast sums for the ARVN as a needless drain on the budget, Congress voted on August 6 to authorize only $700 million in military aid for South Vietnam. The armed forces of the Saigon government had unfortunately acquired expensive habits under American tutelage. During the fighting in 1974, ARVN soldiers used 56 tons of ammunition for every ton used by their enemy. But the cut in American military aid meant that they could no longer afford to employ an endless amount of firepower. Unable to continue fighting a rich man's war, ARVN officers began to doubt their ability to survive a major communist offensive.

At the same time, the movement to impeach President Nixon set the stage for a political crisis in South Vietnam. The House Judiciary Committee charged Nixon with obstructing justice and abusing his power in late July 1974 after the Supreme Court had ordered him to turn over key tapes dealing with the Watergate coverup. Then, on August 9, Nixon resigned in order to avoid the humiliation of impeachment. The departure of his American patron left Thieu vulnerable to his own critics. Tran Huu Thanh, a conservative Catholic priest, led a popular anticorruption campaign against the Saigon government. On September 8, Father Thanh and his associates issued a provocative document that accused Thieu and his family of several specific acts of corruption. Three Saigon newspapers printed the full text of the indictment in defiance of government censors, and many Catholics who had been strong backers of the Thieu regime joined the anticorruption movement. On October 30, in an effort to placate the protesters, Thieu fired three of his four corps commanders. But large anticorruption demonstrations continued to shake the political foundations of the Saigon government.

Amid the growing turmoil in Saigon, the communist leaders in Hanoi decided that the time had arrived for a final offensive to achieve a military victory. Preparations had been made during the past year for a major campaign to topple the Thieu regime and reunite the Vietnamese people under communist rule. Soldiers and supplies had been quietly infiltrated into South Vietnam, roads had been built to carry troops and arms to future battlefronts, and a fuel pipeline running down from North Vietnam had been extended to within 100 miles of Saigon. Members of the Politburo held an important meeting in October 1974 to discuss the situation with the Central Military Committee of the Lao Dong party. After concluding that the possibility of renewed American intervention seemed remote, the conferees unanimously approved a plan for a large-scale offensive that would begin during the next spring. The Politburo members met again to review the situation in January 1975, and they adopted a two-year plan for winning the war. "Large surprise attacks would be launched in 1975," they agreed, "creating conditions for the general offensive and uprising in 1976."

The North Vietnamese offensive for 1975 opened on March 10 with an attack in the Central Highlands of South Vietnam. When Ban Me Thuot fell to the communist forces within two days, a panicky Thieu ordered his troops to withdraw to the coast. The retreat quickly turned into a rout that resulted in the destruction of two ARVN divisions and the loss of six South Vietnamese provinces.

After taking the Central Highlands, the North Vietnamese began advancing down the coast like a hot knife through butter. South Vietnamese army units rapidly disintegrated as soldiers joined civilians in a disorganized flight from the pursuing enemy. Hué capitulated on March 26. Danang was abandoned in anarchy during the next three days. ARVN troops looted the deserted city while frightened refugees crowded aboard departing ships and fishing boats. After capturing Danang without meeting any resistance on March 30, the North Vietnamese forces moved swiftly southward to take Cam Ranh Bay. ARVN soldiers continued to flee rather than fight, and within a few days, the communists were in control of the entire northern half of South Vietnam.

Shocked by the avalanche, President Gerald R. Ford asked Congress on April 10 for $722 million in supplemental military aid for South Vietnam. He argued that the South Vietnamese needed a quick infusion of American assistance to replace the equipment that had been lost during the precipitous retreat from the northern portion of South Vietnam and to organize new ARVN units to defend the remainder of the country. Appearing before Congress to rationalize the request on April 15, Kissinger claimed that the United States had a deep moral obligation to aid the Saigon government and the South Vietnamese people. "Our failure to act in accordance with that obligation," he warned, "would inevitably influence other nations' perception of our constancy and our determination." Kissinger concluded that American credibility would consequently be weakened to the detriment of "the peaceful world order we have sought to build." But his argument fell on deaf ears. Refusing to authorize additional military assistance for South Vietnam, Congress eventually approved $300 million to be used for the evacuation of Americans and to provide relief for hundreds of thousands of homeless refugees.

The aid debate masked the harsh realities in South Vietnam. Kissinger had attributed the collapse of the South Vietnamese army largely to cuts in American military assistance to Saigon after the peace agreement. But intelligence agencies in Washington estimated that North Vietnam had received only $730 million in military aid from Russia and China in 1973 and 1974 compared with the $3.3 billion that South Vietnam had received from the United States in the same years. The hard fact of the matter was that the South Vietnamese army suffered more from a lack of leadership than from a shortage of supplies. ARVN soldiers did not desert to take care of their families until after they had been abandoned by their senior officers. Despite many years of indoctrination and training, American military advisers had failed to build a professional army in South Vietnam. And the military forces supporting Thieu proved to be utterly inadequate in 1975 when the day of reckoning arrived. South Vietnam was too sick to be saved by a last-minute injection of American aid.

Surprised by the sudden collapse of the South Vietnamese army, the communist leaders in Hanoi realized that the historic moment to complete their anticolonial revolution was at hand. Only the badly demoralized forces of the Saigon government stood between them and their long-cherished goal of national reunification. On March 31, the Politburo decided to seize the opportunity to achieve a total military victory before the beginning of the rainy season and to raise the red flag over South Vietnam. The Ho Chi Minh campaign began on April 26 in honor of the great Vietnamese hero, and on May 1, Saigon fell to the communist forces. The Khmer Rouge, with deposed Prince Sihanouk serving as a frontman to help them gain peasant support, had captured Phnom Penh two weeks earlier. After Congress had banned the bombing of Cambodia, Nixon had rushed shiploads of new military equipment to Lon Nol. But his army was just as incompetent and corrupt as the one supporting Thieu, and the Khmer Rouge gradually took control of the Cambodian countryside before making a final assault on Phnom Penh. When the Pathet Lao assumed power in Laos a few months later, the communist triumph in Indochina was at last complete.

DOCUMENT 7-1

Richard Nixon, Address on the War in Vietnam, November 3, 1969

President Richard M. Nixon delivered a public address on the war in Vietnam to the American people on November 3, 1969.

Good evening my fellow Americans: Tonight I want to talk to you on a subject of deep concern to all Americans and to many people in all parts of the world—the war in Vietnam.

I believe that one of the reasons for the deep division about Vietnam is that many Americans have lost confidence in what their Government has told them about our policy. The American people cannot and should not be asked to support a policy which involves the overriding issues of war and peace unless they know the truth about that policy. . . .

Now, let me begin by describing the situation I found when I was inaugurated on January 20.

—The war had been going on for 4 years.

—31,000 Americans had been killed in action.

—The training program for the South Vietnamese was behind schedule.

—54,000 Americans were in Vietnam with no plans to reduce the number.

—No progress had been made at the negotiations in Paris and the United States had not put forth a comprehensive peace proposal.

—The war was causing deep division at home and criticism from many of our friends as well as our enemies abroad. . . .

Now, many believe that President Johnson's decision to send American combat forces to South Vietnam was wrong. And many others, I among them, have been strongly critical of the way the war has been conducted.

But the question facing us today is: Now that we are in the war, what is the best way to end it?

In January I could only conclude that a precipitate withdrawal of American forces from Vietnam would be a disaster not only for South Vietnam but for the United States and for the cause of peace.

For the South Vietnamese, our precipitate withdrawal would inevitably allow the Communists to repeat the massacres which followed their takeover in the North 15 years before.

—They then murdered more than 50,000 people and hundreds of thousands more died in slave labor camps.

—We saw a prelude of what would happen in South Vietnam when the Communists entered the city of Hue last year. During their brief rule there, there was a blood reign of terror in which 3,000 civilians were clubbed, shot to death, and buried in mass graves.

—With the sudden collapse of our support, these atrocities of Hue would become the nightmare of the entire nation—and particularly for the million and a half Catholic refugees who fled to South Vietnam when the Communists took over in the North.

For the United States, this first defeat in our nation's history would result in a collapse of confidence in American leadership, not only in Asia but throughout the world. . . .

For the future of peace, precipitate withdrawal would thus be a disaster of immense magnitude.

—A nation cannot remain great if it betrays its allies and lets down its friends.

—Our defeat and humiliation in South Vietnam without question would promote recklessness in the councils of those great powers who have not yet abandoned their goals of world conquest.

—This would spark violence wherever our commitments help maintain the peace—in the Middle East, in Berlin, eventually in the Western Hemisphere.

Ultimately, this would cost more lives. It would not bring peace; it would bring more war.

For these reasons, I have rejected the recommendation that I should end the war by immediately withdrawing all our forces. I chose instead to change American policy on both the negotiating front and the battlefront.

In a television speech on May 14, in a speech before the United Nations, and on a number of other occasions I set forth our peace proposals in great detail.

—We have offered the complete withdrawal of all outside forces within 1 year.

—We have proposed a cease-fire under international supervision.

—We have offered free elections under international supervision with the Communists

DOCUMENT 7-1 Continued

participating in the organization and conduct of the elections as an organized political force. And the Saigon Government has pledged to accept the result of the elections.

We have not put forth our proposals on a take-it-or-leave-it basis. We have indicated that we are willing to discuss the proposals put forth by the other side. We have declared that anything is negotiable except the right of the people of South Vietnam to determine their own future. . . .

Hanoi has refused even to discuss our proposals. They demand our unconditional acceptance of their terms, which are that we withdraw all American forces immediately and unconditionally and that we overthrow the Government of South Vietnam as we leave. . . .

At the time we launched our search for peace, I recognized we might not succeed in bringing an end to the war through negotiation.

I therefore put into effect another plan to bring peace—a plan which will bring the war to an end regardless of what happens on the negotiating front. It is in line with a major shift in U.S. foreign policy which I described in my press conference at Guam on July 25.

Let me briefly explain what has been described as the Nixon Doctrine—a policy which will not only help end the war in Vietnam but which is an essential element of our program to prevent future Vietnams. . . .

I laid down in Guam three principles as guidelines for future American policy in Asia:

—First, the United States will keep all of its treaty commitments.

—Second, we shall provide a shield if a nuclear power threatens the freedom of a nation allied with us or of a nation whose survival we consider vital to our security.

—Third, in cases involving other types of aggression, we shall furnish military and economic assistance when requested in accordance with our treaty commitments. But we shall look to the nations directly threatened to assume the primary responsibility of providing the manpower for its defense. . . .

In the previous administration we Americanized the war in Vietnam. In this administration we are Vietnamizing the search for peace.

The policy of the previous administration not only resulted in our assuming the primary responsibility for fighting the war but, even more significantly did not adequately stress the goal of strengthening the South Vietnamese so that they could defend themselves when we left. . . .

We have adopted a plan which we have worked out in cooperation with the South Vietnamese for the complete withdrawal of all U.S. combat ground forces and their replacement by South Vietnamese forces on an orderly scheduled timetable. This withdrawal will be made from strength and not from weakness. As South Vietnamese forces become stronger, the rate of American withdrawals can become greater. . . .

It is a plan which will end the war and serve the cause of peace, not just in Vietnam but in the Pacific and in the world.

In speaking of the consequences of a precipitate withdrawal, I mentioned that our allies would lose confidence in America.

Far more dangerous, we would lose confidence in ourselves. Oh, the immediate reaction would be a sense of relief that our men were coming home. But as we saw the consequences of what we had done, inevitable remorse and divisive recrimination would scar our spirit as a people. . . .

I know that it may not be fashionable to speak of patriotism or national destiny these days. But I feel it is appropriate to do so on this occasion.

Two hundred years ago this nation was weak and poor. But even then, America was the hope of millions in the world. Today we have become the strongest and richest nation in the world. The wheel of destiny has turned so that any hope the world has for the survival of peace and freedom will be determined by whether the American people have the moral stamina and the courage to meet the challenge of free-world leadership.

Let historians not record that when America was the most powerful nation in the world we passed on the other side of the road and allowed the last hopes for peace and freedom of millions of people to be suffocated by the forces of totalitarianism.

And so tonight—to you, the great silent majority of my fellow Americans—I ask for your support.

(continued)

DOCUMENT 7-1   Continued

I pledged in my campaign for the Presidency to end the war in a way that we could win the peace. I have initiated a plan of action which will enable me to keep that pledge.

The more support I can have from the American people, the sooner that pledge can be redeemed; for the more divided we are at home, the less likely the enemy is to negotiate at Paris.

Let us be united for peace. Let us also be united against defeat. Because let us understand: North Vietnam cannot defeat or humiliate the United States. Only Americans can do that . . . .

Source: U.S. Government, *Public Papers of the President's of the United States: Richard M. Nixon* (Washington, D.C.: Government Printing Office, 1971), 901–909.

DOCUMENT 7-2

Statement on Vietnam Peace Treaty Negotiations, October 26, 1972

The North Vietnamese government released on October 26, 1972, a public statement that summarized recent negotiations with the U.S. government to conclude a peace treaty that would end the war in Vietnam.

With a view to making the negotiations progress, at a private meeting on October 8, 1972, the DRV side took a new, extremely important initiative: it put forward a draft "agreement on ending the war and restoring peace in Vietnam," and proposed that the Government of the Democratic Republic of Vietnam, with the concurrence of the Provisional Revolutionary Government of the Republic of South Vietnam, and the Government of the United States of America, with the concurrence of the Government of the Republic of Vietnam, immediately agreed upon and signed [as received] this agreement to rapidly restore peace in Vietnam. In that draft agreement, The DRV side proposed a cessation of the war throughout Vietnam, a cease-fire in South Vietnam, an end to all U.S. military involvement in Vietnam, a total withdrawal from South Vietnam of troops of the United States and those of the foreign countries allied with the United States and with the Republic of Vietnam, and the return of all captured and detained personnel of the parties. From the enforcement of the cease-fire to the installation of the government formed after free and democratic general elections, the two present administrations in South Vietnam will remain in existence with their respective domestic and external functions.

These two administrations shall immediately hold consultations with a view to the exercise of the South Vietnamese people's right to self-determination, achieving national concord, ensuring the democratic liberties of the South Vietnamese people, and forming an administration of national concord which shall have the task of promoting the South Vietnamese parties' implementation of the signed agreements and organizing general elections in South Vietnam. The two South Vietnamese parties shall settle together the internal matters of South Vietnam within three months after the cease-fire comes into effect. Thus the Vietnam problem will be settled in two stages in accordance with the oft-expressed desire of the American side: The first stage will include a cessation of the war in Vietnam, a cease-fire in South Vietnam, a cessation of the U.S. military involvement in South Vietnam and an agreement on the principles for the exercise of the South Vietnamese people's right to self-determination. In the second stage, the two South Vietnamese parties will settle together the internal matters of South Vietnam. The DRV side proposed that the Democratic Republic of Vietnam and the United States sign this agreement by mid-October 1972.

The above initiative of the Government of the Democratic Republic of Vietnam brought the negotiations on the Vietnam problem, which had dragged on for four years now, onto the path to a settlement. The American side itself admitted that he draft "agreement on ending the war and

DOCUMENT 7-2 Continued

restoring peace in Vietnam" put forward by the DRV side was indeed an important and very fundamental document which opened up the way to an early settlement.

After several days of negotiations, on October 17, 1972, the Democratic Republic of Vietnam and the United States reached agreement on almost all problems on the basis of the draft agreement of the Democratic Republic of Vietnam, except for only *two unagreed issues*. With good will, the DRV side did its utmost to remove the last obstacles in accepting the American side's proposals on the two remaining questions in the agreement. In his October 20, 1972, message to the premier of the Democratic Republic of Vietnam, the President of the United States appreciated the good will of the Democratic Republic of Vietnam, and confirmed that the formulation of the agreement could be considered complete. But in the same message, he raised a number of complex points. Desirous of rapidly ending the war and restoring peace in Vietnam, the Government of the Democratic Republic of Vietnam clearly expressed its views on this subject. In his October 22, 1972, message, the President of the United States expressed satisfaction with the explanations given by the Democratic Republic of Vietnam. Thus by October 22, 1972, the formulation of the agreement was complete. The main issues of the agreement which have been agreed upon may be summarized as follows:

1. The United States respects the independence, sovereignty, unity and territorial integrity of Vietnam as recognized by the 1954 Geneva agreements.
2. Twenty-four hours after the signing of the agreement, *a cease-fire shall be observed throughout South Vietnam*. The United States will stop all military activities, and end the bombing and mining in North Vietnam. Within 60 days, there will be a total withdrawal from South Vietnam of troops and military personnel of the United States and those of the foreign countries allied with the United States and with the Republic of

Vietnam. The two South Vietnamese parties shall not accept the introduction of troops, military advisers and military personnel, armaments, munitions, and war material into South Vietnam. The two South Vietnamese parties shall be permitted to make periodical replacements of armaments, munitions, and war material that have been worn out or damaged after the cease-fire, on the basis of piece for piece of similar characteristics and properties. The United States will not continue its military involvement or intervene in the internal affairs of South Vietnam.
3. The return of all captured personnel of the parties shall be carried out simultaneously with the U.S. troop withdrawal.
4. The principles for the exercise of the South Vietnamese people's right to self-determination are as follows: The South Vietnamese people shall decide themselves the political future of South Vietnam through genuinely free and democratic elections under international supervision: the United States is not committed to any political tendency or to any personality in South Vietnam, and does not seek to impose a pro-American regime in Saigon: national reconciliation and concord will be achieved, the democratic liberties of the people ensured: an administrative structure called the National Council of National Reconciliation and Concord of three equal segments will be set up to promote the implementation of the signed agreements by the Provisional Revolutionary Government of the Republic of South Vietnam and the Government of the Republic of Vietnam and to organize the general elections, the two South Vietnamese parties will consult about the formation of councils at lower levels; the question of Vietnamese armed forces in South Vietnam shall be settled by the South Vietnamese parties in a spirit of national reconciliation and concord, equality and mutual respect, without foreign interference, in accordance with the post-war situation: . . . the two South Vietnamese parties shall sign a

(continued)

DOCUMENT 7-2 Continued

agreement on the internal matters of South Vietnam as soon as possible and will do their utmost to accomplish this within three months after the cease-fire comes into effect.

5. The *reunification* of Vietnam shall be carried out step by step through peaceful means.

6. There will be formed a four-party joint military commission, and a joint military commission of the two South Vietnamese parties.

An international commission of control and supervision shall be established.

An international guarantee conference on Vietnam will be convened within 30 days of the signing of this agreement.

7. The Government of the Democratic Republic of Vietnam, the Provisional Revolutionary Government of the Republic of South Vietnam, the Government of the United States of America, and the Government of the Republic of Vietnam shall strictly respect the Cambodian and Lao peoples' fundamental national rights as recognized by the 1954 Geneva agreements on Indochina and the 1962 Geneva agreements on Laos, i.e., the independence, sovereignty, unity and territorial integrity of these countries. They shall respect the neutrality of Cambodia and Laos. The Government of the Democratic Republic of Vietnam, the Provisional Revolutionary Government of the Republic of South Vietnam, the Government of the United States of America and the Government of the Republic of Vietnam undertake to refrain from using the territory of Cambodia and the territory of Laos to encroach on the sovereignty and security of other countries. Foreign countries shall put an end to all military activities in Laos and Cambodia, totally withdraw from and refrain reintroducing into these two countries troops, military advisers and military personnel, armaments, munitions and war material. The internal affairs of Cambodia and Laos shall be settled by the people of each of these countries without foreign interference.

The problems existing between the *three Indochinese countries* shall be settled by the Indochinese parties on the basis of respect for each other's independence, sovereignty, and territorial integrity, and non-interference in each other's internal affairs.

8. The ending of the war, the restoration of peace in Vietnam will create conditions for establishing a new, equal, and mutually beneficial relationship between the Democratic Republic of Vietnam and the United States. The United States will contribute to healing the wounds of war and to post-war reconstruction in the Democratic Republic of Vietnam and throughout Indochina.

9. This agreement shall come into force as of its signing. It will be strictly implemented by all parties concerned.

The two parties have also agreed on a schedule for signing of the agreement. On October 9, 1972, at the proposal of the U.S. side, it was agreed that on October 18, 1972, the United States would stop the bombing and mining in North Vietnam; on October 19, 1972, *the two parties* would initial the text of the agreement in Hanoi; on October 26, 1972, the foreign ministers of the two countries would formally sign the agreement in Paris.

On October 11, 1972, the U.S. side proposed the following change to the schedule: On October 21, 1972, the United States would stop the bombing and mining in North Vietnam; on October 22, 1972, *the two parties* would initial the text of the agreement in Hanoi; on October 30, 1972, the foreign ministers of the two countries would formally sign the agreement in Paris. The Democratic Republic of Vietnam agreed to the new U.S. schedule.

On October 20, 1972, under the pretext that there still remained a number *of unagreed points* the U.S. side again put forth another schedule: On October 23, 1972, the United States would stop the bombing and mining in North Vietnam; on October 24, 1972, *the two parties* would initial the text of the agreement in Hanoi; on October 31, 1972, the foreign ministers of the two countries would formally sign the agreement in Paris. Despite the fact that the U.S. side had changed many times what had been agreed upon, the DRV side with its goodwill again agreed to the U.S. proposal while

DOCUMENT 7-2 Continued

stressing that the U.S. side should not under any pretext change the agreed schedule.

Thus, by October 22, 1972, the DRV side and the U.S. side had agreed both on the full text of the "agreement on ending the war and restoring peace in Vietnam" and on a schedule to be observed for the formal signing of the agreement on October 31, 1972. Obviously, the *two sides had agreed upon an agreement* of extremely important significance, which meets the wishes of the peoples in Vietnam, the United States and the world.

But on October 23, 1972, contrary to its pledges, the U.S. side referred to difficulties in Saigon, demanded that the negotiations be continued for resolving new problems and did not say anything about the implementation of its commitments under the agreed schedule. This behavior of the U.S. side has brought about a very serious

situation which risks the signing of the "agreement on ending the war and restoring peace in Vietnam."

The so-called difficulties in Saigon represent a mere pretext to delay the implementation of the U.S. commitments, because it is public knowledge that the Saigon administration has been rigged up and fostered by the United States. With a mercenary army equipped and paid for by the United States, this administration is a tool for carrying out the "Vietnamization" policy and the neocolonialist policy of the United States in violation of the South Vietnamese people's national rights. It is an instrument for the United States to sabotage all peaceful settlement of the Vietnam problem.

Source: Committee on Foreign Relations, U.S. Senate, *Background Information Relating to Southeast Asia and Vietnam* (7th rev. ed.), December 1974, 484–487.

DOCUMENT 7-3

Richard Nixon, Letter to Prime Minister Pham Van Dong, February 1, 1973

President Richard M. Nixon promised American aid for the postwar reconstruction of North Vietnam in a letter to Prime Minister Pham Van Dong on February 1, 1973.

The President wishes to inform the Democratic Republic of Vietnam of the principles which will govern the United States participation in the postwar reconstruction of North Vietnam. As indicated in Article 21 of the Agreement on Ending the War and Restoring Peace in Vietnam signed in Paris on Jan. 27, 1973, the United States undertakes this participation in accordance with its traditional policies. These principles are as follows:

1. The Government of the United States of America will contribute to postwar reconstruction in North Vietnam without any political conditions.

2. Preliminary United States studies indicate that the appropriate programs for the United

States contribution to postwar reconstruction will fall in the range of $3.25 billion of grant aid over five years. Other forms of aid will be agreed upon between the two parties. This estimate is subject to revision and to detailed discussion between the Government of the United States and the Government of the Democratic Republic [of] Vietnam.

3. The United States will propose to the Democratic Republic of Vietnam the establishment of a United States-North Vietnamese Joint Economic Commission within 30 days from the date of this message.

4. The function of the commission will be to develop programs for the United States contribution to the reconstruction of North Vietnam. This United States contribution will be based upon such factors as:

   a. The needs of North Vietnam arising from the dislocation of war;

(continued)

DOCUMENT 7-3   Continued

    b. The requirements for postwar reconstruc-tion in the agricultural and industrial sec-tors of North Vietnam's economy.

5. The Joint Economic Commission will have an equal number of representatives from each side. It will agree [bk1]upon a mechanism to administer the program which will constitute the United States contribution to the recon-struction of North Vietnam. The commission will attempt to complete this agreement within 60 days after its establishment.

6. The two members of the commission will function on the principle of respect for each other's sovereignty, noninterference in each other's internal affairs, equality and mutual benefit. The offices of the commission will be located at a place to be agreed upon by the United States and the Democratic Republic of Vietnam.

7. The United States considers that the imple-mentation of the foregoing principles will prompt economic, trade and other relations between the United States of America and the Democratic Republic of Vietnam and will con-tribute to insuring a stable and lasting peace in Indochina. These principles accord with the spirit of Chapter VIII of the Agreement on Ending the War and Restoring Peace in Vietnam which was signed in Paris on Jan. 27, 1973.

Understanding Regarding Economic Reconstruction Program

It is understood that the recommendations of the Joint Economic Commission mentioned in the President's note to the Prime Minister will be imple-mented by each member in accordance with its own constitutional provisions.

Note Regarding other Forms of Aid

In regard to other forms of aid, the United States studies indicate that the appropriate programs could fall in the range of $1 billion to $1.5 billion, depending on food and other commodity needs of the Democratic Republic of Vietnam.

Source: *Aid to North Vietnam*, Hearing before the Subcommittee on Asian and Pacific Affairs of the Committee on International Relations, House of Representatives, 95th Congress, 1st Session (Washington, D.C.: Government Printing Office, 1979), Appendix 2, 25.

Chronological List of Main Events

March 1969	The beginning of the secret American bombing of Cambodia	**March 1972**	The beginning of the Easter offensive
July 1969	The delivery of an American ultimatum to North Vietnam	**December 1972**	The Christmas bombing of Hanoi and Haiphong
April 1970	The American and South Vietnamese incursion into Cambodia	**January 1973**	The singing of a peace treaty in Paris
		August 1974	The resignation of President Nixon
February 1971	The South Vietnamese invasion of Laos	**May 1975**	The fall of Saigon to communism

Study Questions

1. What was the Madman Theory?

2. What was the Vietnamization policy?

3. What were the military and political consequences of the 1972 Christmas bombing?

4. Would President Nixon have been able to prevent the communist conquest of South Vietnam if he had not been entangled in the Watergate scandal?

8

The War That Nobody Won

We remember sadly now the things that will not be; the weddings never attended; the children never born; the houses never built and the fields not plowed; the books never written and the songs not sung.

AN AMERICAN MOTHER WHO LOST A SON IN VIETNAM

THE UGLY AFTERMATH OF WAR

The Second Indochina War had tragic consequences not only for Vietnam, Laos, and Cambodia but also for the United States. After answering the summons of the trumpet, American soldiers, airmen, sailors, and marines experienced a mountain of misery as they fought in and over the jungles and rice paddies of Vietnam. Nearly 60,000 American servicemen were killed in the conflict, and more than 300,000 were wounded. Some returned to the United States physically disabled after losing an eye, an arm, or a leg as a result of enemy bullets, artillery shells, or land mines. Like Americans who had fought in past wars, many GIs also came home with enduring psychological scars. And few who returned from Vietnam were welcomed as heroes who had fought for a noble cause. Although most Vietnam veterans readjusted to civilian life without great difficulty, many became alcoholics or drug addicts, others ended up homeless or in jail, and a few committed suicide. "I had all the symptoms," one veteran complained, "an inability to concentrate, a childlike fear of darkness, a tendency to tire easily, chronic nightmares, an intolerance of loud noises—especially doors slamming and cars backfiring—and alternating moods of depression and rage that came over me for no apparent reason." Many other combat veterans likewise suffered from what came to be called posttraumatic stress disorder, a new name for a condition that earlier generations had called shell shock or battle fatigue.

Even those Americans who did not fight in Vietnam had to endure the painful economic consequences of the conflict. On top of the massive spending for domestic welfare programs launched under the Great Society banner in the 1960s, the enormous military expenditures during the war helped set the stage for double-digit inflation in the United States. The swift rise in prices during the 1970s, reinforced by the Arab oil embargo, made American products less competitive both at home and abroad. And as exports decreased while imports grew, the United States was plagued by a widening foreign trade deficit. Manufacturers of basic industrial products, like automobiles and steel, laid off workers rather than modernizing their plants by installing expensive machinery in an effort to regain market share. As Americans experienced widespread unemployment in the midst of rampant inflation, economists coined the term "stag-flation" to describe their plight. It was not long before labor unions, especially those representing auto and steel workers, started to demand protection from Japanese competition. At the same time, historians began arguing that the United States was suffering from the effects of "imperial overreach" and could no longer afford to be the policeman of the world.

For decades after the war ended, most Americans agreed that the United States should never again get sucked into another quagmire as it had in Vietnam. Many repeatedly chanted "no more Vietnams" every time policymakers in Washington sought to project American military power overseas. President Ronald W. Reagan felt the full effect of this so-called Vietnam syndrome in 1981, when he began providing military aid to help the government of El Salvador defeat leftist rebels. Critics in every part of the United States immediately warned that Central America might become another Vietnam. Hoping to destroy radicalism in the region without provoking further criticism, Reagan ordered the Central Intelligence Agency to engage in various clandestine opera-tions to help Nicaraguan dissidents overthrow the socialist government in Managua. President George H. W. Bush also faced the ghost of Vietnam in 1991, when he unleashed an international military force to compel Saddam Hussein to withdraw his army from Kuwait. American oppo-nents of the Persian Gulf War predicted that the conflict in the desert, like the fighting in Vietnam, would be long and bloody. Bush was therefore elated after the coalition forces quickly defeated Iraq. "By God," he declared, "we've kicked the Vietnam syndrome once and for all."

Afterward, however, the specter of Vietnam continued to haunt the White House. When eighteen American marines were killed in Somalia in 1993, President William J. Clinton hastily removed the remaining combat troops from that country in order to keep the United States from being drawn into a protracted conflict on the Horn of Africa. Clinton then hesitated for a long time before he finally decided in 1995 to send 20,000 American soldiers as part of a North Atlantic Treaty Organization (NATO) peacekeeping mission to stop ethnic violence in Bosnia. Even when the United States was the target of devastating terrorist attacks in 2001, the Vietnam syndrome did not disappear. Many Americans, fearful that Afghanistan or Iraq might become another Vietnam, opposed President George W. Bush when he dispatched military forces to drive first the Taliban and then Saddam Hussein from power. On the other hand, some who advocated American military intervention in the Middle East argued that the United States could have won the Vietnam War. Thus, at the dawn of the twenty-first century, painful memories of the American experience in Vietnam still helped shape vitally important debates over foreign policy in the United States.

The Second Indochina War had a far more devastating impact on Laos than on the United States. While conducting a secret war against North Vietnamese logistical operations in Laos, the Central Intelligence Agency in 1962 began training and equipping Hmong or Meo tribesmen to attack the Ho Chi Minh Trail winding through the jungles and mountains in the eastern part of their country. More than 17,000 of these Laotian soldiers had been killed by 1973 when the fight-ing ended. Then, two years later, the Hmong became the victims of a great human tragedy when their American patrons abandoned them and the Pathet Lao communists took complete control of Laos. The Pathet Lao and their North Vietnamese allies immediately launched a campaign of extermination against the mountain tribesmen. The communists slaughtered about 100,000 Hmong during the ensuing massacre. To escape from the genocide in their native land, waves of Laotian soldiers fled with their families to the safety of refugee camps in Thailand. Around 100,000 Hmong ultimately found permanent homes in the United States.

Conditions were even more horrendous in Cambodia following the capture of Phnom Penh in April 1975 by the Khmer Rouge under the fanatical leadership of Pol Pot. After proclaiming that it was "Year Zero" of a new age for Kampuchea, his name for Cambodia, Pol Pot immediately began implementing his plans for transforming the country into a preindustrial communist utopia. He first directed his ruthless followers to evacuate the entire population of Phnom Penh, the capital that had ballooned from a half-million to 3 million inhabitants as throngs of frightened peasants left their rice paddies to escape American bombs. After turning Phnom Penh into a ghost town, Khmer Rouge soldiers marched the peasant refugees back to the countryside and forced them to work under terrible conditions in rural communes. Many died of disease and starvation, while those caught stealing food or disobeying rules were severely punished or simply killed. Meanwhile, Pol Pot ordered the systematic execution of unwanted minorities and middle-class Cambodians deemed unfit to participate in a purely agrarian society. Khmer Rouge soldiers herded teachers, businessmen, intellectuals, and other educated people into concentration camps to be tortured, murdered, and buried in mass graves. By December 1978, the population of Cambodia had been reduced by about 2 million from a prewar level of around 7 million.

The people of Vietnam also paid dearly for the long struggle to turn their country into an independent, unified, communist utopia. By the time the war ended in 1975, about 3 million Vietnamese soldiers and civilians had been killed, and hundreds of thousands more had been crippled. Vietnamese cities and towns, in the aftermath of the conflict, burst with orphans and refugees from rural areas. Furthermore, the war left the economy of Vietnam in shambles. The 19 million gallons of herbicides that American planes had sprayed on the Vietnamese countryside defoliated 12 million acres of forests, depleted the soil of 25 million acres of farm land, and killed a great many of the water buffalo that peasants used to plow their rice fields. The lingering effects of Agent Orange, a highly toxic compound that Americans used to strip the jungle and to expose enemy soldiers, could be seen long after the war ended in the unusually large number of Vietnamese people suffering from birth defects and various forms of cancer. In the northern half of Vietnam, the massive American bombardment had destroyed most of the ports, bridges, roads, power plants, and factories. In the southern half, it was almost impossible to obtain spare parts for worn or damaged machines that had been imported from the United States. Indeed, the cascade of American bombs, shells, and toxic chemicals that had blanketed Vietnam for more than a decade had a devastating impact on the entire country.

THE FAILURE OF COMMUNISM IN VIETNAM

After the fall of Saigon in May 1975, the top communist leaders in Hanoi, deluded by their military success, arrogantly embarked on a course of action that added greatly to the misery of those who had survived the war. They mistakenly assumed that the vast majority of Vietnamese people, southerners as well as northerners, were ready to move rapidly toward both the reunification of Vietnam and the establishment of a socialist economy throughout the country. After quickly absorbing the members of the People's Revolutionary Party in the south, the Lao Dong party in the north openly called itself the Vietnamese Communist Party (VCP). The formal reunification of the country took place in July 1976, when a Vietnamese national assembly was created to adopt a constitution that had been drafted in Hanoi. The constitution established the Socialist Republic of Vietnam (SRV) with a government headquartered in Hanoi, and it recognized the communist party as the only legal political organization in the country. Although a few prominent leaders from the southern revolutionary movement were given high positions in the new regime, northern communists remained in full control of the SRV.

Determined to consolidate their political power, the communist rulers in Hanoi made a concerted effort to keep those who had supported the old regime in South Vietnam from challenging their authority. The victorious communists hastily rounded up several hundred thousand army officers and government officials in the defeated south and confined them in reeducation camps, where they were forced to confess to past crimes and to promise to abide by communist doctrines in the future. These political prisoners remained incarcerated for weeks or even years, depending on their rank or importance in the vanquished South Vietnamese government, and upon their release, many were placed under constant surveillance and prevented from obtaining good jobs. At the same time, northern communists stationed in Ho Chi Minh City (formally Saigon) tried to wipe out every aspect of capitalism that had contaminated the local population. They even detained and punished young southerners who displayed the trappings of Western culture by cutting off their long hair and taking away their American clothes.

As a key element in their drive to dismantle capitalism in the south, bureaucrats in Hanoi adopted a Soviet model of centralized planning and imposed their economic doctrines throughout the Socialist Republic of Vietnam. But their highly publicized Five Year Plans failed to achieve their goals of rapid economic growth and sustained prosperity. After nationalizing all commercial and industrial operations above the family level, the communist government paid factory managers according to how many workers they employed rather than with regard to how many goods they turned out. As a result, business efficiency declined abruptly, and industrial production remained stagnant. The decision to collectivize agriculture had equally dismal consequences. Peasants dragged their feet when communist administrators ordered them to take unreasonable actions, such as grow coffee instead of tea on land that was not suitable for coffee production. Peasants also lost their incentive to exert themselves when they were forced to work on collectivized rice plantations in the Mekong Delta and elsewhere. As agricultural production failed to keep pace with population growth in the SRV, the government had to resort to rationing food and importing rice in order to prevent widespread starvation.

Many southerners, even some who had supported the revolution that ousted the Saigon regime, complained that northerners were treating them like a conquered people. "Now, with total power in their hands, they began to show their cards in the most brutal fashion," lamented a former member of the National Liberation Front. "They made it understood that the Vietnam of the future would be a single monolithic bloc, collectivist and totalitarian, in which all the traditions and culture of the South would be ground and molded by the political machine of the conquerors." Angered by the political repression and economic regimentation, more than 1.5 million southerners risked their lives to escape from the SRV. Tens of thousands either drowned when their overcrowded boats sank or were killed by pirates roaming the South China Sea. Many of the survivors found sanctuary in refugee camps in neighboring countries, and about 1 million eventually resettled in the United States. Since most of these "boat people" were either well-educated members of the Vietnamese middle class or ethnic Chinese businessmen, the SRV lost many valuable people with technical skills and administrative experience.

Perhaps the awful shortcomings of the Five Year Plans that had been formulated in Hanoi can best be put in perspective by comparing the enduring impoverishment of the Socialist Republic of Vietnam with the growing prosperity of Asian countries that rejected communist economic principles. Thailand, Malaysia, Indonesia, and the other noncommunist members of the Association of the Southeast Asian Nations (ASEAN) developed flourishing economies and became vigorous competitors in the liberal capitalist world system. So did China after Mao Zedong died in 1976 and Deng Xiaoping assumed the reins of power in Beijing. Deng immediately began moving China toward a market economy, although political repression continued under his rule. During the next twenty years, per capita wealth in the country quadrupled, and China became a major exporter to the United States. The SRV, in sharp contrast, remained one of the poorest countries in the world. Desperately trying to overcome their economic troubles and the destruction that had been caused by American military forces, the communist leaders in Hanoi turned increasingly to the Soviet Union to obtain indispensable financial and technical assistance.

Hoping to prevent communism from spreading throughout Southeast Asia, President Gerald R. Ford took a hard line against the triumphant Vietnamese revolutionaries from the very outset. He did everything in his power to keep the Socialist Republic of Vietnam impoverished while encouraging strong commercial and financial ties with the noncommunist ASEAN countries. Claiming that Hanoi had violated the Paris Peace Treaty of 1973, Ford refused to pay any of the $3.25 billion in reparations that former President Richard M. Nixon had promised for the postwar economic reconstruction of Vietnam. Ford then imposed a trade and investment embargo against Vietnam as well as Cambodia and Laos when these countries fell into the communist orbit. Ford also withheld diplomatic recognition from the SRV, and he vetoed its application for membership in the United Nations. To justify his refusal to normalize diplomatic and economic relations with the communist regime in Hanoi, Ford exploited rumors that nearly 2,500 American servicemen listed as missing in action were actually languishing in Southeast Asian prisons. And he did so despite the fact that the Defense Department had declared after the exchange of prisoners of war in 1973 that no living Americans remained incarcerated anywhere in Southeast Asia.

Prospects for a reconciliation between the United States and the Socialist Republic of Vietnam seemed bright, however, when James E. Carter became president. A month after his inauguration in January 1977, Carter announced that he would be glad to normalize relations with the SRV if Hanoi gave a proper accounting of Americans who were missing in action. Hanoi responded by sending the United States the remains of more than sixty MIAs during the next nine months. In return, the United States stopped opposing the admission of the SRV into the United Nations and permitted academic exchanges between the two countries. Citibank and the Bank of America, eager to explore investment opportunities in Vietnam, contemplated opening branches in Ho Chi Minh City. But when President Carter proclaimed that the U.S. did not owe Vietnam any money for postwar reconstruction, Hanoi angrily demanded that Carter fulfill Nixon's pledge to provide reparations. Congress thereupon voted overwhelmingly to ban all economic aid to the SRV. Although in 1978 the Vietnamese proposed, without any preconditions, the establishment of normal relations with the United States, their hopes were dashed by a major shift in American foreign policy. The Carter administration was moving away from détente and toward a renewal of Cold War confrontations with the Soviet Union. Regarding Vietnam as a Russian proxy, National Security Advisor Zbigniew Brzezinski persuaded Carter to shelve his plans for normalization.

President Reagan, like Presidents Carter and Ford, refused to grant diplomatic recognition to Hanoi or to lift the embargo against the Socialist Republic of Vietnam. During his two terms in the White House from 1981 to 1989, the MIA issue became the major obstacle to the establishment of normal relations between the United States and Vietnam. Agitation from the National League of Families of American Prisoners and Missing in Southeast Asia as well as other vociferous groups, occasional reports that live American soldiers had been sighted in Vietnam or Laos, and a plethora of *Rambo*-like films and other sensationalist Hollywood movies led people throughout the United States to believe that many Americans were still being held captive in Southeast Asia. Although only 4 Americans were listed as missing for every 100 confirmed dead in the Vietnam War (compared to a ratio of 15 to 100 in the Korean War and 20 to 100 in World War II), Reagan insisted that Hanoi provide a full and complete accounting of MIAs. Many Americans, especially those who lost loved ones in Vietnam, strongly applauded his position even though the North Vietnamese could not account for as many as 300,000 of their own soldiers who were listed as missing. Determined to contain the SRV, Reagan continued to use the emotional MIA issue to justify his rejection of repeated proposals from Hanoi for a reconciliation with the United States.

THE VIETNAMESE TURN TOWARD CAPITALISM

After establishing themselves as the masters of Vietnam, the communists in Hanoi renewed their demands for a "special relationship" with Cambodia and Laos. But Pol Pot, a militant Cambodian nationalist, concluded that the Vietnamese were simply using fancy rhetoric to disguise their desire to dominate his country. Recalling that during the seventeenth century Vietnamese imperialists had pushed the Khmer people out of the fertile Mekong Delta, Pol Pot launched military raids across the border into Vietnam in hopes of regaining territory that had traditionally belonged to Cambodia. The dictators in Hanoi became increasingly irate, and in December 1978, they decided to remove the Khmer Rouge government that they had helped take power and replace it with a regime in Phnom Penh that they could control. While preparing for war in Cambodia, the SRV signed a treaty of friendship with the Soviet Union and offered the Russians a naval base at Cam Ranh Bay in exchange for additional economic assistance. Then, in January 1979, Vietnamese soldiers invaded Cambodia, drove Pol Pot into the jungles, and installed a puppet government in Phnom Penh. But Pol Pot regrouped his forces and began a guerrilla war in an effort to keep Cambodia from becoming a satellite of Vietnam.

The invasion of Cambodia spelled disaster for the Socialist Republic of Vietnam. The Chinese colossus to the north did not want the smaller Vietnamese dragon to establish hegemony over Indochina. And after declaring that Hanoi was serving as a Russian puppet, Deng Xiaoping ordered Chinese troops in February 1979 to cross the border and commence a punitive expedition in northern Vietnam. Deng withdrew his forces a month later in the face of heavy battlefield casualties and strong international criticism, but not before they had killed many Vietnamese soldiers and destroyed important railroads and power plants in Tonkin. President Carter, in the wake of the Sino-Vietnamese conflict, established formal diplomatic relations with Beijing. And while the Soviet Union continued to back the SRV, which lost an estimated 50,000 soldiers in Cambodia during the next decade, the United States, several other Western countries, and the noncommunist states of ASEAN worked with China in opposing Vietnamese expansionism. Together, these countries supported a coalition of Cambodians, including Pol Pot and the Khmer Rouge, in their guerrilla war against occupying troops from Vietnam. As had occurred many times in the past, national interests overrode ideological considerations.

The protracted war against the Cambodian guerrillas and the international reaction to Vietnamese imperialism added greatly to the economic difficulties that Hanoi was already struggling to surmount. While stationing 140,000 troops in Cambodia and maintaining a standing army of more than a million soldiers, the SRV found itself spending nearly half of its annual budget to support the fourth-largest military force in the world. And the financial burden on Hanoi only grew after the United States pressured many other countries to stand behind its trade and investment embargo against the SRV. As a result, Vietnam could not obtain large amounts of capital from countries that did not want to alienate Washington, nor could it gain access to the resources of the World Bank, the International Monetary Fund, or the Asian Development Bank. And when China stopped giving Hanoi any economic assistance, the SRV became even more dependent on the Soviet Union. Thousands of Soviet technicians and administrators poured into Vietnam during the 1980s to implement an aid program that cost as much as $2 billion a year. But many Vietnamese resented the presence of arrogant Russian advisers and feared Soviet domination of their country. Moreover, despite the flow of rubles from Russia, the SRV remained an economic basket case.

The economic failure eventually led to a radical change in political leadership in the Socialist Republic of Vietnam. Reformers in the ruling hierarchy in Hanoi began arguing that the government had made a serious mistake by attempting to push the Vietnamese people too rapidly toward socialism. As the economy of the SRV continued to stagnate, many complained that the communist ideologues who remained in power had proven less adept at winning the peace than at waging war. The Sixth Congress of the Vietnamese Communist Party, held in December 1986 amid growing criticism of government officials, marked a major turning point in Vietnamese history. After younger and more pragmatic leaders were elected to top positions in the VCP, Pham Van Dong, Le Duc Tho, and other key members of the Old Guard lost much of their influence. The new general secretary of the VCP, Nguyen Van Linh, had been born in Hanoi but had spent most of his life in the south. Despite the dramatic change in political leadership, however, the VCP retained its monopoly of power in Hanoi, and opposition parties remained illegal.

The new generation of Vietnamese leaders soon indicated a willingness to experiment with capitalist methods in order to promote economic development. For his economic adviser, Linh picked Nguyen Xuan Oanh, who had been trained at Harvard University before he became a governor of the central bank in South Vietnam. Then, Linh cautiously embarked on a program of *doi moi*, or renovation, which permitted an increasing amount of free enterprise. Aiming to stimulate industrial, agricultural, and commercial activity, the new regime in Hanoi provided market incentives to the managers of government businesses, relaxed stringent rules concerning private enterprise, froze the wages of factory workers, curbed the power of labor unions, dismantled farming collectives, and restored the old system of individual land ownership. Vietnamese leaders still claimed to be socialists, but they talked and acted more and more like capitalists. In a public statement in January 1988, Linh himself declared that an "underdeveloped nation such as Vietnam needs even more to look to the capitalist world for lessons."

The *doi moi* campaign produced mixed results. On the positive side, industrial production increased significantly, agricultural output expanded even faster, and Vietnam once more became one of the largest rice exporters in the world. The growth rate of the Vietnamese economy, after remaining around 2 percent for years, jumped by the mid-1990s to about 8 percent. On the negative side, economic improvement came at the expense of social justice. Factory workers toiled long hours for low wages, and wealthy landlords exploited peasants just as they had in the old days when Vietnam was a French colony. During the last decade of the twentieth century, the gap between rich and poor widened in the Socialist Republic of Vietnam. A few Vietnamese entrepreneurs lived in luxury, but many Vietnamese children suffered from malnutrition despite growing food supplies and expanding rice exports. In other words, the class structure that emerged in the SRV resembled the one that had existed in Vietnam before the communists began mobilizing the masses to fight for national liberation and social equality.

As part of his endeavor to revamp the economy, Linh made important changes in Vietnamese foreign policy. He sought to speed the economic development of Vietnam by ending its diplomatic isolation, by enacting a liberal foreign investment code, and by encouraging overseas trade. Hoping to open commercial relations with neighboring countries and to reduce the burden of military spending, Linh decided in 1989 to withdraw Vietnamese forces from Cambodia. International support for the embargo that the United States had organized against the Socialist Republic of Vietnam began to crumble soon after Hanoi ended its long military occupation of Cambodia. The Japanese government, for example, paid only lip service to the boycott against the SRV. Although Tokyo refrained from providing any official economic aid to Hanoi, it did not prohibit Japanese businessmen from trading or investing in Vietnam. Japanese companies did not immediately send large amounts of capital into the SRV, but they did scout the country for lucrative opportunities and sign investment contracts that would go into effect as soon as the embargo against Vietnam ended.

Linh intensified his efforts to attract foreign investment when the Soviet Union collapsed in 1991 and the Socialist Republic of Vietnam lost its only significant benefactor. Responding to his calls for capital, foreign corporations sent increasing quantities of money into Vietnam. They hoped to exploit the abundant supply of natural resources, including the possibly rich oil deposits off the Vietnamese coast. They also wished to take advantage of the low minimum wage ($35 a month), the high literacy rate (88 percent), and the strong work ethic in Vietnam. Between 1989 and 1991, foreign investment in the SRV jumped from less than $600 million to more than $1 billion. Companies from Hong Kong and Taiwan led the way, while firms from Australia, France, Britain, and Holland followed on their heels. By 1992, businessmen from thirty-one different nations were making investments in Vietnam. "The country is being overrun," an American journalist reported, "by a stampede of foreign investors, advisers, traders, oil explorers, real estate developers and entrepreneurial adventurers of every stripe who think they've discovered the world's next money-making hot spot."

Foreign exporters viewed the rapidly growing Vietnamese population of more than 70 million people as a potentially huge market for their products. Although the Hanoi government estimated that the annual per capita income in Vietnam was only $200, the actual figure was probably much higher since a considerable amount of business activity took place outside the official economy. Foreign manufacturers, eager to find customers for their wares, began flooding the SRV with a great variety of consumer goods. "Stores and stalls from Hanoi to Ho Chi Minh City," a foreign visitor observed in 1990, "sell Japanese tape decks, German film, Saudi Arabian bottled spring water, shampoo from Malaysia, toys from China and electric fans from Singapore." Japanese corporations such as Sony, Panasonic, Sharp, Toyota, and Honda plastered Vietnam with billboards advertising their electrical and automotive products. As the scramble for markets accelerated, trade between Japan and the SRV expanded to about $1 billion in 1991, and the Land of the Rising Sun quickly became Vietnam's largest trading partner.

THE ROAD TO RECONCILIATION

The United States and Vietnam, in the meantime, gradually began moving toward a reconciliation. Desiring American capital and technology, Linh and his comrades in Hanoi signaled their willingness to cooperate with the United States regarding the MIA issue. Washington took the opportunity in 1991 to open a special liaison office in Hanoi to work with the Vietnamese in resolving the cases of the 2,265 Americans still listed as missing. But public opinion polls taken over the years indicated that a large majority of Americans opposed normalizing relations with the SRV. Although most Americans probably did not feel strongly about the question, some well-organized groups, like many members of the Vietnamese-American community, actively opposed normalization. President George H. W. Bush did not want to arouse their wrath, but in April 1992, he did allow the sale of American products, mainly grain and medicine, for humanitarian purposes in Vietnam. Hoping that Bush would lift the embargo on trade and investment, Hanoi in October 1992 gave the United States over 5,000 photographs of American servicemen who had been killed in Vietnam. The pictures and accompanying documents helped Washington resolve many of the MIA cases, and before the year ended, Bush granted American companies permission to open offices in Vietnam to investigate business opportunities.

By the time President Clinton took the oath of office in January 1993, American commercial and financial interests were clamoring for the White House to lift the embargo on the Socialist Republic of Vietnam. American corporations, after spending huge amounts of money on computers and reducing the size of their workforce, had regained their ability to compete successfully in foreign markets. But while the United States was reestablishing its global economic supremacy, influential spokesmen for the American business community, such as *The Wall Street Journal*, the U.S. Chamber of Commerce, *Fortune*, the National Association of Manufacturers, and *BusinessWeek*, warned that Japan and other rivals were beating the United States in the race for trade and investment in Vietnam. If the boycott were removed, some argued, American capital and commerce would generate prosperity in the SRV and thereby pave the way for the emergence of a democratic government in Hanoi. And public opinion polls showed for the first time that most Americans favored the establishment of normal relations with Vietnam. Clinton moved cautiously, however, because he did not want to provoke the MIA lobby. In July 1993, Clinton stopped blocking international loans to Vietnam, and finally, in February 1994, he lifted the embargo.

The irony was obvious. As part of their drive to establish a liberal capitalist world system following the surrender of the Axis powers in 1945, American policymakers had decided to bankroll the French war effort in Vietnam. They had aimed to contain the cancer of communism and thereby keep the markets of Southeast Asia open to Japan and the countries of Western Europe. And while Truman and Eisenhower feared that communism might spread throughout the rest of Southeast Asia if the Vietminh gained control of Vietnam, Kennedy and Johnson extended the domino theory to cover the entire Third World. But their worst fears did not materialize. Instead, the members of ASEAN maintained their firm anticommunist orientation, and the Chinese, the Russians, and many others around the world began moving toward capitalism. Even the Vietnamese communists, after emerging victorious in 1975, soon expressed a strong desire to participate in the expanding international trading network. As the dream of a Pax Americana seemed to be coming true during the 1990s, Washington took the first step along the road to reconciliation with Hanoi in order to help American businessmen outmaneuver their Japanese and other economic rivals in Vietnam.

Almost immediately after the boycott ended, American corporations rushed to do business in the Socialist Republic of Vietnam. Caterpillar submitted bids to repair harbors and roads that had been bombed during the war, while Coca-Cola and PepsiCo began producing soft drinks in Vietnam. A year later, Ford invested $120 million in a plant near Hanoi to make cars, midsize trucks, and minivans. American marketing experts noted that about half of the Vietnamese population was under twenty years old. "It is that age group," an advertising agency explained, "that most craves American products, such as blue jeans and athletic footwear." Pleased that the embargo had been eliminated, business leaders throughout the United States wanted the White House to take the next step and normalize diplomatic relations with Hanoi. Normalization would allow the Export-Import Bank to help finance the sale of American products in Vietnam, the thirteenth-largest country in the world. Normalization would also permit the State Department to negotiate trade, investment, and tax agreements with the SRV. In January 1995, more than 100 American companies formed the Coalition for US-Vietnamese Trade to lobby for diplomatic relations with Vietnam. Policymakers in Washington agreed that normalization was necessary. In July 1995, President Clinton extended official diplomatic recognition to the SRV, and a month later, Secretary of State Warren Christopher traveled to Hanoi and expressed his wish that "many more Americans will join companies like Ford, Coca-Cola and Baskin-Robbins in betting on Vietnam's future."

The twin themes of economic liberalization in Vietnam and diplomatic reconciliation with the United States remained in the forefront between 1996 and 2006, when Phan Van Khai served two successive terms as prime minister of the Socialist Republic of Vietnam. With Khai and other economic reformers in Hanoi overseeing the *doi moi* program, Vietnam continued to register one of the fastest growth rates in gross domestic product in Asia. The Vietnamese economy, in fact, grew at an average annual rate of about 7.5 percent during the first five years of the twenty-first century. At the same time, the SRV deepened its involvement in the global economy and strengthened its ties to the United States. American exporters hoped to increase the sale of agricultural and industrial goods to the SRV with its rapidly expanding number of potential customers, while American investors were eager to take advantage of the well-educated workforce and low cost of labor in Vietnam. And in July 2000, during the last year of the Clinton administration, the United States and Vietnam signed a free trade agreement that liberalized economic relations between the two countries. The commercial accord soon yielded substantial benefits to both Vietnam and the United States. As American-Vietnamese trade quadrupled in value to almost $8 billion per annum during the ensuing five years, the United States replaced Japan as the largest market for Vietnamese exports, and the SRV became the fastest-growing market for American products.

Government officials and business leaders in the United States were delighted as Phan Van Khai and his colleagues in Hanoi made the Vietnamese economy more open and promised to abide by global standards that protect intellectual property. Joining other American companies such as Nike and Cargill that were already operating in Vietnam, Intel announced in February 2006 that it would invest $300 million in a semiconductor plant in Ho Chi Minh City. Then, in May 2006, the Bush administration agreed that the SRV should be allowed to join the World Trade Organization (WTO). Although Khai announced his resignation as the prime minister of Vietnam a month later, he wanted to make sure that his liberal economic policies would be

A billboard on the road to Ho Chi Minh City Airport advertising VISA credit cards. From Barry Lewis/Alamy.

continued by his successor. Khai therefore nominated Deputy Prime Minister Nguyen Tan Dung to be his replacement as the top government official in Hanoi. A pro-market reformer from Ca Mau province located at the southern tip of Vietnam, Dung had been very successful in attracting foreign investment both to his home province and to Ho Chi Minh City, the economic engine of the country. And while serving as the head of the SRV's central bank during the 1990s, Dung had supervised the restructuring of the Vietnamese banking system. Dung was determined to pursue a liberal economic agenda when the Vietnamese Communist Party elevated him to the post of prime minister, and he was elated in January 2007 when Vietnam became the 150th member of the WTO.

The Asia-Pacific Economic Cooperation (APEC) summit, held in Hanoi just two months earlier, dramatized the fact that the Socialist Republic of Vietnam was being swiftly integrated into the global economy. A few days before the conference opened, Intel announced that it would triple its investment in Vietnam to $1 billion, expanding the size of the chip assembly and testing plant that it was building in Ho Chi Minh City. Other American corporations, attracted by large tax breaks and the growing demand for their products, made commitments during the APEC forum to invest almost $2 billion in Vietnam. And while government officials from 21 countries gathered for high-profile meetings in Hanoi, more than 1,200 business executives from around the world flooded into the city to hold a shadow summit of their own. Several American companies, such as Microsoft, General Motors, and Citigroup, donated $250,000 each to sponsor the big gathering of business leaders, and multicolored APEC banners featuring the names and logos of these corporate sponsors hung from lampposts and trees that lined the major streets in Hanoi. Underscoring the strong interest in economic questions exhibited by the top political leaders attending the APEC summit, both U.S. Secretary of State Condoleezza Rice and Chinese President Hu Jintao delivered keynote addresses to the business executives who were meeting in the huge auditorium of the National Convention Center in the Vietnamese capital.

American-Vietnamese relations have come full circle in the years since World War II. During the final months of fighting in the Pacific theater, American military and intelligence officers began helping the Vietnamese communists who were opposing the Japanese occupation of their country. But the two allies became adversaries for more than forty years after World War II ended. Then, for both economic and strategic reasons, the United States and Vietnam resumed friendly relations during the last decade of the twentieth century. The two countries wanted not only to develop strong commercial and financial ties with each other but also to block any future efforts by China to dominate Southeast Asia. On many occasions, however, American-Vietnamese relations could have taken a different turn. Truman could have recognized the government established in 1945 by Ho Chi Minh. Eisenhower could have supported the Geneva Accords that had called for national elections in 1956 to reunify Vietnam. Kennedy could have terminated rather than expanded the American military advisory program in Vietnam. Johnson could have rejected the recommendations of his civilian and military advisers to dispatch American combat troops to Vietnam. And Nixon could have abandoned rather than perpetuated the long American struggle to defeat the Vietnamese communists.

The protracted American military involvement in Vietnam raises several provocative questions. If the United States had maintained a friendly policy toward Ho Chi Minh, would he have become an Asian Tito and steered his country away from the Sino-Soviet camp? If the United States had not fought in Vietnam, would all the other dominoes in Southeast Asia have fallen into communist hands? Did the American intervention in Indochina help stem the rising tide of revolution that threatened to swamp the Third World? Or was the bloody ordeal in Vietnam a needless war that had no lasting benefits? Such questions can be answered only by speculation and not by

A placard at the facade above the entrance of the World Trade Organization headquarters in Geneva, Switzerland, welcomes Vietnam as the organization's 150th member on January 11, 2007. From AP Photo/Keystone, Martial Trezzini.

historical evidence. But one thing is clear: The Vietnam conflict was a war that nobody won. After the fall of Saigon in 1975, the triumphant communists renamed the former capital of South Vietnam in honor of Uncle Ho, the father of their revolution. Yet within fifteen years, the residents of Ho Chi Minh City returned to calling their home Saigon, just as if the war had never happened. And most people in the Socialist Republic of Vietnam exhibited friendly attitudes toward American visitors, even though the winds of war that had swept across their country and into Laos and Cambodia left nothing but death and destruction in their path.

The Second Indochina War also produced great suffering in the United States. An American mother expressed her own sorrow as well as the grief of all other mothers who lost a son in Vietnam: "We remember sadly now the things that will not be; the weddings never attended; the children never born; the houses never built and the fields not plowed; the books never written and the songs not sung." The Vietnam Veterans Memorial, dedicated in 1982 and located on the mall in Washington, D.C., continues to remind millions of Americans of the terrible consequences of the conflict. The memorial is a somber black granite structure consisting of two long wings cut into the earth. Many visitors, as they approach the granite slabs containing the names of the nearly 60,000 Americans who died in Vietnam, feel as though they are descending into an open graveyard. Soldiers come to run their fingers across the names of fallen buddies, parents come to touch the names of lost children, and widows come to feel the names of dead husbands. Even those who do not come to mourn the loss of a loved one are deeply moved by the long list of names etched into the black wall that starkly dramatizes the tragedy of Vietnam.

DOCUMENT 8-1
Report on POW/MIAs, January 13, 1993

A Senate committee issued a report on January 13, 1993, on the controversial POW/MIA question.

Summary of Findings and Recommendations
Americans "last known alive" in Southeast Asia

Information available to our negotiators and government officials responsible for the repatriation of prisoners indicated that a group of approximately 100 American civilians and servicemen expected to return at Operation Homecoming did not. Some of these men were known to have been taken captive; some were known only to have survived their incidents; others were thought likely to have survived. The White House expected that these individuals would be accounted for by our adversaries, either as alive or dead, when the war came to an end. Because they were not accounted for then, despite our protests, nor in the period immediately

following when the trail was freshest and the evidence strongest, twenty years of agony over this issue began. This was the moment when the POW/MIA controversy was born.

The failure of our Vietnam war adversaries to account for these "last known alive" Americans meant that families who had good reason to expect the return of their loved ones instead had cause for grief. Amidst their sorrow, the nation hailed the war's end; the President said that all our POWs are "on the way home," and the Defense Department, following standard procedures, began declaring missing men dead . . . .Nixon, Ford, and Carter Administration officials all dismissed the possibility that American POWs had survived in Southeast Asia after Operation Homecoming.

This Committee has uncovered evidence that precludes it from taking the same view. We acknowledge that there is no proof that U.S. POWs survived, but neither is there proof that all those who did not return had died. There is evidence, moreover, that

(continued)

DOCUMENT 8-1 Continued

indicates the possibility of survival, at least for a small number, after Operation Homecoming. . . .

Given the Committee's findings, the question arises as to whether it is fair to say that American POWs were knowingly abandoned in Southeast Asia after the war. The answer to that question is clearly no. American officials did not have certain knowledge that any specific prisoner or prisoners were being left behind. But there remains the troubling question of whether the Americans who were expected to return but did not were, as a group, shunted aside and discounted by government and population alike. The answer to that question is essentially yes.

Inevitably the question will be asked: who is responsible for that? The answer goes beyond any one agency, administration or faction. By the time the peace agreement was signed, a decade of division, demonstrations and debate had left our entire nation weary of killing and tired of involvement in an inconclusive and morally complex war. The psychology of the times, from rural kitchens to the Halls of Congress to the Oval Office, was to move on; to put the war out of mind; and to focus again on other things. The President said, and our nation wanted to believe, that all of our American POWs were on the way home. Watergate loomed; other crises seized our attention. Amidst it all, the question of POW/MIA accountability faded. In a sense, it, too, became a casualty of war. . . .

When the war shut down, so, too, did much of the POW/MIA related intelligence operations. Bureaucratic priorities shifted rapidly and, before long, the POW/MIA accounting operation had become more of a bureaucratic backwater than an operation center for matters of life and death. . . .

Still, the families wait for answers and still, the question haunts, is there anyone left alive? The search for a definite answer to that question prompted the creation of this Committee.

As much as we would hope that no American has had to endure twenty years of captivity, if one or more were in fact doing so, there is nothing the Members of the Committee would have liked more than to be able to prove this fact. We would have recommended the use of all available resources

to respond to such evidence if it had been found, for nothing would have been more rewarding than to have been able to re-unite a long-captive American with family and country.

Unfortunately, our hopes have not been realized. This disappointment does not reflect a failure of investigation, but rather a confrontation with reality. While the Committee has some evidence suggesting the possibility a POW may have survived to the present, and while some information remains yet to be investigated, there is, at this time, no compelling evidence that proves that any American remains alive in captivity in Southeast Asia.

The Committee cannot prove a negative, nor have we entirely given up hope that one or more U.S. POWs may have survived. As mentioned above, some reports remain to be investigated and new information could be forthcoming. But neither live-sighting reports nor other sources of intelligence have provided grounds for encouragement, particularly over the past decade. The live-sighting reports that have been resolved have not checked out; alleged pictures of POWs have proven false; purported leads have come up empty; and photographic intelligence has been inconclusive, at best.

In addition to the lack of compelling evidence proving that Americans are alive, the majority of the Committee Members believes there is also the question of motive. These Members assert that it is one thing to believe that the Pathet Lao or North Vietnamese might have seen reason to hold back American prisoners in 1973 or for a short time thereafter; it is quite another to discern a motive for holding prisoners alive in captivity for another 19 years. The Vietnamese and Lao have been given a multitude of opportunities to demand money in exchange for the prisoners some allege they hold but our investigation has uncovered no credible evidence that they have ever done so. . . .

Finally, there is the question of numbers. Part of the pain caused by this issue has resulted from rumors about hundreds or thousands of Americans languishing in camps or bamboo cages. The circumstances surrounding the losses of missing Americans render these reports arithmetically impossible. . . .

DOCUMENT 8-1 Continued

Only in a few cases did the U.S. Government know for certain that someone was captured;

In many of these cases, there is only an indication of the potential of capture; and

In a large number of the cases, there is a strong indication that the individual was killed.

The Committee emphasizes that simply because someone was listed as missing in action does not mean that there was any evidence, such as radio contact, an open parachute or a sighting on the ground, of survival. We may make a presumption that an individual could have survived, and that is the right basis upon which to operate. But a presumption is very different from knowledge or fact, and cannot lead us—in the absence of evidence—to conclude that someone is alive. Even some of the cases about which we know the most and which show the strongest indication that someone was a prisoner of war leave us with certain doubts as to what the circumstances were. The bottom line is that there remain only a few cases where we know an unreturned POW was alive in captivity and we do not have evidence that the individual also died while in captivity.

There is at least one aspect of the POW/MIA controversy that should be laid to rest conclusively with this investigation and that is the issue of conspiracy. Allegations have been made in the past that our government has had a "mindset to debunk" reports that American prisoners have been sighted in Southeast Asia. Our Committee found reason to take those allegations seriously. But we also found in some quarters a "mindset to accuse" that has given birth to vast and implausible theories of conspiracy and conscious betrayal. Those theories are without foundation.

Yes, there have been failures of policy, priority and process. Over the years, until this investigation, the Executive branch's penchant for secrecy and classification greatly contributed to perceptions of conspiracy. In retrospect, a more open policy would have been better. But America's government too closely reflects America's people to have permitted the knowing and willful abandonment of U.S. POWs and a subsequent coverup spanning almost 20 years and involving literally thousands of people.

The POW/MIA issue is too important and too personal for us to allow it to be driven by theory; it must be driven by fact. Witness after witness was asked by our Committee if they believed in, or had evidence of, a conspiracy either to leave POWs behind or to conceal knowledge of their fates—and no evidence was produced. The isolated bits of information out of which some have constructed whole labyrinths of intrigue and deception have not withstood the test of objective investigation; and the vast archives of secret U.S. documents that some felt contained incriminating evidence have been thoroughly examined by the Committee only to find that the conspiracy cupboard is bare.

The quest for the fullest possible accounting of our Vietnam-era POW/MIAs must continue, but if our efforts are to be effective and fair to families, they must go forward within the context of reality, not fiction.

Source: *Report of the Select Committee on POW/MIA Affairs*, United States Senate, 103 Congress, 1st Session (Washington, D.C.: Government Printing Office, 1993)

DOCUMENT 8-2

Free Trade Agreement, July 13, 2000

The United States and the Socialist Republic of Vietnam signed a free trade agreement on July 13, 2000.

AGREEMENT BETWEEN THE UNITED STATES OF AMERICA AND THE SOCIALIST REPUBLIC OF VIETNAM ON TRADE RELATIONS

Chapter 1 Trade in Goods

Article 1

MOST FAVORED NATION (*NORMAL TRADE RELATIONS*)

1. Each Party shall accord immediately and unconditionally to products originating in or exported to the territory of the other party treatment no less favorable than that accorded to like products originating in or exported to the territory of any third country in all matters relating to:

   a. customs duties and charges of any kind imposed on or in connection with importation or exportation, including the method of levying such duties and charges;

   b. method of payment for imports and exports, and the international transfer of such payments;

   c. rules and formalities in connection with importation and exportation, including those relating to customs clearance, transit, warehouses and transshipment;

   d. taxes and other internal charges of any kind applied directly or indirectly to imported products;

   e. laws, regulations and other requirements affecting the sale, offering for sale, purchase, transportation, distribution, storage and use of products in the domestic market; and

   f. the application of quantitative restrictions and the granting of licenses. . . .

Article 2

NATIONAL TREATMENT

1. Each Party shall administer tariff and nontariff measures affecting trade in a manner which affords meaningful competitive opportunities for products of the other Party with respect to domestic competitors.

2. Accordingly, neither Party shall impose, directly or indirectly, on the products of the other Party into its territory, internal taxes or charges of any kind in excess of those applied, directly or indirectly, to like domestic products.

3. Each party shall accord to products originating in the territory of the other Party treatment no less favorable than that accorded to like domestic products in respect to all laws, regulations and other requirements affecting their internal sale, offering for sale, purchase, transportation, distribution, storage or use. . . .

Article 3

GENERAL OBLIGATIONS WITH RESPECT TO TRADE

1. The Parties shall seek to achieve a satisfactory balance of market access opportunities through the satisfactory reciprocation of reductions in tariffs and nontariff barriers to trade in goods resulting from multilateral negotiations. . . .

Article 4

EXPANSION AND PROMOTION OF TRADE

Each Party shall encourage and facilitate the holding of trade promotion events such as trade fairs, exhibitions, missions and seminars in its territory and in the territory of the other Party. Similarly, each Party shall encourage and facilitate the participation of its respective nationals and companies in such events. Subject to the laws in force within their respective territories, the Parties agree to allow the import and re-export on a duty free basis of all articles for use in such events, provided that such articles are not sold or otherwise transferred.

Article 5

GOVERNMENT COMMERCIAL OFFICES

1. Subject to its laws and regulations governing foreign missions, each Party shall allow government commercial offices of the other

DOCUMENT 8-2 Continued

Party to hire host-country nationals and, subject to immigration laws and procedures, third-country nationals.

2. Each Party shall ensure unhindered access of host-country nationals to government commercial offices of the other Party.

3. Each Party shall allow the participation of its nationals and companies in the commercial activities of the other Party's government commercial offices.

4. Each Party shall allow access by government commercial office personnel of the other Party to the relevant host-country officials, and to representatives of nationals and companies of the host Party.

Article 6

EMERGENCY ACTION ON IMPORTS

1. The Parties agree to consult promptly at the request of either party whenever either actual or prospective imports of products originating in the territory of the other Party cause or threaten to cause or significantly contribute to market disruption. Market disruption exists within a domestic industry whenever imports of an article, like or directly competitive with an article produced by such domestic industry, are increasing rapidly, either absolutely or relatively, so as to be a significant cause of material injury. The consultations provided in this paragraph shall have the objectives of (a) presenting and examining the factors relating to such imports that may be causing or threatening to cause or significantly contributing to market disruption, and (b) finding means of preventing or remedying such market disruption. Such consultations shall be concluded within sixty days from the date of the request for such consultations, unless the parties agree otherwise.

2. Unless a different solution is mutually agreed upon during the consultations, the importing Party may (a) impose quantitative import limitations, tariff measures or any other restrictions or measures it deems appropriate,

and for such period of time it deems necessary, to prevent or remedy threatened or actual market disruption, and (b) take appropriate measures to ensure that imports from the territory of the other Party comply with such quantitative limitations or other restrictions introduced in connection with market disruption. In this event, the other Party shall be free to deviate from its obligations under this Agreement with respect to substantially equivalent trade. . . .

Article 7

COMMERCIAL DISPUTES

For the purposes of Chapter 1 of this Agreement:

1. Nationals and companies of either Party shall be accorded national treatment with respect to access to all competent courts and administrative bodies in the territory of the other Party, as plaintiffs, defendants or otherwise. . . .

2. The Parties encourage the adoption of arbitration for the settlement of disputes arising out of commercial transactions concluded between nationals or companies of the United States of America and nationals or companies of the Socialist Republic of Vietnam . . . .

Chapter II Intellectual Property Rights

Article 1

OBJECTIVES, PRINCIPLES AND SCOPE OF OBLIGATIONS

1. Each party shall provide in its territory to the nationals of the other Party adequate and effective protection and enforcement of intellectual property rights.

2. The Parties recognize the underlying public policy objectives of national systems for the protection of intellectual property, including developmental and technological objectives, and ensure that measures to protect and enforce intellectual property rights do not themselves become barriers to legitimate trade. . . .

(continued)

DOCUMENT 8-2   Continued

Chapter III Trade in Services

Article 2

MOST-FAVORED-NATION TREATMENT

1. With respect to any measure covered by this Chapter, each Party shall accord immediately and unconditionally to services and service suppliers of the other party treatment no less favorable than that it accords to like services and service suppliers of any other country . . . .

Chapter IV Development of Investment Relations

Article 2

NATIONAL TREATMENT AND MOST-FAVORED-NATION TREATMENT

1. With respect to the establishment, acquisition, expansion, management, conduct, operation and sale or disposition of covered investments, each Party shall accord treatment no less favorable than that it accords, in like situations, to investments in its territory of its own nationals or companies (hereafter "national treatment") or to investments in its territory of nationals or companies of a third country (hereafter "most favored nation treatment"), whichever is most favorable (hereafter "national and most favored nation treatment")....

Article 4

DISPUTE SETTLEMENT

1. Each party shall provide companies and nationals of the other Party with an effective means of asserting claims and enforcing rights with respect to covered investments.
2. In the event of an investment dispute, the parties to the dispute should attempt to resolve the dispute through consultation, which may include the use of non-binding third-party procedures....

Source: U.S. House of Representatives, 107th Congress, 1st Session, House Document 107-85, (Washington, D.C.: Government Printing Office, 2001).

DOCUMENT 8-3

Condoleezza Rice, Remarks at Asia-Pacific Economic Summit, November 18, 2006

Remarks made by Secretary of State Condoleezza Rice at the Asia-Pacific Economic Cooperation CEO Summit on November 18, 2006, in Hanoi.

Fellow ministers, distinguished guests, ladies and gentlemen: It is my great pleasure to join all of you here in Hanoi for this year's APEC summit. The United States views APEC as the premier multilateral organization in the Asia-Pacific region. And here in this room today, we see the true spirit of APEC—in people like you, and millions of other entrepreneurs across the Asia-Pacific, who work every day to create jobs, to expand opportunity, and to unleash the energy of the imagination of the Asia-Pacific community.

The United States has always been a Pacific power, and we are proud to support and be part of Asia's success. We have opened our markets to Asia's entrepreneurs. We have opened our schools and universities to Asia's students. . . . In 1989, we and our Asian partners joined together to create this great organization, APEC.

The results of our cooperation have been dramatic: Since the creation of APEC, the combined wealth of our economies has grown by 66 percent. Today, nearly two-thirds of all U.S. trade occurs with our friends in the Asia-Pacific. And the benefits on this side of the ocean are plain for all to see: People in this region are lifting themselves out of poverty, in greater numbers and with greater speed, than ever before in human history.

The lesson, ladies and gentlemen, is clear: The economies of the Asia-Pacific region are completely and inextricably linked together. We share the benefits, as well as the burdens, of expanding prosperity. For this reason, APEC, and the free economies of the Asia-Pacific, should know that

DOCUMENT 8-3 Continued

they have no better friend, and no stronger supporter, than the United States of America.

Today, I would like to share America's vision for APEC with you. It is a vision that transcends simple cooperation, and looks to the emergence of a true Asia-Pacific Economic Community, spanning the public sphere and the private sector. I see several principles that must define that sense of community.

We must create opportunities for sustainable growth. There is simply no better way to achieve this goal than free trade, and the United States has a comprehensive trade policy in Asia-Pacific.

. . . We are working with our APEC partners and with you in the business community, to promote regional economic integration, including the possibility of a Free Trade Area of the Asia-Pacific.

In order to foster trade, we must also facilitate interaction and travel. Therefore, the United States has decided this year to recognize the APEC Business Travel Card, as the first step toward joining the program. This will enable entrepreneurs like you to gain visas, to move through our immigration lines, and to visit America—in a faster, safer, and easier manner. . . .

Our sense of economic community must promote well-governed societies. Just as APEC is increasingly recognizing that prosperity depends on security, we are also acknowledging the connection between development and good governance. More and more entrepreneurs are sick and tired of bearing the economic risks of political malfeasance—and for good reason. Who wants to do business in an economy where the rule of law is enforced by whim or perhaps not at all? Or where the state is compromised by corruption? Or where the intellectual products of innovation can be pirated at any cost?

This is an area in which we must work together, because corruption and the absence of the rule of law will most certainly retard economic growth, both for growing, developed economies and also for those who wish to enter the international economic system and gain benefit and prosperity for their people.

Finally, our sense of economic community must strengthen our shared institutions. On this front, the United States will lead by example. Over the next two years, President Bush plans to increase America's funding for APEC—to empower this organization to meet the challenges of the 21st century.

Let me say one more thing about the idea of a community in the Asia-Pacific. I find it really remarkable, as the American Secretary of State, to be standing here in Hanoi, barely three decades after the tragic war between our countries, and yet our conversation today is not about conflict, it's about community, it's about progress. (Applause) One has to ask: How is this possible?

Well, in fact, the answer is really pretty simple and it is an answer about the triumph of the human spirit and an answer about the human desire to overcome difficulty: Twenty years ago, the leaders of Vietnam took a hard look at their isolated economy, and made a strategic choice to begin reforms. As Vietnam sought to create opportunities for its people, it found a friend in the United States—a friend who has continued, and will continue, to raise our issues of concern, issues of human rights and religious freedom, but a friend nonetheless. We have supported Vietnam's good decisions and worked to bind up old wounds. We have opened our markets to Vietnamese goods and joined in the fight against AIDS. We are helping Vietnam to enter the World Trade Organization and, hopefully very soon, we will extend Permanent Normal Trade Relations to Vietnam. (Applause) But most of all, the United States and Vietnam, of course, have restored diplomatic relations, but they have restored more than that. They restored a hopeful partnership and a hope for the people of Vietnam and America to work towards a better future. . . .

Source: State Department, http://2001-2009.state.gov/secretary/rm/2006/76277.htm.

Chronological List of Main Events

July 1976	The establishment of the Socialist Republic of Vietnam
January 1979	The Vietnamese invasion of Cambodia
February 1979	The Chinese invasion of Vietnam
December 1986	The change in leadership in the Vietnamese Communist Party
October 1992	The dispatch from Hanoi of information about 5,000 American MIAs
February 1994	The lifting of the American embargo against Vietnam
July 1995	The resumption of U.S.-Vietnamese diplomatic relations
July 2000	The signing of a U.S.-Vietnamese free trade agreement
January 2007	Vietnam joins the World Trade Organization

Study Questions

1. What was the Vietnam syndrome?
2. What was the *doi moi* program?
3. Why did the United States and the Socialist Republic of Vietnam establish friendly relations during the 1990s?
4. Would many of the countries in Southeast Asian have fallen into communist hands if the United States had not fought in Vietnam?

SELECTED BIBLIOGRAPHY

DOCUMENTS

The best place to begin is the *Pentagon Papers,* a collection of primary sources prepared by the Department of Defense and eventually published in several editions. U.S. Congress, Senate, Subcommittee on Building and Grounds, *The Pentagon Papers (The Senator Gravel Edition),* 4 vols. (Boston, 1971) is an orderly and easy-to-use set. For the documents concerning peace initiatives, see George C. Herring, *The Secret Diplomacy of the Vietnam War: The Negotiating Volumes of the Pentagon Papers* (Austin, Tex., 1983). *The Foreign Relations of the United States,* a series of official documents prepared by the Department of State, contains valuable material dealing with Vietnam. William Appleman Williams et al., *America in Vietnam: A Documentary History* (New York, 1985) is a superb collection. Gareth Porter, *Vietnam: The Definitive Documentation of Human Decisions,* 2 vols. (Stanfordville, N.Y., 1979) is also excellent.

GENERAL WORKS

The following books provide the most comprehensive accounts: Stanley Karnow, *Vietnam: A History* (New York, 1983); Gabriel Kolko, *Anatomy of a War: Vietnam, the United States, and the Modern Historical Experience* (New York, 1985); Marilyn B. Young, *The Vietnam Wars, 1945–1990* (New York, 1991); William J. Duiker, *Sacred War: Nationalism and Revolution in a Divided Vietnam* (New York, 1995); George C. Herring, *America's Longest War: The United States and Vietnam, 1950–1975,* 4th ed. (New York, 2002); Robert D. Schulzinger, *A Time for War: The United States and Vietnam, 1941–1975* (New York, 1997); George D. Moss, *Vietnam: An American Ordeal,* 5th ed. (Upper Saddle River, N.J., 2006); James S. Olson and Randy Roberts, *Where the Domino Fell: America and Vietnam, 1945–1995,* 5th ed. (St. James, N.Y., 2006); Gerard J. DeGroot, *A Noble Cause? America and the Vietnam War* (New York, 2000); David Anderson, *The Vietnam War* (New York, 2005); and Charles E. Neu, *America's Lost War: Vietnam, 1945–1975* (Wheeling, Ill., 2005). For an analysis of developments in an important region, see David Elliot, *The Vietnamese War: Revolution and Change in the Mekong Delta, 1930–1975* (Armonk, N.Y., 2006). On the Vietnamese side, see the excellent works of Joseph Buttinger, *The Smaller Dragon: A Political History of Vietnam* (New York, 1958); *Vietnam: A Dragon Embattled,* 2 vols. (New York, 1967); and *A Dragon Defiant: A Short History of Vietnam* (New York, 1972). See also Ang Cheng Guan, *The Vietnamese War from the Other Side: The Vietnamese Communists' Perspective* (London, 2002); and Ang Cheng Guan, *Ending The Vietnamese War: The Vietnamese Communists' Perspective* (London, 2004).

ORIGINS–1941

For the establishment of the French Indochina empire, see John Cady, *The Roots of French Imperialism in Asia* (Ithaca, N.Y., 1954); Milton E. Osborne, *The French Presence in Cochinchina and Cambodia: Rule and Response, 1859–1905* (New York, 1969); Martin J. Murray, *The Development of Capitalism in Colonial Indochina, 1870–1940* (Berkeley, Calif., 1980); and Peter Zinoman, *The Colonial Bastille: A History of Imprisonment in Vietnam, 1862–1940* (Berkeley, Calif., 2001). Ngo Vinh Long, *Before the Revolution: The Vietnamese Peasants under the French* (New York, 1973) provides an excellent analysis of the exploitation of the peasant masses in French Indochina. For an analysis of Vietnamese culture, see Neil L. Jamieson, *Understanding Vietnam* (Berkeley, Calif., 1993). On the rise of Vietnamese nationalism, see John T. McAlister, Jr., *Vietnam: The Origins of Revolution* (New York, 1971); William J. Duiker, *The Rise of Nationalism in Vietnam, 1900–1941* (Ithaca, N.Y., 1976); and David G. Marr, *Vietnamese Anti-Colonialism 1885–1925* (Berkeley, Calif., 1971); David G. Marr, *Vietnamese Tradition on Trial, 1920–1945* (Berkeley, Calif., 1982); Phan Boi Chau, *Overturned Chariot: The Autobiography of Phan-Boi-Chau* (Honolulu, 1999); and Troung Buu Lam, ed., *Colonialism Experienced: Vietnamese Writings on Colonialism, 1900–1931* (Ann Arbor, Mich., 2002). On the roots of Vietnamese communism, see Douglas Pike, *History of Vietnamese Communism* (Stanford, Calif., 1978); Huynh Kim Khanh, *Vietnamese Communism, 1925–1945* (Ithaca, N.Y., 1981); and Shawn F. Mc Hale, *Print and Power: Confucianism, Communism, and Buddhism in the Making of Modern Vietnam, 1920–1945* (Honolulu, 2003). For biographies of Ho Chi Minh, see Jean Lacouture, *Ho Chi Minh: A Political Biography* (New York, 1968); David Halberstam, *Ho* (New York, 1987); and William J. Duiker, *Ho Chi Minh* (New York, 2000).

1942–1952

On American plans for the establishment of a liberal capitalist world system, see Patrick J. Hearden, *Architects of Globalism: Building a New World Order During World War II* (Fayetteville, Ark., 2002). For American attitudes toward the colonial question and the trusteeship scheme embraced by Franklin D. Roosevelt, see Christopher Thorne, *Allies of a Kind: The United States, Britain, and the War Against Japan, 1941–1945* (New York, 1978); William Roger Louis, *Imperialism at Bay: The United States and the Decolonization of the British Empire* (New York, 1978); and Gary R. Hess, *The United States' Emergence as a Southeast Asian Power, 1940–1954* (New York, 1987). Archimedes L. Patti, *Why Vietnam? Prelude to America's Albatross* (Berkeley, Calif., 1980) is a firsthand account by an Office of Strategic Services agent who dealt with the Vietminh during World War II. On the origins of the First Indochina War, see Stein Tonnesson, *The Vietnamese Revolution of August 1945: Roosevelt, Ho Chi Minh, and de Gaulle in a World at War* (Oslo, 1991); David G. Marr, *Vietnam 1945: The Quest for Power* (Berkeley, Calif., 1995); and Martin Shipway, *The Road to War: France and Vietnam, 1944–1947* (Providence, R.I., 1996). For the American decision to support the French war effort in Indochina, see Andrew J. Rotter, *The Path to Vietnam: Origins of the American Commitment to Southeast Asia* (Ithaca, N.Y., 1987); and William S. Borden, *The Pacific Alliance: United States Foreign Economic Policy and Japanese Trade Recovery, 1947–1955* (Madison, Wis., 1984). Ronald H. Spector, *Advice and Support: The Early Years of the U.S. Army in Vietnam, 1941–1960* (New York, 1985) analyzes the American military assistance program in Vietnam. Giang Zhai, *China and the Vietnam Wars, 1950–1975* (Chapel Hill, N.C., 2000) shows the importance of Chinese military aid to the Vietnamese struggle for national liberation. Lloyd C. Gardner, *Approaching Vietnam: From World War II Through Dienbienphu, 1941–1954* (New York, 1988) places American involvement in Southeast Asia in a broad global perspective. Also see Robert M. Blum, *Drawing the Line: The Origin of the American Containment Policy in East Asia* (New York, 1982); John L. Gaddis, *Strategies of Containment: A Critical View of Postwar American National Security Policy* (New York, 1982); and Steven H. Lee, *Outposts of Empire: Korea, Vietnam, and the Origins of the Cold War in Asia* (Montreal, 1995). The standard account of the First Indochina War is Ellen Hammer, *The Struggle for Indochina, 1945–1955* (Stanford, Calif., 1966). Bernard B. Fall, *Street Without Joy* (New York, 1972) describes the French military operations in Vietnam. For detailed discussions of the French defeat at Dien Bien Phu, see Jules Roy, *The Battle of*

Dienbienphu (New York, 1965); Bernard B. Fall, *Hell in a Very Small Place* (Philadelphia, 1966); Howard R. Simpson, *Dien Bien Phu: The Epic Battle America Forgot* (Dulles, Va., 1994); and Martin Windrow, *The Last Valley: Dien Bien Phu and the French Defeat in Vietnam* (New York, 2004). For accounts of the peace settlement that ended the First Indochina War, see Robert F. Randle, *Geneva 1954: The Settlement of the Indochina War* (Princeton, N.J., 1969); and James Cable, *The Geneva Conference of 1954 on Indochina* (New York, 1986).

1953–1963

In addition to the excellent study by Spector listed above, good works to begin with are David Anderson, *Trapped by Success: The Eisenhower Administration and Vietnam, 1953–1961* (New York, 1991); David Halberstam, *The Best and the Brightest* (New York, 1969); Lawrence Freedman, *Kennedy's Wars: Berlin, Cuba, Laos, and Vietnam* (New York, 2000); and David Kaiser, *American Tragedy: Kennedy, Johnson, and the Origins of the Vietnam War* (Cambridge, Mass., 2000). For an analysis of the relationship between American policymakers and Ngo Dinh Diem, see Seth Jacobs, *Cold War Mandarin: Ngo Dinh Diem and the Origins of America's War in Vietnam, 1950–1963* (Lanham, Md., 2006). On the origins of the insurgency against the Diem regime, see Jeffery Race, *War Comes to Long An* (Berkeley, Calif., 1972); William J. Duiker, *The Communist Road to Power in Vietnam* (Boulder, Colo., 1981); and Carlyle Thayer, *War by Other Means: National Liberation and Revolution in Vietnam, 1954–1960* (Sydney, 1989). Truong Nhu Tang, *A Vietcong Memoir* (New York, 1985) is a revealing firsthand account by a Vietnamese participant in the National Liberation Front. Roger Hilsman, *To Move a Nation* (New York, 1967), a memoir by an American diplomat, sheds light on the development of the counterinsurgency program. See David Halberstam, *The Making of a Quagmire* (New York, 1964) for an account by a dissident American journalist whose reports from Saigon challenged the official line during the Kennedy administration. On the difficulties encountered by American military advisers in their effort to help the South Vietnamese army, see Neil Sheehan, *A Bright Shining Lie: John Paul Vann and America in Vietnam* (New York, 1988). George M. Kahlin, *Intervention: How America Became Involved in Vietnam* (New York, 1986) is especially good in analyzing the American response to the Buddhist movement and the subsequent political turmoil in South Vietnam. On the overthrow of Diem, see Ellen Hammer, *A Death in November: America in Vietnam, 1963* (New York, 1987); and Philip E. Cantton, *Diem's Final Failure: Prelude to America's War in Vietnam* (Lawrence, Kan., 2002).

1964–1968

In addition to the penetrating study by Kahlin listed above, see the following works on American policy during the Johnson administration: Larry Berman, *Planning a Tragedy: The Americanization of the War in Vietnam* (New York, 1982); Larry Berman, *Lyndon Johnson's War: The Road to Stalemate in Vietnam* (New York, 1989); Lloyd C. Gardner, *Pay Any Price: Lyndon Johnson and the Wars for Vietnam* (Chicago, 1995); Michael H. Hunt, *Lyndon Johnson's War: America's Cold War Crusade in Vietnam, 1954–1968* (New York, 1996); Brian Van De Mark and Robert S. Mc Namara, *In Retrospect: The Tragedy and Lessons of Vietnam* (New York, 1996); and H. R. McMaster, *Dereliction of Duty: Lyndon Johnson, Robert McNamara, the Joint Chiefs of Staff, and the Lies that Led to Vietnam* (New York, 1997). For an account of the Tonkin Gulf affair, see Edwin E. Moise, *Tonkin Gulf and the Escalation of the Vietnam War* (Chapel Hill, N.C., 1996). George C. Herring, *LBJ and Vietnam: A Different Kind of War* (Austin, Tex., 1994) analyzes the limited war strategy employed by Johnson in Vietnam. For American ground operations in Vietnam, see Shelby L. Stanton, *The Rise and Fall of an American Army: U.S. Ground Forces in Vietnam, 1965–1973* (New York, 1985); and David Maraniss, *They Marched into Sunlight: War and Peace Vietnam and America October 1968* (New York, 2003). The American air war in Vietnam is covered in the following studies: James C. Thompson, *Rolling Thunder: Understanding Policy and Program Failure* (Chapel Hill, N.C., 1980); Mark Clodfelter, *The Limits of American Air Power: The American Bombing of North Vietnam* (New York, 1989); Craig C. Hannah, *Striving for Air Superiority: The Tactical Air Command in Vietnam* (College Station, Tex., 2002); and Ronald B. Frankum, Jr., *Like Rolling Thunder: The Air War in Vietnam, 1964–1975* (Lanham, Md., 2005). For the Tet offensive, see Don Oberdorfer, *Tet! The Turning Point in the Vietnam War* (New York, 1971); Keith W. Nolan, *The Battle for Hue: Tet, 1968* (Novato, Calif., 1983); James J. Wirtz, *The Tet Offensive: Intelligence Failure in War* (Ithaca, N.Y., 1991); Robert Pisor, *The End of the Line: The Siege of Khe Sanh,* rev. ed. (New York, 2002); and David F. Schmitz, *The Tet Offensive: Politics, War, and Public Opinion* (Lanham, Md., 2005). For critical studies of American military policy in Vietnam, see Dave R. Palmer, *Summons of the Trumpet: A History of the Vietnam War from a Military Man's Viewpoint* (San Rafael, Calif., 1978); Guenter Lewy, *America in Vietnam* (New York, 1978); Harry G. Summers, Jr., *On Strategy: A Critical Analysis of the Vietnam War* (San Rafael, Calif., 1982); Bruce Palmer, Jr., *The 25-Year War: America's Military Role in Vietnam* (Lexington, Ky., 1984); Andrew F. Krepinevich, Jr., *The Army in Vietnam* (Baltimore, 1986); and Eric Bergerud, *Dynamics of Defeat* (Boulder, Colo., 1991). The work listed above by Zhai shows that Johnson had good reason to worry about the possibility of Chinese intervention to prevent the defeat of North Vietnam. On the relationship between the Vietnam War and American politics, see Walter LaFeber, *The Deadly Bet: LBJ, Vietnam, and the 1968 Election* (Lanham, Md., 2005). On the role of the media, see Kathleen Turner, *Lyndon Johnson's Dual War: Vietnam and the Press* (Chicago, 1985); Daniel C. Hallin, *The Uncensored War: The Media and Vietnam* (New York, 1986); Clarence R. Wyatt, *Paper Soldiers: The American Press and the Vietnam War* (New York, 1993); Melvin Small, *Covering Dissent: The Media and the Anti-War Movement* (New Brunswick, N.J., 1994); and William M. Hammond, *Reporting Vietnam: Media and Military at War* (Lawrence, Kan., 1999). For the antiwar movement in the United States, see Nancy Zaroulis and Gerald Sullivan, *Who Spoke Up? American Protest Against the War in Vietnam, 1963–1975* (Garden City, N.Y., 1984); Thomas Powers, *Vietnam, The War at Home: The Antiwar Movement* (Boston, 1984); Todd Gatlin, *The Sixties: Years of Hope, Days of Rage* (New York, 1987); Charles De Benedetti, *An American Ordeal: The Antiwar Movement of the Vietnam War* (Syracuse, N.Y., 1990); Kenneth J. Heineman, *Campus Wars: The Peace Movement at American State Universities in the Vietnam Era* (New York, 1993); Tom Wells, *The War Within: America's Battle Over Vietnam* (Berkeley, Calif., 1994); Melvin Small, *Antiwarriors: The Vietnam War and the Battle for America's Hearts and Minds* (Wilmington, Del., 2002); Michael S. Foley, *Confronting the War Machine: Draft Resistance during the Vietnam War* (Chapel Hill, N.C., 2003); Joseph A. Fry, *Debating Vietnam: Fulbright, Stennis, and their Senate Hearings* (Lanham, Md., 2006); and Mark H. Lytle, *America's Uncivil Wars: The Sixties Era from Elvis to the Fall of Richard Nixon* (New York, 2006).

1969–1975

Jeffrey P. Kimball, *Nixon's Vietnam War* (Lawrence, Kan., 1998) is a good place to start. See also Jeffery P. Kimball, *The Vietnam War Files: Uncovering the Secret History of the Nixon Era Strategy* (Lawrence, Kan., 2003). For highly critical accounts of Nixon and Kissinger, see

William Shawcross, *Sideshow: Kissinger, Nixon, and the Destruction of Cambodia* (New York, 1979); Seymour M. Hersh, *The Price of Power: Kissinger in the White House* (New York, 1983); and Larry Berman, *No Peace, No Honor: Nixon, Kissinger, and Betrayal in Vietnam* (New York, 2001). For a different view, see Henry A. Kissinger, *Ending the Vietnam War: A History of America's Involvement in and Extrication from the Vietnam War* (New York, 2002). For the fighting in Vietnam after the Tet offensive, see Ronald H. Spector, *After Tet: The Bloodiest Year in Vietnam* (New York, 1993). Among the many excellent accounts depicting the combat experience of American infantrymen in Vietnam, see especially Philip Caputo, *A Rumor of War* (New York, 1977); Michael Herr, *Dispatches* (New York, 1977); James Webb, *Fields of Fire* (New York, 1978); Frederick Downs, *The Killing Zone* (New York, 1978); Al Santoli, *Everything We Had* (New York, 1981); Robert Goff and Robert Sander, *Brothers: Black Soldiers in Nam* (Novato, Calif., 1982); Wallace Terry, *Bloods: An Oral History of the Vietnam War by Black Veterans* (New York, 1984); and Christian G. Appy, *Working Class War: American Combat Soldiers and Vietnam* (Chapel Hill, N.C., 1993). For an analysis of the performance of the military forces deployed by the Saigon government, see Robert K. Brigham, *ARVN: Life and Death in the South Vietnamese Army* (Lawrence, Kan., 2006). For discussions of the role of women on both sides of the Vietnam War, see Karen G. Turner, *Even the Women Must Fight: Memories of War from North Vietnam* (New York, 1998); Olga Gruit-Hoyt, *A Time Remembered: American Women in the Vietnam War* (Novato, Calif., 1999); and Karen Zeinert, *The Valiant Women of the Vietnam War* (Minneapolis, 2000). For accounts of the My Lai massacre, see James S. Olson and Randy Roberts, eds., *My Lai: A Brief History with Documents* (Boston, 1998); and Michael R. Belknap, *The Vietnam War on Trial: The My Lai Massacre and the Court-Martial of Lieutenant Calley* (Lawrence, Kan., 2002). Gareth Portor, *A Peace Denied: The United States, Vietnam, and the Paris Agreements* (Bloomington, Ind., 1975) is an excellent analysis of the 1973 peace treaty. For the communist negotiating strategy, see Robert K. Brigham, *Guerrilla Diplomacy: The NLF's Foreign Relations and the Vietnam War* (Ithaca, N.Y., 1999). On the organization and strength of the North Vietnamese army, see Douglas Pike, *PAVN: People's Army of Vietnam* (Novato, Calif., 1986). For the role of the Soviet Union, see Ilya V. Gaiduk, *The Soviet Union and the Vietnam War* (Chicago, 1996). The best overall interpretation of the situation in Indochina during the two years following the Paris peace treaty is Arnold R. Isaacs, *Without Honor: Defeat in Vietnam and Cambodia* (Baltimore, Md., 1983). Frank Snepp, *Decent Interval: An Insider's Account of Saigon's Indecent End Told by the CIA's Chief Strategy Analyst in Vietnam* (New York, 1975) describes the disintegration of the South Vietnamese army prior to the fall of Saigon.

THE POSTWAR ERA

For general discussions of the postwar era, see Robert D. Schulzinger, *A Time for Peace: The Legacy of the Vietnam War* (New York, 2006); and Arnold R. Isaacs, *Vietnam Shadows: The War, Its Ghosts, and Its Legacy* (Baltimore, 1997). For conditions in Vietnam after the war ended, see William J. Duiker, *Vietnam since the Fall of Saigon* (Athens, Ohio, 1989); Neil Sheehan, *After the War Was Over: Hanoi and Saigon* (New York, 1991); Edward P. Metzner, Huynh Van Chinh, and Tran Van Phuc, *Reeducation in Postwar Vietnam: Personal Postscript to Peace* (College Station, Tex., 2001); Trin Yarborough, *Surviving Twice: Amerasian Children of the Vietnam War* (Dulles, Va., 2005); and Thomas J. Vasseur, *Touch the Earth: An Aftermath of the Vietnam War* (Macon, Ga., 2005). On the legacy of the Second Indochina War in Laos and Cambodia, see Jane Hamilton-Merrit, *Tragic Mountains: The Hmong, the Americans, and the Secret Wars for Laos, 1942–1992* (Bloomington, Ind., 1993); William Shawcross, *The Quality of Mercy: Cambodia,*

Holocaust, and Modern Conscience (New York, 1984); David P. Chandler, *The Tragedy of Cambodian History* (New Haven, Conn., 1992); David P. Chandler, *Brother Number One: A Biography of Pol Pot* (Boulder, Colo., 1999); and Ben Kiernan, *The Pol Pot Regime: Race, Power, and Genocide in Cambodia under the Khmer Rouge, 1975–1979*, 2nd ed. (New Haven, Conn., 2000). For accounts of the bitter conflicts in Indochina after the fall of Saigon, see Nayan Chanda, *Brother Enemy: The War after the War* (New York, 1986); King C. Chen, *China's War with Vietnam, 1979: Issues, Decisions, and Implications* (Stanford, Calif., 1987); Robert S. Ross, *The Indochina Tangle: China's Vietnam Policy 1975–1979* (New York, 1988); and Joseph L. Zasloff, *Postwar Indochina: Old Enemies and New Allies* (Washington, D.C., 1988). For discussions of the POW/MIA issue, see Bruce H. Franklin, *M.I.A. or Mythmaking in America* (New Brunswick, N.J., 1992); and Susan K. Keating, *Prisoners of Hope: Exploiting the POW/MIA Myth in America* (New York, 1994). For discussions of the impact of the Vietnam War on the United States, see Anthony S. Campagna, *The Economic Consequences of the Vietnam War* (New York, 1991); Keith Beattie, *The Scar that Binds: American Culture and the Vietnam War* (New York, 1998); and Arnold Gordon, *The Afterlife of America's War in Vietnam: Changing Visions in Politics and on Screen* (Jefferson, N.C., 2006).

CREDITS

Page 16: Laure Albin-Guillot/Roger-Viollet/The Image Works; page 37: Peter Newark Military Pictures/ The Bridgeman Art Library International; page 59: National Archives (Still Pictures Branch), U.S. Air Force; page 84: AP Photo; page 111: Bettmann/Corbis; page 128: AP Photo/Phuoc; page 147: National Archives (Nixon Collection); page 178: Barry Lewis/Alamy; page 180: AP Photo/Keystone, Martial Trezzini.

INDEX